Fifty Years a H

Trapper

Autobiography, experiences and observations
of Eldred Nathaniel Woodcock during his
fifty years of hunting and trapping.

Eldred Nathaniel Woodcock

Alpha Editions

This edition published in 2021

ISBN : 9789355894786

Design and Setting By
Alpha Editions
www.alphaedis.com
Email - info@alphaedis.com

Contents

PREFACE.

Sometime early in the spring of 1903, a letter was received from a man in Pennsylvania and published in H-T-T, which a few weeks later brought to light one of the truest and best sportsmen that ever shouldered a gun, strung a snare or set a trap--E. N. Woodcock.

Some of the happenings are repeated and all dates may not be correct, for be it remembered that Mr. Woodcock has written all from memory. It is doubtful if he kept all copies of H-T-T, therefore was not sure if such and such incidents had been written before. In most cases these are somewhat different and as they all "fit in" we have used them as written and published from time to time.

Much information is also contained in the writings of Mr. Woodcock and whether you use gun, steel traps, deadfalls or snares, you will find something of value. The articles are also written in a style that impresses all of their truthfulness, but, so written that they are very interesting.

Those of our readers who have read his articles will be glad of this opportunity to get his writings in book form, while those that have only read a few of his more recent articles will be pleased to secure all.

Perhaps the following editorial which appeared in H-T-T will be in place here:

"Although crippled with rheumatism, there is an old hunter and trapper living in Potter County, Pa., whose enthusiasm is high and his greatest desire is still to get out over the trap lines a few seasons before the end of the "trail" of life's journey is reached. May that desire be fulfilled is the earnest wish of the H-T-T as well as thousands of our readers, who have read the writings of this kind-hearted and wide experienced hunter and trapper, as they have been penned from his home near the Allegheny Mountains.

It is with pleasure that we publish in this issue the "Autobiography of E. N. Woodcock as a Trapper." During his half century with trap and gun, he has had some narrow escapes and experiences, but not the many "hair-breadth escapes" that some claim, but which only occur on paper. Mr. Woodcock is a truthful man, and you can read his autobiography knowing that it is the truth even to the minutest detail."

The autobiography was written by Mr. Woodcock at the request of the Editor of Hunter-Trader-Trapper in the spring of 1908 and published July of the same year. We are glad to add that since that time, Mr. Woodcock has enjoyed several hunting and trapping expeditions. Some were in his home state--Pennsylvania--on same grounds, or at least near those he camped on many, many years ago. He also took a couple of trips into the south--fall of 1911 and 1912. He was in Tennessee, Alabama, Georgia and the Carolinas. An account of these hunts is given in Chapters XXX, XXXI and XXXII.

In May, 1912, the Editor of Hunter-Trader-Trapper visited Mr. Woodcock and family at their home some four miles from Coudersport, Pennsylvania. Mr. Woodcock, though physically not large, is a wonderful man in the "ways of the woods." He is not given to exaggeration or boasting like many a man who has followed the Trail and Trap Line. Every word that he says or writes can be put down as truthful beyond a doubt.

At this time, (May, 1912) he was afraid he would never be able to get out on the trap line again, as he was suffering from rheumatism and heart trouble. Towards fall he became better, and enjoyed the sport, which for more than fifty years has been his--may he be spared to enjoy many more.

By noting the dates as given in connection with various articles published, it will be seen that Mr. Woodcock shortly after 1900 began to point out the need of protection to game and fur animals. After a life on the trap and trail of more than fifty years, such advice should be far reaching. Mr. Woodcock is a man of unusual foresight and knowing that he is nearing the end of the trail, wishes to forcibly impress the needs of protection.

By referring to a good map, you will be able to see the location of many of Mr. Woodcock's hunting, camping and trapping trips, as he generally mentions State, County and Streams.

Very few men have had wider experience than Mr. Woodcock. He knows from more than a half century much of the habits and characteristics of animals. He gives his reasons why marten are plentiful in one section and are gone in a few days. His reason too, looks plausible. He describes trapping wolves in Upper Michigan about 1880, also beaver. Tells how he caught the "shadow of the forests" as wolves are often called by trappers-- they are so hard to trap. By reading of his many experiences you will not only enjoy what he says, but will get facts about bear, deer, fox, wolves, mink, marten and other fur bearers that you had never thought of.

This man, while on the "trail" upwards of fifty years, so far as known never killed out of season or trapped unprime furs.

A WORD FROM MR. WOODCOCK.

The editor of HUNTER-TRADER-TRAPPER has requested a foreword of introductory to FIFTY YEARS A HUNTER AND TRAPPER OR EXPERIENCE OF E. N. WOODCOCK, saying that so many have enjoyed my articles, which have appeared from time to time in HUNTER-TRADER-TRAPPER, extending over a period of some ten years, 1903 to 1913, that same are to be published in book form.

I was born at Lymansville, Potter County, Pennsylvania, August 30, 1844. From early childhood, my nature led me to the Forests and Streams. I have hunted in many of the states of the Far West including the three Pacific States--California, Oregon and Washington. I killed my first panther or cougar in the mountains of Idaho on the headwaters of the Clearwater river. My first real experience in wolfing was in Southeastern Oregon. I met my greatest number of deer in Northwestern California.

I have trapped of late years, in nearly all of the states east of the Mississippi river and also on the White River of Arkansas; also trapped bear and other fur bearing animals and hunted deer in Northern Michigan, also forty years ago.

Another sport which I enjoyed was the "pigeon days." I have netted wild pigeons from the Adirondack Mountains in New York state to Indian Territory--now Oklahoma--trapping them in the states of Michigan, Indiana, Missouri, Pennsylvania and New York.

My nature led me to the Trail and Trap line from early childhood and I have trapped bear and hunted deer in the mountains of Pennsylvania for more than 50 years--half a century--and my picture with my two foxes on my shoulder shows me on the trap line for the season of 1912-13.

March 1, 1913.
E. N. WOODCOCK.

CHAPTER I.
Autobiography of E. N. Woodcock.

I was born on the 30th day of August, A. D. 1844, in a little village by the name of Lymansville, Potter County, Pennsylvania. Lymansville was named after my grandparent, Isaac Lyman, or better known as Major Lyman, having held office of that rank in the Revolutionary War. It is from this limb of the family that I inherited that uncontrollable desire for the trap, gun and the wild.

At a very early age it was my greatest delight to have all the mice, squirrels and groundhogs and in later years young raccoons, young fox and every other varmint or wild animal that I could catch or could get from other sources, and at times I had quite a menagerie.

I began trapping at a very early age, the same as many boys do who live out in the country where they have an opportunity. My father owned a grist mill and a sawmill. These mills were about one-half mile apart and it was about these mills and along the mill races and ponds of these mills that I set my first traps for muskrats, mink and coon. Before I was stout enough to set a trap which was strong enough to hold the varmint, it was necessary for me to get some older person to set the trap. I would take the trap to the intended place and set for the particular animals I was in quest of, whether mink, coon or rat.

In those days clearings were small, woods large and full of game. Deer could be seen in bunches every morning in the fields and it was not uncommon to see a bear's track near the house that had been made during the night. Wolves were not plenty though it was a common thing to see their tracks and sometimes hear them howl on the hills.

Like other boys who lead an outdoor life, I grew stronger each year and as I grew older and stronger my trap lines grew longer and my hunts took me farther into the woods. Finally as game became scarcer my hunts grew from a few hours in length to weeks and months camping in a cabin built in the woods in a section where game was plenty.

At the age of thirteen while out with a party of men on a hunting and fishing trip, I killed my first bear. While I had now been out each fall with my traps and gun, it was not until I was about eighteen years old that I took my first lesson from an old and experienced trapper, a man nearly eighty years old and a trapper and hunter from boyhood. The man's name was Aleck Harris. We made our camp in the extreme southeastern part of this

(Potter) County in a section known as "The Black Forest" and it was here that I learned many things from an experienced trapper and hunter that served me well on the trap line and the trail, in the years that followed.

It was here that I made my first bed in a foot or more of snow with a fire against a fallen tree and a few boughs thrown on the ground for a bed. At other times perhaps a bear skin just removed from the bear for covering, or I might have no covering other than to remove my coat and spread it over me. This I have often done when belated on the trail so that I was unable to reach the cabin and was happy and contented.

It was here I first learned to do up the saddles or the carcass of a deer in the more convenient way to carry. It was here that I took my first practical lessons in skinning, stretching, curing and handling of skins and furs. I also learned many things of traps and trapping and to do away with sheath knives and other unnecessary burdens on the trap line. In my younger days I preferred to "go it alone" when in a country that I was familiar with and many a week I have spent in my cabin alone save for my faithful dog, but as I grew older and became afflicted with rheumatism I have found a partner more acceptable.

I have met with many queer circumstances while on the trap line and trail, yet I have never met with any of those bloodcurdling and hair-breadth escapes from wild animals which are mostly "pipe dreams". Perhaps the nearest I ever came to being seriously hurt by a wild animal was from a large buck deer. It was in November and on a stormy day. I had killed a doe and was in the act of dressing the doe and was leaning over the deer at work. I was within a few feet of a fallen tree. Hearing a slight noise, I raised up to see what caused it, when with the speed of a cannon ball a buck flew past me, barely missing and landed six or eight feet beyond me.

The deer had come up to this fallen tree on the track of the doe and seeing me at work over the doe, became angered and sprung at me and only my straightening up at the very instant that I did saved me from being seriously hurt or perhaps killed. I sprang over the log. The deer stood and gazed at me for a moment. His eyes were of a green hue and the hair on his back all stuck up towards his head. After gazing at me for a moment the deer walked slowly away. The suddenness of the occurrence so unnerved me that I was unable to shoot for some minutes though my gun was standing against the tree within reach.

At another time I was somewhat frightened by what I supposed was a dead bear suddenly coming to life. I had caught the bear in a trap and it had got fastened in some saplings growing on the steep bank of a small brook. I shot the bear in the head, as I thought, and it fell over the bank in such a manner that his whole weight was held by the leg that was fast in the trap. I was unable to release it from the trap where it was hanging as I had no clamp to put the trap springs down with, to release the bear's foot. I had set my gun, a single barrel rifle, against a tree without reloading it.

I cut the bear's paw off close to the trap which allowed the animal to roll down the bank to level ground. I had begun to rip down the leg that had been caught in the trap. A lad of about ten years was with me having accompanied me to attend the traps that day. The lad stood looking on when all of a sudden he said, "See him wink." I stopped my work and glanced at the bear's eyes and sure enough he was winking and winking fast, too, and almost before I knew it the bear was trying to get onto his feet. My gun was unloaded and the lad was screaming at the top of his voice, "Kill him! Kill him!" But what was I to kill him with? Nothing came to my mind at first except to use my gun as a club but I did not like to break it.

In a moment I thought of my hatchet which I had taken from the holster and laid on the bank where I had cut the bear's foot off to release him from the trap. I grabbed the hatchet and one good blow on the head put a stop to the rumpus and nobody harmed, although the boy was badly frightened.

At another time I might have got into trouble with a bear also caught in a trap. I was quite young at this time. I had gone some ten or twelve miles from home and set a trap for a bear. The trap was rather a poor one with a very light chain for a bear trap. I had only set the trap a few days before yet I thought I must go and look after it, but it was more the desire to be in the woods than it was of expecting to have a bear in the trap at that time. I did not take a gun with me, only a revolver loaded as I had no more balls and this was before the days of fixed ammunition.

When I came to the trap there was an ugly bear in it and he had the clog fast in some roots and among some fallen trees. After firing one shot at the Bear's head, which I missed, I then shot the two remaining balls into the bear's body with the only effect of making him more determined to get at me. I now cut a good club determined to put a quietus on Bruin in that manner but after landing several blows my knees began to feel weak. I gave up the job and returned home leaving Bruin in the trap feeling as well as he did when I first found him, so far as I was able to see. But when I returned the next morning with help and now with a regular gun we found Bruin nearly dead and helpless from the shots that I had given him the day before from the revolver.

I have met with other circumstances not quite so fascinating as those just related. At one time a young companion and I were camping and trapping several miles from home and several miles from a road. One day while we were some ways out from camp setting traps my friend became suddenly very ill. It required no skilled doctor to see that it was a case that must have help at once. I started with my friend to get to camp. While my companion was not as old as I, he was larger and heavier. I worked along with him, half carrying him, while he would support himself as best he could. I got him within about a mile of the cabin when he completely gave out and could go no farther and with all my pleadings I could not get him to try to go any farther, but he promised that if I went after help that after resting he would work his way to camp.

Seeing that there was no other way to do, I left him and started for help. It was now dark. My way was over a road of about twelve miles and nearly all the way through a thick woods and part of the way without a road other than a path. When I reached the cabin I stopped long enough to build a fire so that the cabin would be warm when my companion got there if he did get there at all, which I doubted.

I took a lunch in my hand and started for help. I would take a trot whenever the woods were sufficiently open to let in light enough so that I could see my way. I got to my companion's home about midnight and we were soon on the way back with a team and wagon while my companion's father went after a doctor to have him there when we got back with the patient. We drove with the wagon as far as the road would allow, then we left the wagon and rode the horses to the camp.

When we reached the cabin, contrary to expectations, we found my companion there but very sick. We lost no time in getting him onto a horse and starting for the wagon where we had a bed for the patient to lie down on. We got home about eight o'clock in the morning. The doctor was waiting for us and he said as soon as he looked at the man that it was a bad case of typhoid fever. He was right, for it took many weeks before my friend was able to be out again.

When game began to get scarce, that is when game was no longer found plenty right at the door, I began to look for parts where game was plentiful and accordingly, with three companions, I arranged to hunt and trap on Thunder Bay River in Michigan, where deer and all kinds of game, we had been told, were plenty and also lots of fur bearers. This we found to be quite true but the state had passed a law forbidding the shipment of deer. We did not know this when we left home and two of the boys soon got discouraged and returned.

It was while hunting here that I had another trip of twenty miles through the woods over rough corduroy tote road in the night after a team to take my companion (Vanater by name) out to Alpena to have a broken leg set. He was carrying a deer on his shoulder and when near camp it was necessary to cross a small stream to get to the cabin. We had felled a small tree across the creek for the purpose of crossing. There was three or four inches of snow on the log and after my companion was across the creek and just as he was about to step from the log he slipped and fell, striking his leg across the log in some manner so that it broke between the knee and ankle.

After getting my companion to camp and making him as comfortable as possible, I took a lunch in my knapsack and with an old tin lantern with a tallow candle in it, which gave about as much light as a lightning bug, I started over the longest and roughest twenty miles of road that I ever traveled in the night. Sometimes I would trip on some stick or log and fall and put out my light but I would get up, light the candle in the lantern again and hurry on all the faster to make up for lost time. I made the journey all right and was back to camp the next day before noon where we found my companion doing as well as could be expected under the circumstances.

We got my companion out to Alpena where the doctor set the leg and in the course of two or three weeks he was so far recovered that he was able to return to camp and keep me company until he was able to again take up the trap line and trail.

Some years later I again went back to Michigan and hunted deer and trapped on the Manistee, Boardman and Rapid Rivers, but I found game and furs had become somewhat scarce in that part so I next went with a partner to upper Michigan. At that time there was no railroad in Upper Michigan and but few settlers, after leaving the Straits, until near Lake Superior and near the copper and iron mines.

I have tried my luck in three of the states west of the Rocky Mountains. In the Clear Water regions of Idaho there was a fair showing of big game, with a good sprinkling of the fur bearers, including a bunch of beaver here and there. (Beaver protected.) I heard men tell of there being plenty of grizzly and silver tip bear but I saw no signs of them. In California a trapper told, me of a large grizzly coming to his shack in the night. He said that he was cooking venison and that he had the fresh meat of a deer in the shack and he thought that the bear smelled the meat was what brought him there. The man said the bear smelled around the shack awhile and then began to dig at one corner of the shack and soon pulled out the bottom log. The man kept quiet until the bear pulled out the next log and put his head in through the hole when he put a ball between the bear's eyes that fixed Bruin too quick. (A bad case of nightmare.) I think it doubtful if there is a grizzly bear or at least very few now to be found south of the British Columbia line.

My best catch of bear in one season with a partner was eleven. Years ago I caught from three to six bear each season but late years I have not caught more than one to three. I think that of late the heavy lumbering going on through Northern Pennsylvania had something to do with the catch of bear.

The timber in Pennsylvania is largely cut away now leaving bark slashings which make fine shelter for bear and wildcats and both animals were apparently quite plenty I would judge from the number caught in this section, fall of 1907. Deer are very scarce in this state, perhaps the most to be found are in Pike County.

I can lay claim to one thing that but few hunters and trappers can do, that is for forty years I lost only two seasons from the trap line and the trail and each time I was detained by rheumatism. Once being taken down with sciatica while in the camp trapping and hunting, and it held me to my bed for several months hard and tight. I still have the greater part of my trapping and hunting outfit, and am still in hopes to be able to get out on the line and pinch a few more toes.

CHAPTER II.
Early Experiences.

As I promised to write something of my early experience at trapping and hunting, I will begin by saying that I am now living within one mile of where I was born sixty years ago (this was written in 1904), and that I began my trapping career by first trapping rats in my father's grist mill with the old figure four squat trap. I well remember the many war dances that I had when I could not make the trap stay set; but I did not trap long inside the mill for father also ran a blacksmith shop and always kept a good man to do the work in the shop. I was soon coaxing the smith to make me a steel trap, which he did. I now began catching muskrats along the tail race and about the mill dam, but the spring on my trap was so stiff that when I found the trap sprung or found game in it, I was obliged to bring the trap to the house and have some one older than I to set it. Then I would carry it back to the creek and set it. Well this was slow work and I was continually begging the blacksmith to make me more traps with weaker springs so I could set them myself. After much coaxing he made me three more which I was able to set and then the muskrats began to suffer. Let me say at that time a muskrat skin was worth more than a mink skin.

Boys, I was like a man in public office, the more of it they have, the more they want. So it was with me in regard to the traps, but I could not coax the blacksmith to make any more. An older brother came to my aid in this way: he told me to go to town and see the blacksmith there and see if I could not sell some charcoal to him for traps, and he, (my brother) would help me burn the coal. Now this burning the coal was done by gathering hemlock knots from old rotten logs and piling them up and covering them like potato holes, leaving a hole open at the bottom to start the fire. After the fire was well started the hole was closed and the knots smoldered for several days. Well, the plan worked and by the operation I became the possessor of five more traps. By this time the vicinity of the mill dam and race was no longer large enough to furnish trapping grounds, and I ventured farther up and down the stream and took in the coon and mink along with the muskrat.

WOODCOCK, WIFE, SISTER-IN-LAW, RESIDENCE AND HIS DOG MACK.

We had a neighbor, Washburn by name, who was considered a great trapper, for he could now and then catch a fox. As time passed by, I began to have a great desire to get on an equal with Mr. Washburn and catch a fox. I began to urge him to allow me to go with him to see how he set his trap, and after a long time coaxing, he granted my request. I found what everyone of today knows of the chaff bed set. You may now know that it was not long before I had a bed made near a barn that stood well back in the field, and after much worry and many wakeful nights I caught a fox and I thought myself Lord Jonathan. As time went by, and by chance I learned that by mixing a goodly part of hen manure with plenty of feathers in it, and mixing it with the chaff, it was a great improvement on chaff alone. Next I learned of the well known water set. However, I perhaps set different from the most of trappers in making this set. Well as all trappers learn from long years of experience, so have I, and those old-fashioned sets are like the squat traps, not up-to-date. I will now drop the trapping question for a time and tell you how I killed my first deer.

Just outside of the clearing on father's farm and not more than fifty rods from the house was a wet place, such as are known to these parts as a "bear wallow." This wet place had been salted and was what is called a "salt lick." In those days it was not an uncommon thing to see six or eight deer in the field any morning during the summer season--the same as you will see them in parts of California today. It was not an uncommon thing for my older brother to kill a deer at this lick any morning or evening, but that was not making a nimrod of me. I would beg father to let me take the gun (which was an old double barreled flintlock shot gun) and watch the lick. As I was only nine years old, they would not allow me to have the gun, so I was obliged to steal it out when no one was in sight, carry it to the barn and then watch my opportunity and "skipper" from the barn to the lick. All worked smoothly and I got to the lick all right. It was toward sundown and I had scarcely poked the gun through the hole in the blind and looked out when I saw two or three deer coming toward the lick. I cocked the old gun and made ready but about this time I was taken with the worst chill that any boy ever had and I shook so that I could scarcely hold the gun to the peep hole. It was only a moment when two of the deer stepped into the lick, and I took the best aim I could under the condition, and pulled the trigger. Well of all the bawling a deer ever made, I think this one did the worst, but I did not stop to see what I had done but took across the field to the house at a lively gait, leaving the gun in the blind.

The folks heard the shot and saw me running for the house at breakneck speed (this of course was the first that they knew I was out with the gun). My older brother came to meet me and see what the trouble was. When I told him what I had done, he went with me to the lick and there we found a fair-sized buck wallowing in the lick with his back broken, one buck shot (or rather one slug, for the gun was loaded with pieces cut from a bar of lead); one slug had struck and broken the spine and this was the cause of the deer bawling so loud as this was the only one that hit.

The old shotgun was now taken from its usual corner in the kitchen and hung up over the mantle piece above the big fire place and well out of my reach. This did not stop my hunting. We had a neighbor who had two or three guns and he would lend me one of them. I would hide away hen eggs and take them to the grocery and trade them for powder and shot. Of course the man who owned the gun got the game, when I chanced to kill any, for I did not dare to carry it home. It was not long until father found that I was borrowing Mr. Abbott's gun, and he thought that if hunt I would, it would be better that I use our own and then he would know when I was out with it. He took the old flintlock to the gunsmith and had it fixed over into a cap lock, and now I was rigged out with both gun and traps.

I will now tell you about the first bear that I killed. I was about thirteen years old, and it was not so common a thing for one to kill a bear in those days as it is now (1904), for strange as it may seem, bears are far more plentiful here today than they were at that time.

Two of my brothers and three or four of the neighbors went into the woods about twelve miles and bought fifty acres of land. There was no one living within six or seven miles of the place. They cleared off four or five acres and built a good log fence around it. They also built a small barn and cabin. Each spring they would drive their young cattle out to this place, stay a few days and plant a few potatoes, and some corn. About once a month it was customary to go over to this clearing and hunt up the cattle and bring them to the clearing and salt them, then have a day or two of trout fishing, watch licks and kill a deer or two, jerk the meat and have a general good time.

I was allowed to go on one of these expeditions, and the first night the men watched one or two licks and one of the men killed a deer, but I had to stay in camp that night with a promise that I should watch the second night.

During the first night we heard wolves howl away upon the hills. The next morning the men talked very mysteriously about the wolves and said that it would not be safe to watch the licks that night, that no deer would come to the licks as long as the wolves were around. I took it all in and said nothing, but was determined to watch a lick that night. Finally one of the men, John Duell by name, said that I could watch the lick that he had and he would stay in camp. The one that I was to watch was only a short distance from the clearing. When the sun was about one-half hour high, I took the old shot gun, this time loaded with genuine buck shot and climbed the Indian ladder to the scaffold which was built about twenty feet from the ground in a hemlock tree.

I sat quiet until sundown and no deer came. I thought I would tie the gun in the notches in the limbs, which brought the gun in proper range to kill the deer in the lick, should it come after dark. I got one string tied around the barrel and the limb when a slight noise to my left caused me to look in that direction and I saw a dark object standing in the edge of the little thicket, which I took to be a black creature I had seen down near the clearing when I came to the lick. My thoughts were that I would tie the breech of the gun fast to the limb, and then I would climb down and stone the animal away, so I went on tying the gun fast. On looking up I saw that the supposedly black heifer had turned out to be a black bear, and that it was going to go above the lick and not into it. My knife was out in an instant and the next moment I had the strings that held the gun cut. I raised it carefully to my face and about this time the bear stopped, turned his head around and looked back in the direction he had come. This was my chance, and I fired both barrels at his head and shoulders, and immediately there was a snorting, snarling, rolling and tumbling of the bear, but the maneuvers of the bear was no comparison to the screams and shouts that came from me. I was still making more noise than a band of Indians when Mr. Duell arrived on the scene and took in the situation. The other men who were watching other licks thought I had surely been attacked by the wolves by the unearthly yell I was making and the whole party were soon on the ground. The bear was soon dressed and the men gave me the cognomen of the "The Great Hunter of Kentucky" and so ended the killing of my first bear.

I am still in hopes to take the pelts from one or two this fall and winter and later, I will tell of some of the incidents I have seen and experienced while trapping and hunting among them. Perhaps, how a brother of mine got a tenderfoot to ride the carcass of a deer down a steep and hard frozen mountain when there was about two inches of snow on would be interesting.

CHAPTER III.
My First Real Trapping Experience.

When I was about eighteen, I received a letter from a man by the name of Harris, who lived in Steuben County, New York, wherein he stated that a Mr. Lathrop had suggested me as a suitable party to go with him to the region known as Black Forest. This section extends through four counties, the southern part of Potter and Tioga counties, and northern part of Clinton and Lycoming counties, Pa. Every reader knows or has heard of the Black Forest region.

This section was and is still (1910) known as a good bear country. I thought it strange that Mr. Lathrop, a man of much note as a hunter, would recommend me, merely a boy, to go with Mr. Harris and into a region like the Black Forest. As Mr. Lathrop lived about four miles from our place I lost no time in going there to learn who this Mr. Harris was. I was informed that he was an old hunter and trapper about eighty years old and that he wanted a partner more for a companion than a hunter or trapper. Mr. Lathrop had met Mr. Harris while on a fishing tour on the Sinnamahoning waters during the summer and said that he knew nothing of Mr. Harris otherwise than what he saw of him at this meeting and to all appearances he was a fine old gentleman. I showed the letter to father and asked what I should do about it and he replied that he thought I could spend my time to a better advantage in school, but he did not say that I could not go with Mr. Harris. I therefore wrote him that I would be ready at the time mentioned which was the twentieth of October.

Mr. Goodsil, the gunsmith in town, had been at work for some time on a new gun for me. Now that I was going into the woods to hunt in earnest, I was at the gun shop nearly every day, urging Mr. Goodsil to finish my gun which he did and in plenty of time. After I got my gun the days seemed like weeks and the weeks like months. I was constantly in fear that Mr. Harris would not come. But promptly at the time set, in the evening just before sundown, a man with a one horse wagon loaded with bear traps and other traps of smaller size and with one of the worst old rack-of-bones of a horse that I had ever seen, drove up to father's place, stopped and inquired if Mr. Woodcock lived there. I immediately asked if he was Mr. Harris, as I had already guessed who the man was. He replied that he was and said that he took it that I was the lad who was going with him.

Mr. Harris said that "often an old horse and a colt" worked well together and that we would make a good team. While we were putting his horses away I asked him what he intended to do with the old horse and he replied that he brought him along so that if we got stuck he could hitch him on and help out. The other horse was a fine horse and I was at a loss to know what Mr. Harris meant.

During the evening I thought father and Mr. Harris talked on every other subject rather than hunting but I managed to put in a few questions now and again as to what we were to do when we arrived at the great Black Forest.

Mr. Harris was a tall, broad-shouldered man with a long beard nearly as white as snow. We were up early the next morning and on our way before daylight. Our route was over the road known as the Jersey Shore turnpike but after the first four miles we went through an unbroken wilderness for twenty miles, save only one house, then known as the Edcomb Place, now called Cherry Springs. The next place, ten miles farther on, was a group of four or five shacks called Carter Camp, but known now as Newbergen. This was in the year 1863 and the conditions over this road are the same today only the large timber has been mostly cut away and there is no one living at Cherry Springs. Five miles farther on we came to Oleana, where there was a hotel and store, owned by Henry Anderson, a Norwegian, who came to this country as the private secretary of Ole Bull, the great violinist, and it was here where the much talked of Ole Bull Castle was built.

Beg pardon, I guess I am getting off the trap line. We stopped at the hotel for the night and the next morning purchased supplies sufficient to last during the entire campaign, consisting of lard, pork, flour, corn meal, tea, coffee, rice, beans, sugar and the necessary salt, pepper, etc. I remember well when Mr. Harris ordered fifty pounds of beans and asked me if I thought that would do? I replied that I thought it would. In my mind I wondered what we would do with all those beans. But now I wish to say to the man going into camp on a long hunting and trapping campaign, don't forget the beans as they are bread and meat.

We are now within about ten or twelve miles of where we intended to camp, which was at the junction of the Bailey and Nebo Branches of Young Woman's Creek. It was about the middle of the afternoon of the second day we were out and Mr. Harris said that here would be a good place to build the camp. We got the horses out as soon as we could and Mr. Harris picked out a large rock; one side had a straight, smooth side and was high and broad enough for one end of the shanty and there was a fine spring close by. Mr. Harris pointed to the rock and said that there we had one end of our camp already as well as a good start towards the fire place.

He told me to begin the cutting of logs for the other two sides and the other end. We cut the logs a suitable size to handle well and about twelve and fourteen feet long. Mr. Harris did the planning while I did the heavy part of the work.

That night we slept under a hemlock tree and were up the next morning and had breakfast before daylight and ready for the day's work. We could see scuds of clouds away off in the southwest which Mr. Harris said did not show well for us. He had brought a good crosscut saw and it was not long until we had logs enough cut to put up the sides, about four feet high and logs for one end. We hauled the logs all up with the horse so they would be handy. Then we began the work of notching and putting up the logs.

About noon a drizzling rain started and kept it up all the afternoon. We covered our provisions and blankets the best we could to keep them dry and continued to work on the camp. We got the body up, the rafters and a part of the roof on. We put up a ridge roof as Mr. Harris said it would not be necessary to have the sides quite so high with a steep ridge roof. We got our supplies under shelter and had a dry place to sleep that night. It was still raining in the morning but we continued to work on the camp like beavers all day and we got shakes split from a pine stub to finish the roof and chinking blocks to chink between the logs.

The next morning Mr. Harris said that he would go and take the horse out to a farm house that was about six miles out the turnpike, known as the Widow Herod Place, or better known as Aunt Bettie. Mr. Harris said he would go while there was food enough to last the old horse a day or two until we were ready to use him. Then I knew that the old horse was doomed to be used for bear bait.

When Mr. Harris started away with the horse he cautioned me not to go off hunting, but to stick to work on the shanty which I did like a "nailer." When Mr. Harris returned I had the roof on, the chinking all in and the gable end boarded up with shakes and all ready to begin calking and mudding. It was some time in the afternoon when he got back and after looking over the shack to see what I had done he said that he thought I had done so well that I was entitled to a play spell and suggested that we take our guns and go down along the side of the hill and see if we could kill a deer, remarking that we could use a little venison if we had it. He told me to go up onto the bench near the top of the hill while he would take the lower bench and he would hunt the side hill along down the stream until dark.

Mr. Harris had a single barrel gun with a barrel three or four feet long which he called Sudden Death, and it weighed twelve or fourteen pounds. As for me I had my new double barrel gun which I have mentioned before. We had not gone far until I heard the report of a gun below me and soon I heard Mr. Harris "ho-ho-hoa," and I hurried to where the howling came from and found him already taking the entrails out of a small doe. I suggested to Mr. Harris that we take the deer down to the creek before we dressed it and that by so doing we probably could catch a mink or coon with the entrails. He consented to do so and after we had taken out the entrails Mr. Harris noticed a fine place to catch a fox or some other animal and pointed to a large tree that had fallen across the stream.

The tree had broken in two at the bank, on the side of the stream where we were. The water had swung the trunk of the tree down the stream until there was a space of three or four feet between the end of the tree and the bank. Mr. Harris took a part of the offal from the deer and carried it across to the opposite bank and placed the remainder on the side where we were. He then placed an old limb for a drag to the trap at the place where he wanted to set the trap. As we had no traps with us we went to camp and early the next morning we took two traps and went to this place and set them.

We put in that day finishing the camp, putting in the door and fixing the chimney to the fireplace and calking all the cracks between the logs and mudded tight between the logs and all the joints. Now the camp being completed we began setting the bear traps. The old horse was taken onto a chestnut ridge and shot, cut up into small pieces suitable for bear bait, and hung up in small saplings such as we could bend down. After the bait was fastened to the tree we let it spring up so as to keep it out of the reach of any animal until we had a trap set.

The way Mr. Harris set a bear trap was to build a V shaped pen about three feet long and about the same in height, place the bait in the back end of the pen and set the trap in the entrance. We had eleven bear traps and after they were all set on different ridges where bears were most likely to travel, we began the work of setting the small traps which was not a long job, as we had only about forty.

The next morning Mr. Harris said that I had better go down and see if the traps we had set had been disturbed and he said that he would rest while I was gone.

When I came in sight of the traps I could see a fox bounding around in one of the traps. I could see on looking at the trap we had placed across the creek that the drag had been moved closer to the log but I could see nothing moving. I cut a stick and killed the fox when I crossed over to see what was in the other trap and to my disgust there was a skunk. I was not particularly in love with skunks in those days, for while they scented just as loud at that time as now they were vastly lacking in the money value. I took hold of the clog and carefully dragged the skunk to the creek and sank him in the water. I now went back to the other side of the creek and set the fox trap and when I had the trap set the skunk was good and dead. I reset the trap and took the fox and skunk to camp without skinning. When I got to camp I found Mr. Harris busy making stretching boards of different sizes for different animals from shakes that we had left when covering the roof. Mr. Harris laughed and said that he knew that we would need them when I got back. The fox and skunk were skinned, stretched and hung up on the outside of the gable of the shack, and that was the starting point of our catch of the season.

We set the most of our small traps along the streams for foxes and mink, taking a few to the ridges to set in likely places to catch a fox, and at thick laurel patches where we were likely to catch a wild cat as there was a bounty of $2 on them.

After the small steel traps were set we began building a line of deadfalls for marten and fisher. After the deadfalls were built we divided our time between hunting deer and tending the traps.

We caught three bears, two fisher, which were very scarce, as I do not think that fishers were ever very plentiful in this state, a good bunch of marten, foxes, four or five wildcats and killed twenty-two deer. The last days of December Mr. Harris said that we would prepare to go home as the deer season closed the first of January. Although the law gave until the fifteenth to get your deer we had dragged the most of ours up to the Bailey Mill at various times. We got all those around the mill and sent them to Jersey Shore by freight teams to the railroad, then shipped them to New York. We got 15 cents for saddles and 10 cents for the whole deer.

Mr. Harris had brought an auger with him so that he could make a sleigh to go home with and from birch saplings we made one and on the thirteenth of January I went and got the horse. He was as fat as a pig and felt like a colt. We hitched him up to the sleigh and got our stuff up to the Bailey Mill where we loaded the wagon onto the sleigh and piled on the furs and the rest of our outfit and early on the morning of the fourteenth we started for home. This ended my first real experience as a hunter and trapper.

I received two or three letters from Mr. Harris, the last one in which he stated that he was not feeling very well and I never heard from him again.

CHAPTER IV.
Some Early Experiences.

In 1871 or 1872 I had several bear traps made by our local blacksmith and I started in as a bear trapper and went it alone. After being out with Mr. Harris I had taken some valuable lessons on trapping bear and other animals. I built a good log camp on the West Branch of Pine Creek and went to trapping and hunting without either partner or companion, but after being in camp the first season I bought a shepherd dog that was a year old and broke him for still hunting and trapping. I found that a good intelligent dog was not only a companion but also a valuable one. I have noticed that some trappers do not want a dog on the trap line with them, claiming that the dog is a nuisance. This is because the dog was not properly trained.

To get back to the bear trapping: In the locality where I was trapping, bear were not very plentiful except in season, when there was a crop of beechnuts, although there was but little other shack, such as chestnuts and acorns. However, some seasons there would be an abundance of black cherries which the bears are very fond of. I set three traps at the head of a broad basin where there were three or four springs and the next day I set the balance of my bear traps; then I built a few deadfalls for coons and set a few steel traps for fox.

As I had seen several fresh bear tracks crossing the stream, where I had been setting the coon traps, on the morning of the third day after I had set the first three bear traps, I thought that I would go and look after them. They were about a mile and a half from camp and when I came in sight of the first trap I saw that I had a bear. You may be sure that I again felt like a mighty hunter. I was more pleased over this one bear than I was over the eight bear we had caught when I was with Mr. Harris, because now I was the trapper and not Mr. Harris. The bear was a good sized female. She had become fast only a short distance from where the trap was set. I shot and skinned the bear then cut the carcass into quarters, bent down a sapling and hung a quarter of the bear on this. With a forked pole I raised the sapling up until the meat was out of the way of small animals that might happen along.

After hanging up three of the quarters in this manner, leaving one to take to camp, I took the lungs and liver and put them in the bait pen. The bait had all been eaten and I was quite sure it had been done after the bear was caught, as a bear immediately loses its appetite after placing its foot in a good, strong trap. I really expected to find another bear in one of the other traps as they were not far away, but the other traps were undisturbed.

The next morning I thought I would take some bait from camp and bait the trap where I had put the offals from the bear, fearing that should a bear come along it might not eat the bait that was in the pen. You may imagine my surprise when I came in sight of the trap to see another bear fast in the trap.

After killing the bear I removed the entrails and started to carry the bear to camp. It was a cub and I could carry it without cutting it in parts. I was just about to start for camp when I decided I would go to the other traps. If I was surprised at seeing the first cub, I was doubly so, for there was another cub tangled up in the trap. Do you think I felt gay? Well, that was no name for it.

I shot this cub and without waiting to dress it I took a lively gait to the other trap to see if there were any more bears but there was nothing there. The last two bears, I think were the cubs of the old bear that I had caught the night before. I spent the entire day getting the bears to camp. I did not get any more bear for some time although I had an opportunity to learn a whole lot about them.

Some days after I got the old bear and the cubs, I found the bait pen in one of the traps torn down by a bear, which had taken the bait and had not sprung the trap. Right here I will say that I learned a great deal more about the habits of Bruin. After finding the bait gone I thought that all I would have to do was to make the bait pen a little stronger so Bruin could not tear it down so readily to get at the bait. I did not think that a bear knew anything about "trapology," for the experience I had so far in bear trapping was that bears knew but little more about a trap than a hog, though later I found I was very much mistaken.

SETTING A LARGE STEEL TRAP FOR BEAR.

The trap was set in a small brook where there were plenty of rocks of all sizes. I rolled several of these rocks, as large as I could handle, up about the bait pen to strengthen it to such an extent that Bruin would not think of tearing it down. I figured the bear by going over the trap would take the bait from the entrance of the pen as a good bear should; though in this I was greatly mistaken. The second day I went to the trap with full expectation of finding Bruin fast in the trap, but again I was disappointed-- Bruin had again gone to the back of the pen and torn the top of the pen off, rolling away some of the stones, taking the bait.

Now I saw that if I was to get my friend Bruin, I would have to work a little strategy. I removed the trap from the clog, leaving the clog undisturbed and making all appear just the same as it did when the trap was set. I was very careful to have the covering of the trap left just the same as when the trap was set. Then I got another clog and set the trap at the back of the pen at the place where the bear had torn off the top of the bait pen. Here I concealed the trap and clog as completely as I knew how and being very careful to make all appear just as before the trap was set, flattering myself that Bruin would surely put his foot in it this time.

I went early the next morning, being sure that I would find Bruin, but no bear had been there. I went again early the next morning with high expectations of finding Bruin waiting for me, but again nothing had been disturbed. Thinking that Bruin had left that locality altogether, or that he would not be back again for several days, I thought I would go and have a team come and take out the furs and game I had, and give Bruin time to get back after more bait. As I had caught no bear at the other traps, I felt quite certain that Bruin was still somewhere in the neighborhood and would be around again after more bait.

When I reached home an old gentleman by the name of Nelson who was a noted hunter and trapper and who lived near us, came to see me. Let me explain who this Mr. Nelson was, as I shall have more to say of him.

Mr. Nelson was one of the early settlers in this county, moving here at an early date from Washington County, New York State. He was known here as Uncle Horatio and by many as Squire Nelson, as he was a Justice of the Peace here for thirty years.

Mr. Nelson would always come to our house as soon as he found that I was at home, to see what luck I had in the way of trapping and hunting. On this occasion, Mr. Nelson, or Uncle Horatio, as we always called him, was soon over to learn what luck I had and when I told him what sort of a time I had trying to outwit the bear, he said I had better build a deadfall and let the bear kill himself. Uncle said that Bruin would give me much trouble and was likely to leave and I would not get him at all. This idea I did not like, for I had, before this, been put to my wit's end to outwit a cunning old fox, but finally succeeded in catching him and I thought I could outwit such a dumb thing as a bear. I thought if I could not get the bear in a steel trap, there would be but little use trying to get him in such a clumsy thing as a deadfall--however, Uncle had trapped bear long before I was born and knew what he was talking about.

As soon as I got back to camp I went to the bear trap to relieve Bruin of his troubles, but it was not the bear that was in trouble, but myself, for Bruin had been there and torn out a stone at one side of the pen and had taken the bait. Well, the case was getting desperate, so I got another trap and set it at the side where the bear took the bait the last time, taking all the pains possible in setting the trap, but the result was no better than before.

I had made it a habit to hang on a small bait near the bear traps, believing that the bear would be attracted by the scent of the bait hanging up from the ground more than it would from the bait in the pen. At this trap I had hung up the bait in a bush that extended out from the bank over the brook and each time the bear had taken this bait. I now took one of the traps at the pen, leaving the clog and all appearances as though the trap still remained there. Getting another clog I concealed it under the edge of the bank and set the trap under the bait that I had hung in the bush. I was certain this time that I would outwit Bruin, but instead, the bear went onto the bank, pulled the bush around, took the bait and went about his business. Now I was getting pretty excited and began to think of the advice of Uncle Horatio but I was not willing to give up yet.

Up the brook, fifty or sixty feet from the bait pen, there had fallen a small, bushy hemlock tree which stood on the right hand bank of the spring, and the top of the tree reached nearly over to the opposite bank. I had noticed that when the bear had come to the trap he had come down the brook and went back the same way. The water was shallow in the brook, barely covering the stones and fallen leaves all over the bed of the brook. Going to the top of the hemlock tree, I saw that the bear had passed between the top of this tree and the bank of the brook. Here was a fine place to conceal the trap and I said, "Old fellow, here I will surely outwit you." I took the trap from the bait pen and set it in the open space between the top of the tree and concealing all the very best I could, I again put more bait in the bait pen and hung up more on the bush.

I waited two days and then went to the traps again, wondering all the way what the result would be. Well, it was the same as before. The bear had gone to the bush on the bank, taken the bait, and had also taken the bait from the bait pen as usual. Now I thought it quite time to try Uncle's plan, though I had but little faith in it.

It was several miles to Mr. Haskins', the nearest house, but I lost no time in getting there for I was now feeling desperate. Mr. Haskins readily consented to help me build a deadfall. We cut a beech tree that was about fourteen inches through, that stood back in thick undergrowth some rods from the bait pen. We cut a portion about four feet long from the large end of the tree for the bed-piece and placing it against the small tree for one of the stakes. With levers we placed the tree on top of the bed-piece and with three other good stakes driven at each side of the logs fastened the tops of the stakes together with withes to strengthen them, we soon had a good, strong deadfall made, as every boy who is a reader of the H-T-T, knows how to build. We baited the trap and set it, getting done in time for Mr. Haskins to get home before dark.

I again put bait back in the bait pen and on the bush as before and patiently awaited results. The second day I looked after the traps but there were no signs of bear being about either the deadfall or the steel traps and I feared that I had frightened Bruin out of the country in building the deadfall. I put in three or four days looking after other traps, thinking but little about the bear that had, so far, been beyond my skill.

After three or four days, I again went to the deadfall, wondering and imagining all kinds of things. When I came to the steel traps the bait was still undisturbed and I was now sure that that particular bear was not for me, but when I stepped into the thicket so that I could see the deadfall, there was Bruin, good and dead. When I looked at the bear I found that he had three toes gone from one foot and this I thought to be the cause of his being so over-shy of the steel traps.

I learned a lesson that has since served me more than one good turn.

* * *

In later years it was customary for many of my friends to come to my camp and spend a few days with me. It was of one of these occasions that I will relate. Two young men, named Benson and Hill, had sent me word that they were coming out to my camp and hunt a few days; also to go with me to my bear traps but added that they did not suppose that I would get a bear while they were in camp, even if they would stay all winter.

It had been drizzling sort of a rain for several days and every old bear hunter knows that dark, lowery weather is the sort bears like to do their traveling in. I had set the time to go out on a stream known as the Sunken Branch, to look after some fox traps and also two bear traps that I had in that section the day I got word from Benson and Hill that they would be over to camp the next day. I thought I would put off going to look after the traps in that locality until the boys came over and should I have the luck to find a bear in one of the traps it would come very acceptable to have the help to get the bear to camp for it was some four or five miles to the farthest trap.

The boys came as they said but the next morning after they got there it was raining very hard and they did not want to go out and did not want me to go until it slacked up. Well, the next morning it was raining hard and the boys were in no better mood to go out than the day before. It had been several days since I had been to the traps, in that direction, and there were some chestnuts in that locality where the bear traps were set. The storm had knocked the chestnuts out and it was probable that bears would be in that locality. I told the boys I did not like to let the traps go any longer without looking after them and they could stay in camp and I would go to the traps. When I was about ready to start, Hill said that he would go with me, notwithstanding the rain, though Benson tried to persuade us not to go, stating that no bear was fool enough to travel in such a rain and that all we would get would be a good thorough soaking.

I was determined to delay no longer looking at the traps and started off when Hill said, "Well, I'm with you." So we took the nearest cut possible to reach the traps. Hill was continually wishing we would find a bear in one of the traps and that he could shoot it so that he could joke with Benson.

Our route took us along the top of a ridge for about three miles when we dropped off to the first trap. When we were still half way up the side of the ridge I saw that Hill had got his wish for I could see a bear rolling and tumbling about down in the hollow and knew that it was fast in the trap. I tried to point it out to Hill but he could not get his eye on it, so we went farther down the hill when Jim (that was Hill's given name) could see the bear. He said there was no need of going closer, that he could shoot it from where we were, but I said we must go closer as I did not like to make holes in the body of the skin unnecessarily. We had only taken a few steps farther when Jim said we were plenty close, that he could, shoot it from where we were and that if we should go closer the bear might break out of the trap and escape.

With all my urging I could not get Hill closer so I told him to be sure that he shot the bear in the head and not in the body. I discovered that Hill was very nervous and told him to take all the time necessary to make a sure shot. When the gun cracked I saw a twig fall that the gun had cut off fully three feet above the bear's head. I urged Hill a few yards closer when he tried again with no better results than the first shot. After making the third shot Hill said he guessed that I had better shoot the bear as he thought something had gone wrong with the sights on his gun. It was raining hard so I killed the bear and took the entrails out, set the trap again and left the bear lying on the ground. As it was a small bear we concluded to take the bear to camp whole.

We hurried on to the next trap which was about a mile farther down the stream. When we got to where the trap was set it was gone, but the way things were torn up we could see that we had a bear this time that was no small one.

The bear had worked down the stream, first climbing the hill on one side of the stream until it became entangled in a jam of brush or old logs, then back down the hill and up on the other side until it became discouraged, when it would try the other side again. The bear was continuously getting the clog fast under the roots of trees or against old logs when it would gnaw the brush and tear them out by the roots. It was also noticed where he would rake the bark on the trees in trying to climb them, in hopes of escaping the drag that was following him. The bear would gnaw and tear old logs to pieces whenever the clog became fast against them.

This was all very interesting and exciting to Hill and he said he would give Benson the laugh when we got to camp. Hill had made me promise not to tell Benson how he had shot three times at the bear's head and missed it.

The bear had worked his way down the stream nearly a mile from where the trap was set, when we came upon him and shot him at once. Hill declaring that it was getting too near night and raining too hard for him to practice on shooting bear any more that day.

We skinned the bear, hung up the meat, took the trap and skin and went back up the creek and set the trap in the same place again. Taking the bear skin we started back to where we left the other bear. After carrying the whole bear and bear skin until it was dark, we hung the bear skin up in the crotch of a tree, taking the bear and hurrying to camp at as lively a gait as we were able to make.

Hill said that while we had had a pretty rough day of it he would make it all up in getting the joke on Benson if I would not give him away on shooting the bears, as Hill was to tell Benson all about how he did it.

Before we came to camp I said to Hill that if he cared to we would play a joke on Benson. He wished to know what the plan was. I said that we would fix the bear up in the path that led from the shack to the spring and get Benson to go after a pail of water and run onto the bear. So we planned to have Benson think that we got no bear and after supper was over I was to take the pail and start to the spring after a pail of fresh water when Hill was to interfere and insist that Benson should go for the water as he had been in camp all day and needed exercise.

It was about a hundred feet from the shack to the spring and down quite a steep bank and about half way from the shack to the spring was a beech log across the path. When we got near camp we made no noise and when we came to the spring we washed our hands carefully to remove any blood that might be on them. Then we took the bear to the log that was across the path and placed the forepaws and shoulders up over the log leaving the hind parts on the ground, then with a small crotched stick placed under the bear's throat to hold up its head we had it fixed up to look as natural as we were able to in the dark.

We went into the shack looking as downcast as a motherless colt. It was unnecessary to deny getting any bear for Benson told us almost before we were inside that we should have known that we would get no bear in any such weather as we were having and none but simpletons would have gone out in such rain.

We ate our supper which Benson had waiting for us. We had little to say farther than to talk of what a fearful rain we were having. After supper was over I took the water pail, though it was nearly full of water, and threw the water out the door before Benson had time to object, saying that I would get a pail of fresh water. Hill said that we should let Benson go after the water as he had not been out of the shanty all day and needed some fresh air. Benson consented to go after another pail of water although he said that he had brought the water that we had thrown out just before we came. I told Benson that I would hold the light at the door so he could see but Benson replied that I need not bother, all that was necessary was to leave the door of the shack open so that he could see his way back.

About the time that Benson reached the log he gave a terrible howl and we heard the water pail go rattling through the brush and when we got to the door Benson was coming on all fours, scrambling as fast as he could and yelling "Bah--bah--bear--bear!"

Hill nor I could not keep from roaring with laughter, and finally Hill managed to say, "Oh, you didn't see any bear."

Benson made no reply but was as white as a sheet and shook as though he had the ague. We could not conceal our feelings and when Benson found his speech he said, "You think you are mighty cunning; if you got a bear why didn't you say so and not act like two dumb idiots."

We had laughed so hard that Benson caught on and the game was up.

Well, after Benson was onto our joke, nothing would do but we must get the bear in and skin out the fore parts so we could have some bear meat cooked before we went to bed. Every time Hill awoke during the night he would burst out laughing while Benson would hurl a few cuss words at him.

The next day we brought in the skin and saddles of the other bear, leaving the fore quarters for fox and marten bait.

The rain now being about over with and the ground and leaves thoroughly soaked, it was a good time for still hunting deer, so we were all out early the next morning. We started out together and soon became separated and it so happened that I was the only one to get a deer during the day. When I got to camp I found Benson was not in yet, so I did not tell that I had killed a deer, but thought I would wait until Benson came in and see what luck he had. If he had not killed anything I would give him the hint and let him have the credit of killing the deer that I got as a sort of off-set on Hill on the bear hunt. I stayed outside gathering dry limbs for wood until I saw Benson coming and I planned to meet him before Hill got to talk to him. I learned that Benson had not killed anything, so I told him where I had killed the deer and that if he cared to he could claim the deer as his game. Benson was much pleased with the idea and as I had told him just where I had killed the deer it was easy for Benson to explain to Hill where the deer was shot. Hill did not believe that Benson had killed a deer and said he would not believe he (Benson) had killed one if he did not know that he had been alone and anyway he must see the deer before he would believe it. I took the first opportunity when Hill was out to tell

Benson which way to go so that he would be sure to find the deer and the next morning the boys went out and brought in the deer while I went to look after some traps. The boys stayed a day or two longer and then went home declaring that they had had the best hunt of their lives.

I will now tell of some of my hunting and trapping with Mr. Nelson and my first experience with a big cat. About 1860, when I was a mere chunk of a boy, a man by the name of Perry Holman was camping on the extreme headwaters of Pine Creek, hunting and trapping. Early one morning Mr. Holman came out of the woods after groceries and other necessaries. On his way out he saw where a small bear had crossed the road just at the top of the hill on the old Jersey Shore turnpike and about five miles from Mr. Nelson's place. Mr. Nelson at that time always kept one or two good bear dogs. Mr. Holman told Mr. Nelson of the bear's track and said that the bear had gone into a laurel patch on the west side of the road and that the track was very fresh. He thought if Mr. Nelson would take his dogs and go out that he could get the bear without much trouble as he believed the bear would still be in the laurels close to the road.

Mr. Nelson told Mr. Holman to get his groceries while he would come to see if I would go along to look after the team while Mr. Nelson and Mr. Holman went into the laurels after the bear. Of course, I was ready for anything that had hunt in it. The sleighing was good and Mr. Nelson was soon ready, taking his dogs into the sleigh so that they would not break off on the track of a deer or some other animal.

When we came to where Mr. Holman saw the bear or cub, Mr. Nelson, or Uncle as we always called him, said to Mr. Holman before he got out of the sleigh:

"Perry, that is no cub's track; that is a big cat and I think we will find him in the laurel patch."

Uncle told me to stay with the team and that they would not be gone long; that if the track led off he would come back to the sleigh and I could go back with the team and he would go to Mr. Holman's camp and stay over night and come home the next day.

The dogs were anxious to take the trail, but Uncle held them in to the laurels. They had not been gone more than ten minutes when the dogs began to give tongue like mischief. I could see that the dogs were coming towards the road and in about a minute saw the biggest cat that I had ever seen at that time, shinning up a large tree that was not further than fifty yards from the sleigh. The dogs were soon at the tree barking their best and in a few minutes I heard the crack of a gun and the big cat seemed to fly out into the air. I could hear the cat go threshing down through the limbs on the trees and the dogs doubled their howling and I could hear the men laugh. I called to the men to see if they got the cat. Uncle told me to watch the horses and they would soon be there, and they were soon in sight dragging a large panther instead of either a cub or cat. Uncle drove down to where Holman's path left the road to go down to his camp and we then drove back home. Uncle was greatly pleased over Perry's cat hunt as Mr. Nelson called it.

* * *

In or about the year '67 or '68, Uncle Horatio Nelson, whom I have spoken of before, had for years been accustomed to going to Edgecomb Place, later known as Cherry Springs, to hunt and trap. Wolves were then more plentiful than foxes are at the present time.

I will explain that Cherry Springs was simply a farm house built of logs. This house was located about half way through, or in the center of a dense forest of about twenty miles square. The Jersey Shore turnpike ran through this vast forest and the stage or any traveler going through this region were obliged to stop at this house to feed at noon, or to stop over night, this being the only house on the road.

From where this house was located there was easy access to the waters of Pine Creek, which flowed east, to the waters of the Cross Fork of Kettle Creek, which flowed south and to the waters of the East Fork of the Sinnamahoning which flowed west. There was no one living on any of these streams for many miles. This was the point where Mr. Nelson, or Uncle, as I shall call him, hunted for many years.

At the time I am writing of, it had been a noted place for many hunters to stop from all parts of the country. There were almost too many hunters stopping at Cherry Spring to suit Uncle as he was getting pretty well along in years and did not like so much company. I had been camping a greater part of the time for several seasons about five miles north of Cherry Springs and one day Uncle said, if I cared to, he would go on to Crossfork and build a cabin and we would hunt and trap, more particularly trap. This was satisfactory to me although I had a good camp where I was trapping and in a fairly good locality for game, but the Crossfork country was a little farther in the tall timber so I thought that the change might be a good thing.

About the first of October we took a team, went into the woods and cut out a sort of a turkey trail from the wagon road down to Boon Road Hollow to the Hog's Back branch of the Crossfork, where we selected a sight for the camp. We felled a large hemlock tree and cut off four logs of suitable length to make the body of the camp about ten by twelve feet inside. We worked them around in shape fitting the two shorter logs in between the ends of the two longer logs; then placing rafters at about half pitch, put on the covering, chinked and calked all the cracks and built a chimney of stones, sticks and clay and put in a door.

We were now ready for the trap line. We set the bear traps on different ridges where we thought would be the most likely places for bears to travel. Then we put out two lines of deadfalls for marten. We then took the different branches and spring runs, building more deadfalls for mink and coons, setting the greater part of our steel traps for foxes. After all the steel traps but three or four were set, Uncle said that if I would go down the creek and set the balance of the steel traps, he would go and look after the first of the bear traps that we had set. I set the steel traps for foxes and built one or two more deadfalls farther down the creek. I think that I found a mink and one coon in the deadfalls that we had set in that section.

I got to camp about dark but Uncle had not come yet. I hustled supper to have it ready when he came, but when supper was ready I could neither see nor hear anything of him. After waiting some time I concluded to eat and then if he did not come I would go in the direction he had taken as I now suspected that he had gotten a bear and was bringing in what he could carry and that I would meet him and help him in with his load. Before I started out to see if I could find him I gave several long and loud "coohoopes," but got no answer. I concluded I would fire a couple of gunshots and see if I could get an answer, but got no reply save the hoot of an owl.

I now began to feel alarmed, fearing that some misfortune had happened Uncle as he knew every rod of the ground in that section. I had no lantern so I made two good torches from fat pine, having a good supply in camp, and followed the stream until I came to a little draw where we had a bear trap set. This trap had not been disturbed, so I climbed the hill to the top of the ridge when I fired two more gunshots but still got no response. I was now thoroughly alarmed as I knew that a gunshot on the still night air could be heard a long ways from the high ridge I was on.

With the aid of another torch I hurried on to the next bear trap and upon arriving at the second trap I saw that the clog was gone and that there was a trail leading off through the leaves and undergrowth. I now knew that it was something in connection with the bear that was detaining Uncle, but what it was I could not tell.

I followed the trail with the aid of the torch for fifty yards when I came to a fallen tree that lay up about a foot from the ground. Here I found the clog that had been fastened to the trap. I could see that the trap ring had been moved from the clog by the aid of a hatchet. I searched about but could find no signs of the trap nor of the bear and I could no longer follow the trail by the aid of the torch, the last one being now pretty well burned out. There was nothing for me to do but go back to camp and wait until morning.

When I was within a mile or less of camp, I heard the report of a gun in the direction of camp and knew that Uncle had arrived and was firing his gun to let me know that he was in camp. I answered the call by firing my gun and hurried on to camp to see what had detained him.

The bear had gone over the fallen tree while the end of the clog had caught under the log and a weak link in the trap chain had given away, Bruin going off with the trap. Uncle had followed the bear several miles when dark came on. He followed down the stream to where it came in to the branch that the camp was on, and being over a ridge and so far from the camp was the cause of him not hearing the gunshots that I had fired. Uncle followed the bear until dark so as to know about where he was in case a snow should fall to fill up the trail.

It was after midnight when we turned in but we were up in good season the next morning and taking a lunch in our knapsacks and each a blanket, we started for the wind jam to see if we could find the bear. Uncle took me to the bear's trail at the edge of the wind jam where I waited, giving him time to get around on the opposite side of the jam, at a point, where the bear was likely to come out, provided I should start him. I had not followed the trail far into the jam before I came to where the bear had made a bed by breaking down briers and gnawing down saplings, but he did not stay long at this place when he again went on.

I soon came to another such bed and after finding several more, came to one that was fresher than the others. I could see that the bed had been made during the night. I now began to work my way along the trail very cautiously with my gun in hand ready for action and my heart in my mouth for I knew that Bruin would soon be on the move. I worked my way through the jam at a snail's pace and soon heard the rattle of the trap and could see the brush move not more than a hundred feet away.

The undergrowth was so thick that I could get no distinct sight of the bear but fired a shot more to let Uncle know that Bruin was on the move than of any expectation of hitting him. When the gun cracked the bear gave a snort like that of a frightened hog and I could hear him tearing through the brush at a great rate. It was not long until I heard Uncle shoot and in the course of two or three minutes I heard him shoot again and knew that Bruin had given up the trap.

After I had gone along the trail quite a ways, I saw a few drops of blood now and then and when I reached Uncle he was already skinning the bear. We found three holes in the bear. Uncle's second shot which was the finishing shot, hit the bear in the head. The shot that I fired caught Bruin just forward of the hips and undoubtedly would have killed him in time.

We skinned the bear and took the hind quarters, the skin and trap and started for camp. I must say that I think this was the hardest stunt of packing that I remember and every old trapper knows what sort of a job of toting he often runs up against. We went down the run about two miles before coming to the stream that our camp was on, and then we had to go up this stream about four miles to camp. When we reached the stream it was dark; there was no path and there was a great deal of fallen timber and undergrowth along the creek, the creek winding around from one side of the valley to the other. It was a continual fording of the creek, climbing over fallen timber, through undergrowth and what not. You know no one but a trapper would be silly enough to do such a stunt in the dark. We arrived at camp about 9 o'clock, wet, tired and hungry. The next morning Uncle was still a little sore but I was as good as new and ready for another job of the same kind.

Some days later we had a fall of snow of several inches and the second or third day after the snow came we heard a number of gunshots south of the camp on the ridge in the direction that we had a bear trap set. It was near sundown and as we were not aware that there was anyone camping or living in the direction of the gunshots, we concluded it was hunters shooting at deer. The shots were at such long intervals that Uncle said he did not think it was anyone shooting at deer and that the shots sounded like they were right where we had a bear trap set and that he thought hunters had run onto a bear in our trap and were shooting at it. It was then too late to go to the trap. Uncle said we would get up early in the morning for he was sure the gunshots were close in the neighborhood in which our trap was set, and he thought it likely that we had a bear in the trap.

We were on the way before it was fairly daylight but when we came to the place where the trap had been set we found it gone. We followed the trail a short distance when the tracks of three men came onto the trail. The men had stamped and tracked about where they came onto the trail as though they were holding a council and then all started off on the trail of the bear. They did not go far before they came up with the bear where the trap clog had become fast between two saplings. The trap was nowhere to be seen. The men had made many tracks where they killed the bear.

Uncle said it looked as though the men intended to steal the bear trap and all. We saw where the track of a man led off towards a large log and returned. Uncle told me to follow that man's tracks and see what he went out there for, as probably he hid the trap behind the log. I found the trap clog behind the log but there was no trap. It was snowing some at the time the men killed the bear.

When we found that the men had taken the trap and hid the trap clog Uncle exclaimed, "The varmints intend to steal our bear." We followed the trail of the men as fast as we could for we were quite sure they must have stopped over night not far from there for it was nearly dark when they killed the bear. Their trail led down the hillside to the main stream, then down the creek and we hustled after them as fast as we could go. After going down the creek a mile or more we saw a smoke and Uncle said, "There the varmints are," and he was right. We were none too soon as the men were already hitching the horses to the sleigh ready to start off. We could see that the bear was already on the sleigh, although it was covered over with a blanket. The men started at us but did not say a word.

Uncle walked up to the end of the sleigh, caught a corner of the blanket, threw it back and uncovered the bear. Then taking the bear by the foreleg he gave it a flop onto the ground saying, "You have a bear, haven't you," and the bear rolled to the ground and uncovered the trap; Uncle said, "You have a trap, too, haven't you." Not a word did any of the men say and when Uncle asked them who they were and where they lived, one of them said that they did not intend to steal the bear but were going to take it to the first house and leave it for us.

Uncle told them that we did not care to have the bear go in that direction and told the men they must take the bear to our camp and their intentions were to steal the bear and trap and that they had better settle the matter at once. The men were ready to settle and asked what it would cost and Uncle told them if they would take the bear to our camp and then leave the woods and not be caught in that section again, that he would let them go. This they readily consented to do and insisted that we take a part of a cheese they had brought in with them. Uncle told them that we did not care for their cheese or anything else they had--all that we wanted was that they take the bear to our camp and get out of the woods. This they did and one of them also took the cheese along and left it at the camp. Then they left, begging that we would not say anything farther about the matter.

We learned that the men did not live down the creek but instead lived in New York State. They had come for a few days' deer hunting and had only made a shelter of hemlock boughs. The first day out they ran across the bear and as it was snowing they thought it would snow enough to cover up their tracks and they would take the bear and get back to New York State. Well, they did get back but it happened they left the bear behind.

I would like to ask the old liners who have grown too old on the trail and trap line to follow it longer with profit and pleasure, if they keep bees? I find it a great pleasure to watch these little, industrious and intelligent fellows work.

CHAPTER V.
Some Early Experiences (Concluded.)

I will state that I began my career as a trapper and hunter at a very early age. The woods extended to the very door of my father's house and deer were more numerous than sheep in the fields at the present day. Bear were also quite plentiful and wolves were to be found in considerable numbers in certain localities. Panthers were much talked of and occasionally one would be killed by some hunter or trapper of which I will speak later.

It was not long before I found my way further up the stream into the woods where mink and coon tracks were in real paths, and here was where father taught me how to make the deadfall, which was the trap principally used in those days.

The guns that father had were one double barrel shotgun and a single barrel rifle, both flintlocks, and with much anxiety I watched those guns and begged of the older members of the family to let me shoot the gun but mother was ever on the watch to see that I was not allowed to handle the guns.

About this time a man moved into the place by the name of Abbott from Schuylkill County, Pa., who brought two guns with him, a double barrel shotgun and a double barrel rifle. After doing some hard begging Mr. Abbott said that I could take the shotgun but that he could not furnish the ammunition. I later thought that Mr. Abbott thought that the problem of getting ammunition would put me up the tree. But again the will was good and I soon found a way. I began to watch the hen's nests pretty close and hide away the eggs and mother began to complain that the hens were not laying as many eggs as usual. Well, three dozen of eggs would get a pound of shot, a fourth of a pound of powder and a box of G. D. gun caps.

I had some fine times out with the gun and I always gave Mr. Abbott whatever game I killed. I did not dare to take it home fearing that I would be compelled to explain how I came by the game. One day I had been out after wild pigeons and had got quite a number or more than I liked to give away and go without ourselves. I thought I would resort to one of those white lies that we have all heard tell of. I told my parents that Mr. Abbott gave me the pigeons but the plan did not work, although it was the making of me so far as a gun is concerned.

When father inquired of Mr. Abbott as to how I got the pigeons it brought out the whole thing as to the gun business and also why the egg basket had not filled up as usual. The result was that father and mother held a council of war and decided that if I was to have a gun the better way was to let me have one of my own. Father told me that I must not borrow a gun any more but take one of our own guns and that he (father) would take the gun to the gunsmith and have the locks changed from a flint lock to a cap lock.

You may be sure that this was the best news that this kid ever heard. I picked up double the usual stone piles that day and went and got the cows without being told a half dozen times.

Well, as every hunter and trapper who is born and not made is always looking for taller timber and trying to get farther and farther from the ting-tong of the cow bells, so it was in my case. I had seen some whelp wolves that friends of ours (Harris and Leroy Lyman, who were noted hunters) had got. They had gone onto the waters of the Sinnemahoning and taken five pup wolves not much larger than kittens, from their den. The puppies were brought out alive but they killed the old mother wolf. On their way home they stopped at our house so that we could see the young wolves.

I heard these hunters tell how they discovered the wolf den; how they had howled in imitation of a wolf to call the old wolves up; how they had shot the old female and had then taken the young wolves from the den; heard them tell of the money that the bounty on wolves would bring them (there was $25 bounty on all wolves then, the same as now). All of this made me long for the day when I would be old enough to do as these noted hunters had done.

I had already found a den of young foxes and had kept five of them alive, which father finally killed all but one because he said they were a nuisance. I had seen some Indians bring a live elk in with ropes, dogs and horses, which they had roped in, after the dogs had brought it to bay, on a large rock on Tombs Run (Waters of Pine Creek).

All this made me hungry for the day that I too could hit the trail and trap line that I might get some of those wolves and with the bounty money buy traps and guns to my satisfaction.

A number of persons at our place (Lymansville) had gone several miles into the woods to the headwaters of the Sinnamahoning and taken up fifty acres of land. An acre or two was cleared off and the timber from this clearing was drawn and put in an immense pile to be used for the camp fire. The camp was simply a shed or leanto, open on one side, and in front of this shed the fire was built of beech and maple logs. Brook trout and game of all kinds were in abundance. Two or three times during the summer a party of six or eight persons would go out to this clearing and camp a week, killing as many deer as they could make use of, jerking a good portion to take home with them and having a general good time feasting on trout, venison and other game, and amusing themselves shooting at marks, pitching quoits, etc. I will add that the main reason they went to this camp was for a good time rather than the game, as game was plentiful right at their homes in those days.

Well, it was at one of these outings that I killed my first bear. I was about thirteen years old, and, of course, in my own mind, it made a mighty hunter of me, not to be compared with Esau of old. It was in June and shortly after we got to camp there was a heavy thunder storm, but it all passed over before sundown, the sun coming out nice and bright. I was determined to go with some of the men to watch a lick (there were three or four licks not far away), but none of the men cared to have my company, and they said it was likely to rain again and made many excuses why I should not go to watch a lick with them. Just before they were ready to start out to the lick we heard a wolf howl away off on the hills and they (the men) put up the wolf scare on me and said that there would be no deer come to the lick so long as wolves were in the neighborhood. I took their stories all in but insisted that I would watch a lick all the same. There was a lick only a few hundred yards from camp, but for some cause deer rarely ever worked it. When they saw that I was going to watch a lick in spite of thunder storms, wolves or all the rest of the excuses that they could make, they finally said that I could watch the lick which I have mentioned and get eaten up by wolves.

There was a blazed line from camp to the lick and when the men started for the licks that each one had decided on watching, I started to the lick that was given me to watch.

There was one man left in camp to watch the horses and to keep camp. This man said that when he heard me shoot he would come up and help me bring in the deer.

The blind at the lick was a scaffold built up in a tree twenty or thirty feet from the ground. I climbed to the scaffold and placed the old gun in the loops that were fastened to limbs on the tree to give the gun the proper range to kill the deer, should one come to the lick after it was too dark to see to shoot.

Nothing came round the lick before dark, but as soon as it got dark I could hear animals walking and jumping on all sides of me and one old inquisitive porcupine came up the tree to see what I was doing. He perched himself on a limb not more than two feet from my face and sat there and chattered his teeth until I could stand it no longer. I took the large powder horn that I had strung over my shoulder with a cord and gave the porcupine a rap on the nose that sent him tumbling down the tree. I remember well how other animals scampered from under the tree when the porcupine tumbled down. At that time I wondered what it all was, but later I learned that all these animals were only flying squirrels, rabbits and porcupines, but I imagined that the noises were made by anything but squirrels and rabbits.

Well, about eleven o'clock I heard something coming towards the lick with a steady tread like that of a man and again I was taken with a chill that caused the scaffold to shake, but the chill only lasted for a moment. Soon I heard the animal step in the soft mud and directly it began to suck the salt from the dirt and I was sure that it was a deer and that it was the right time to pull the trigger, which I did. When the report of the gun died away all that I could hear were the same noises that were made when I knocked the old porcupine from the tree. I now feared that I had pulled the gun on some other animal rather than a deer. I thought the report of the gun would frighten all the deer in the woods, so that no deer would go to the licks the men were watching. I was afraid I would get a terrible scolding by the men who were watching the other licks when they came to camp in the morning.

After waiting some time and hearing no noise of any kind, I concluded to get down and go to camp. Upon getting down from the tree I decided that I would go and look in the lick and see if I could tell what it was that I had heard there and had shot at. As it was so dark that I could not see from the blind, you can imagine my surprise when I got to the lick to see a large buck deer lying broadside as dead as could be.

I immediately lost all fear of being scolded by the other men, so I claimed first blood. I began calling for the man who remained in camp but could get no answer from him so I went down to camp and found him fast asleep. I awakened him and we immediately made a torch and went to the lick and dragged the deer to camp. Then we took out the entrails and bunked down for the rest of the night.

The next thing that I knew, one of the men who had watched a lick not far away was kicking me and saying, "Get out of this, you old deer slayer, you, and get some venison frying for breakfast." We were soon up for the sun was shining brightly and more than an hour high. Soon the other watchers came in and reported that not a sound of a deer had they heard about their licks. Two or three of us (I say "us" because I was now counted as one of them) went to catch trout for breakfast, while the others were at work taking care of the venison and preparing breakfast, boiling coffee, frying venison and trout. And so the day was spent, sleeping, cocking and eating until it was again time to go to the licks, as the men wished to get another deer so as to have plenty of venison to take home with them. When the men were about ready to start to their watching places, one of them inquired of me what I would do as there was no further use of watching the lick where I had killed the deer, as it was blooded from the deer I had killed.

The man who had watched the lick nearest the camp, and quite an old man, said that I could watch the lick that he had watched and he would stay in camp. (The men now acknowledged me as a thoroughbred hunter, you see.) Well, I was getting there pretty lively, I thought, when an old hunter would give up his lick to me, when only the evening before none of the men thought that I was up to watching a lick at any price.

I was pleased to again have a place to watch. Taking some punk wood to make a little smoke to keep off the gnats and mosquitoes, I started for the lick and climbed the Indian ladder to the scaffold, built in a hemlock tree.

I had barely got fixed in shape to begin to watch when I chanced to look towards a small ravine that came down from the hill a few yards to my left and saw what I took to be a black yearling steer. I will add that the woods in that locality were covered with a rank growth of nettles, cow cabbage and other wood's feed, and people would drive their young cattle off into that locality to run during the summer. I thought I would get down from the scaffold and throw stones at it and drive it off lest it might come into the lick after dark and I might take it for a deer and shoot it.

As I started to climb down I again looked in the direction of the steer, and this time I saw what I thought was the largest bear that ever traveled the woods. He had left the ravine and was walking with his head down, going up the hill and past the lick. I cocked both barrels of the gun and raised it carefully to my shoulder, and, breaking a little dry twig I had in my hand caused the bear to stop and turn his head around so as to look down the hill. This was my time so I leveled on his head and shoulders and let go both barrels of the gun at once.

The bear went into the air and then began tumbling and rolling down the hill towards the tree that I was in, bawling and snorting like mad. But if the bear made a howl from pain he was in, it was no comparison to the howl that I made for help and it did not cease until the men in camp came on the run thinking that I had accidentally shot myself. Well, this was my first bear and it was the greatest day of my life.

We took the bear to camp, skinned and dressed it and then went to bunk for the night, but it was very little I slept for I could only think what a mighty hunter I was (in my mind).

The men came in in the morning with no better luck than they had the night before, and they all declared that if I had not been with them they would have had to go without venison.

The men said that we had meat in plenty now and that we would not watch the licks any more that time, so they put in their time jerking the venison and also some of the bear meat. They built a large fire of hemlock bark, and when it was burned down to a bed of coals so that there was no longer any smoke, they made a rack or grate of small poles, laid in crotches driven in the ground, so as to have the grate over the coals, and then laid the slices of venison on this grate and stood green bark about the grate to form a sort of an oven. The strips of meat were first sprinkled with salt and wrapped up in the skin from the deer and allowed to remain wrapped in the skin for a few hours until the salt would strike through the meat so as to make it about right as to salt.

The men remained in camp about a week. They would shoot at a mark, pitch quoits and have jumping contests and other amusements, including fishing, eating trout, venison and bear meat along with toasted bread and coffee and potatoes roasted in the ashes.

* * *

The time had arrived when I thought that I must take to the taller timber to trap and hunt. I searched among the boys of my age, in the neighborhood, for a partner who would go with me to the Big Woods, as the section where I wished to go, was called. I finally found a pard who said he would go with me and stay as long as I cared to.

The middle of October came. We packed our knapsacks with a grub stake, a blanket or two, and taking our guns started for the Big Woods, with a feeling that is not known to those who are not lovers of the wild.

As we only had a limited number of steel traps it was our intention to spend the first week in camp, building deadfalls for coon and mink and use the steel traps for fox. Our intention was to build as many deadfalls as we would be able to attend to before we baited and set any of them. We had built our traps on many of the small brooks and streams to the south and east of the camp, and had built traps on the stream on which the camp was located nearly a mile below camp.

About a mile and a half below camp there was another branch coming in from the north. Pard and I started early one morning to finish the line of traps on the camp stream and then go up the stream that came from the north and build as many traps as we could during the balance of the day. We had finished the line of traps on the camp stream, and had built a trap or two on the other branch, when pard complained of having a bad headache, but refused to go to camp. We built another trap or two, when pard consented to go to camp, if I would build another trap on a little spring run where coon signs were plentiful, which I readily consented to do. When I got the trap done it was nearly sundown.

It was about three miles to camp so I hurried to see how pard was feeling. I had not gone more than a half mile on my way from where pard turned back to go to camp, when I found him lying on the ground. He said that he was feeling so sick that he was unable to go any further and complained that every bone in his body ached.

After explaining to pard the conditions under which we were placed, it was with difficulty that I managed to get him up, and by supporting and half carrying him I managed to get him along a few rods at a time. I could see that he was continually growing worse. After I had helped until we were within about three-quarters of a mile of camp, he begged me to let him lie down and rest. I tried to urge him along by explaining that I must go for a team to get him out of the woods, and that I could not leave him lying there on the damp ground. It was of no use; I could not get him to go any further. While I was somewhat older than pard, he was much the heavier, and I was unable to carry him.

Taking in the situation, there was only one thing for me to do and that was to leave him and go for help. After making him promise that as soon as he rested he would work his way to camp I took off my coat, and put it under him, again making him promise to get to camp, I started for help.

The night was dark and it was miles through the woods to the first house. When I came to camp I stopped long enough to get a bite to eat which I took in my hand. After lighting a fire so if pard did manage to get to camp he would have a good fire, I started for help. Wherever the light would get through the trees enough so that I could see the path, I would take a trot. After the first mile and a half I came to the turnpike road where I could make better time although it was dense woods. After about six or seven miles I reached the first clearing and from there the rest of the way was more or less clearings and I could see the road better and was able to make better time.

I reached pard's home about a mile before I came to my home, rattled at the door and called for pard's father. I told him the condition of his son. He requested me to go to my home and get some of my family to take a team and start back at once after his son; he would go after a doctor and have the doctor there when we got back with the boy. I lost no time in getting started back. We could not get nearer than a mile and a half to the camp, as we were obliged to leave the wagon road at that point, and go down a very steep hill and only a trail cut through the woods. When we reached the camp, contrary to expectations, we found Orlando (that was pard's name) lying in the bunk in camp but he said that he was feeling no better. It was after midnight and we lost no time in getting him on one of the horses and started back to the wagon which we reached with some difficulty. On reaching the wagon we laid him on a straw bed which we had brought for the purpose and got back to his home sometime after daybreak.

The doctor was there and after examining pard said he feared it was a bad case of fever. I waited a few days to see if he would be able to go back to camp and then the doctor told me that he would not be out of bed in two months and advised me to keep out of the woods or I would be brought out on a stretcher. I had my mind on all those deadfalls that we had built and all the coon, mink and fox that we could catch, and was determined to go back to camp notwithstanding our friend's advice to the contrary. After looking around for another partner which I was unable to find as no one wished to go and stay longer than a day or two (what we call summer trappers), I again packed my knapsack and went back to camp. The next morning, after catching a good lot of trout for coon and mink bait, I began the work of setting the hundred or more deadfalls that pard and I had built. As soon as I had all the deadfalls set I hunted up good places to set the traps that we had. I was so busy all the time that there was no chance to get lonesome. Every day there were coon and mink to skin and stretch. Now and then a big, old coon was so strong that he would tear the deadfall to pieces and I would be compelled to build it all over and make it stronger.

What a difference there is now with the many styles of traps and the H-T-T to guide the young hunter and trapper. If I could have had a couple dozen of the No. 1 1/2 Victor traps made as at the present time, I would have been as proud as a small boy with a new pair of boots, although I think what was lacking in modern traps was fully made up by the number of furbearing animals.

I had been so busy during the two weeks I was in camp that I had forgotten the day of the week; neither did I take time to kill a deer or to go up to the road to see if anyone had written, to see if I was dead or alive. There was a stage passed over the road twice a week. I had nailed a box with a good tight lid on a tree by the road so that I could send a line out home for anything I wanted or my family could write to me.

I had two or three traps set for foxes up towards the road along the edge of a laurel patch where there were plenty of rabbits and the foxes worked around to catch rabbits. I thought I would go to the road and be there about the time the stage passed along and see if I could hear anything from pard and the folks at home and then I could tend the traps on my way back to camp.

WOODCOCK AND SOME OF HIS CATCH.

I was at the road shortly before the stage came along and was surprised as well as delighted to see a neighbor boy by the name of Frank Curtis aboard the stage as he had said he would come over and stay a day or two with me in camp. Frank had not been allowed to spend much time with a gun or traps, but like most boys, he liked a gun. My mother died before I was eleven years old and father allowed me to trap and hunt about as I liked.

When we got down near the traps we set our packs down--I say we, for my folks had sent me a new supply of provisions--and went to look after the traps. The first one had a rabbit leg in it and it was plain to be seen that some animal had eaten the rabbit. We reset the trap and went on to the next trap which was set in a little gorge or hollow. A few yards below the trap two large trees had blown down across the little hollow. The tree on the side farthest down the hill from the trap had broken in two where it fell over the hollow and dropped down so that it laid close to the ground while the tree on the upper side, the side nearest the trap, lay a foot from the ground in the hollow.

The trees were two or three feet apart right at the hollow but were close together on one side. When we came to where the trap had been set we found trap and drag gone and nothing in sight. We soon discovered the animal which we supposed was a coon, had gone down the ravine toward the two large trees that had fallen across the hollow. We went to the logs and looked between them. There we could see the clog but the animal was crowded back under the logs so we could see but little of it.

Frank said that he would get between the logs and poke the coon out. I told him that he had better let me go, as I was afraid that he would take a hold of the clog and pull the trap loose from the coon's foot, but Frank grabbed a stick and jumped between the logs. He had hardly struck the ground when he gave a fearful yell and there was a spitting, snarling animal close at his heels. He scrambled out from between the logs, as white as a sheet. I then saw that it was a wildcat and a mad one. I cut a good stout stick and while Frank stood on the bank with his gun, I poked the cat from under the log by punching it, until Frank could see it enough to shoot it. We pulled the cat out from between the logs, took the trap from its foot, reset it and took the cat with our traps and went to camp, declaring in our minds that there was no other such mighty trappers as we.

Frank declared that he was nearly famished with hunger so we had supper and then skinned the cat. We did not sleep much that night as Frank had to tell me all about things at home. He also told me that pard was no better. Every time an owl would hoot, or a rabbit or porcupine or a mouse would make a noise in the leaves, Frank would give me a punch and ask what it was. Frank remained three days in camp and then he took the stage back home, that being as long as his parents would allow him to stay. I went to the road to see him off. When leaving he made many declarations that he would come back to camp, although he never did.

The snow now began to lie on the ground as it fell and it began to get cold at night. Coon did but little traveling and some way, after Frank had been over to camp and stayed those three days, I seemed to get homesick. I had not become expert enough to make a business of deer hunting and marten and bear trapping, so I sprung the deadfalls and took up the few steel traps that I had and began to take my furs and other plunder to the road to take the stage home. After going home I went to school for a few weeks.

I no longer remember how many coon, mink and other furs I caught, but it was quite a bunch for furs were very plentiful in those days.

CHAPTER VI.
A Hunt on the Kinzua.

Comrades, as I have not been able to trap any for the past two years--1905 and 1906--and as I have previously served for more than 50 years almost without cessation, along the trap line, I beg to be admitted to your ranks as one of the "Hasbeens."

I will therefore tell of one of my trips on a hunting and trapping expedition in the fall and winter of 1865-6, a party of two besides myself. My two companions' names were Charles Manly and William Howard. We started about the 15th of October for Coudersport with a team of horses and wagon loaded with the greater part of our outfit and went to Emporium, Cameron County, where we hit the Philadelphia and Erie Railroad. The only railroad that touched Northwestern Pennsylvania at that time. Here we took the railroad to Kane, a town in Southwestern McKean County, where we stopped one day and made purchases for three months' camping. We hired a good team here to take our outfit about seven or eight miles on to Kinzua Creek.

Almost the entire distance was through the woods and over the rock. There was no sign of a road only as we went ahead of the team and cut a tree or log here and there. The outfit was lashed onto a bobsled, and as we had bargained with the man to make the trip for a stated price, he did not seem to care whether there was any road or not, so that he got through as quickly as possible.

We reached the stream about noon. The man fed his team some oats, swallowed a few mouthsful himself and was soon on his way back to town, while we began laying plans for our camp. We selected a spot on a little rise of ground near a good spring of water, and where there was plenty of small yellow birch trees handy to cut logs out of for camp. We placed a good sized log down first at the end of the shanty that we intended to build the fire place in. Another was placed at the end that was to be the highest, so to give the right slope to the roof, which was a shed roof. We always kept the large ends of the logs one way, so that when we had the logs rolled up it made the lower or eaves end of the camp about five feet high.

There was a slope of about two feet for the roof. We felled bass wood trees which we split in half, and then dug or scooped them out so as to make a trough. We notched the two end logs down and then placed the scoops or troughs in these notches so that they would lay firm with the hollow side up.

After placing these scoops across the entire width of the shack we then placed another layer of the scoops (reverse) on the first set. That is to say, the rounding side up. This made a very good roof but required a good deal of chinking at the ends to keep the cold out, but as moss was plenty, it was not a long job. The second day after we got into the woods we had the camp in pretty good shape, well chinked and calked.

The third day we worked on the fire place, laying it up to the jam of stone, then we finished the chimney with logs and mud. We had a fairly comfortable camp with but two exceptions. These were, no windows, and for a door we had what I called a "hoghole," that was a door so small that one had to get down on all fours to get in or out. On the fourth day we intended to cut wood all day, and were at it before it was fairly light, but before 10 o'clock it began to snow. In a couple of hours there was a good tracking snow and the boys were bound to go out and see if they could not kill a deer. I tried hard to get them to stick to the wood job, but it was no use, they must go hunting.

There was no partnership business in this hunt. It was every man for himself, and the dogs, take the hindermost. I told the boys I would stay in camp and do something at the wood job.

I had been along the creek a little the day before, poking my nose under the banks and old drifts to see what manner of signs I could see, and I had noticed several mink tracks. The boys had no more than gone when I had a fishing tackle rigged out. It consisted of a line braided from horsehair, out of a horse's tail, and a hook baited with some bits of fat pork. It did the business, for the stream fairly swarmed with trout. Taking three or four trout for bait, I was soon at work building deadfalls. It was not long before I had three or four built close up under the banks and behind logs where I thought the boys would not see them.

I then scampered back to camp and went to cutting wood like a good boy. I had only just got to camp when I heard a gun shot away up the creek, and in about an hour Charley came dragging a yearling deer. Will did not show up for some time after dark, but had nothing, though he said that he had a fair standing shot at a large buck, but his gun snapped on him and he lost.

The next morning we were out at the peep of day, each one going his own way. I went down the creek so that I could take a peep at my traps. None had been disturbed until I came to the last one. There, to my satisfaction, I found a mink. As I had passed a small run that emptied into the main creek I noticed that some animal had gone over a pole that lay across a little run and partly in the water. The animal had brushed the snow off the pole in going over it. I gave it no particular attention, thinking that it was a coon, but when I got the mink I thought I would go back to camp, make a stretching board and stretch the mink skin and get a trap and set at the run for the coon, as I supposed.

I will mention that furs were bringing about the same prices then as at the present time, 1907, a good No. 1 mink being worth about $10.

Near the camp was a large elm tree that was hollow, and the fire had burned a hole out on one side up the tree, nearly as high as a man's head. After I had stretched the mink skin I hung it up in this hollow tree, and it was a very good place to dry the pelts that I caught. The boys never mistrusted that I was doing any trapping for small game.

To get back to my job, I took one out of three steel traps No. 3, and all the traps that we had brought with us. In fact, the other boys did not care to trap. When I got back at the run I gave more attention to the trail of the supposed coon, and discovered that it was an otter. With greater caution I waded up the run until I found a suitable place to set the trap, knowing that he would be back that way again sooner or later.

After setting the trap I climbed the ridge to look for deer and got two shots during the afternoon but missed both. All came to camp that night without killing any deer. I had seen a number of marten tracks during the afternoon. The next morning it was thawing and the boys feared they would lose the tracking snow, so Charley and Will hurried to localities where they expected to find deer. I sliced some strips of venison from the fore-quarters, or rather what was left of the fore-quarters, of the deer Charley had killed the first day out. I made tracks to the ridge where I had seen the marten tracks, and I lost no time in putting up deadfalls at the best pace I was capable of getting into.

In the afternoon on my way to camp I came to the creek some ways below where I had set the mink traps, so I put up two or three more deadfalls for mink. I also found a big flood drift which otter were using for their feeding grounds. I selected places to set the other two steel traps which were in camp, and then went to camp, looking at the mink traps on the way, but found that none had been disturbed.

When I got to camp I found both Charley and Will there, and each had killed a deer. Will had killed a good sized buck close to camp, so he dragged it down to the shanty to dress and hang up. The boys gave me the laugh because I had not killed any deer. I told them to hold their breath and I would get into the harness after a bit. In the morning the snow was all gone and the boys were afraid that it was going to get so warm that their venison would spoil. Cuts were drawn to see which one of them should go to Kane to get a team to take out their venison. It fell on Charley. They tried to have me join in the draw, but I told them that I did not see where I came in as I had no venison to spoil.

The weather kept warm for several days, so I kept building deadfalls on the different ridges for marten and along the creek for mink and coon. Charley and Will continued to still hunt, killing several deer. When the snow came again I had all the traps up I intended to build, but it turned out that later I built two deadfalls for bear. I now put in my time still hunting, shaping my course as much as possible so as to tend to my traps. I killed a deer occasionally as did the other boys. I set the two steel traps on the drift where I had seen the otter signs, and the second time I looked at them I found an otter tangled up in one of the traps.

I was also getting mink, marten and coon now and then, and occasionally I would get two mink or marten in one day. I would cut a long slender withe to stretch the skins over, bending them in the form of a stretching board the best I could and hang the pelts in the old elm tree and kept mum. I remembered the old adage, "he that laughs last, laughs best," and was bound to have the last laugh.

One night Will came in and said that a bear had eaten up the offal where he had dressed a deer. I asked him if he was going to set a trap for him, and he said that he had no trap to set. I told him to build a deadfall. Will said that I could have that job if I wanted it. I told him all right if he would tell me where to find the place. He said that he would go with me in the morning and show me. In the morning I took the best axe, some bait and went with Will to the place where the bear had eaten the offal. We saw that the bear had been back there during the night and cleaned up the remains left the previous night.

I selected a good sized beech tree, where I could fell it so that I could cut a piece from the butt for the bottom piece and have the remainder of the tree come so that I could use a small tree for one of the stakes or posts. When I pulled off my coat and began chopping on the tree Will gave me the laugh again, and said that I had more days' work in me than brains, or something to that effect.

It was my intention to get the trap all ready and then get one of the boys to help me set it. I got the trap done and saw that by using a long lever or pry I could set the trap without the aid of another. With the pry I raised the dead piece up as high as I wanted it. Then tied the lever to a sapling to hold the dead log in place, using the figure four trigger. I placed a bit of log in the bait pen to rest the bait spindle on. I then placed the trigger in place and pressed them between the logs to steady them until I could release the lever and let the weight onto the trigger. I then put some poles onto the dead log to make doubly sure that I had weight enough to kill any bear that traveled those woods. I now went to camp giving myself credit of doing a good job.

When the boys came in the night of the day I built the first deadfall for bear, they both reported seeing bear tracks and they said the tracks all seemed to be going south. I told the boys that the bear were looking up winter quarters, and that if we would all go at it and put up several deadfalls we would stand a fair chance to get a bear or two, but it was no go.

They said they would give me a clean title to all the bear I could catch, but they did not care to invest. So I took the axe and some bait and went to the head of a small draft where the boys had seen the bear tracks. I found at the head of this hollow what seemed to be a bear runway or crossing, for three or four bears had passed around the head of this basin in the past few days.

With some hard work and heavy lifting I got another good deadfall built that day. The next day I went the rounds of the marten and mink traps, and I think I killed a deer and got two marten. I remember that at this time we had a good snow to hunt on, and that it was not an uncommon thing for us to cut wood for the camp long after dark, and sometimes it was pretty scant at that. I think it was the third day after I had set the first bear trap when Will came in, shortly after Charley and I had got to camp, and as he stuck his head through the hoghole (as I called the substitute for a door) he says, a fool for luck.

I suspicioned what was coming and said, "Well, what kind of luck have you had?"

Will said, "It is not me that has had the luck, but you have got one of the Jed-blasted bears up there in that rigging you built, you ever see."

I remember that I had some kind of a hipo that night, so that I would laugh every now and then "kindy" all by myself. I do not think that I slept much that night, though it was not the first bear I had ever caught. I thought it was beginning to look as though the laugh was coming my way all right.

In the morning the boys went to the trap with me and helped get the bear out of the trap and helped set the trap again, and then went on with their deer hunting. I went to skinning the bear, and it was all I did that day to skin that bear and stretch the skin on the shanty. I told the boys when they came in that night that I thought we were going to have a hard winter, and so I concluded to weatherboard the camp with bear skins. The carcass of the bear was, of course, a complete loss, and that is a serious objection to the deadfall as a bear trap.

I think that it was about this time that Will met with an accident in his foot gear, so he went out to Kane after a pair of gum shoes. At this time we had several deer so thought it best to have the team come in and take them out and ship them.

When Will came back that evening he said that some kind of an animal had crossed the path about one-half mile from camp, dragging something. He said that he could not make up his mind what it was, but thought it was some kind of an animal in a trap, but we knew of no one trapping in that locality.

I did not know but it might be possible that some animal had gotten in one of my otter traps and had broken the chain and gone off with the trap. Early in the morning I went down the creek to look at the traps and see if they were all right. When I came to the Spring Run I saw that my otter (or at least I called it my otter), had again gone up the run, on his usual round of travel. When I came to where the trap was it wasn't there at all.

I had fastened the trap to a root that was two or three inches under water and a root that I supposed sound. I was mistaken, for the root was pretty doty and the otter had broken the root and gone with my trap. I lost no time in taking up the chase. The trail led up this run to its source, then over a spur of ridge and down the hill again into a branch of the main stream, then up this branch for a distance of a mile or more, where I came up with him.

He had gone under the roots of a large hemlock tree, and it took me two or three hours to get him out with nothing to work with only my belt axe and a sharpened stake. It was nearly night when I got to camp. I made a stretching board from a spault I split out of a basswood log and stretched the otter skin, and put in the balance of the day in chopping wood. One of the boys killed three deer that day. I do not remember which one it was.

The next day I made the rounds of nearly all the traps and got what I have many a time before--nothing. I put in three or four days still hunting and had the luck to kill a deer or two, but Charley and Will killed more than I did. I remember, during this time, they were all the time joking me because they were getting more deer than I did. I claimed that they had the best grounds to hunt on, they hunting east of the camp and up nearer the head of the stream, while I hunted west of the camp.

We would see bear tracks nearly every day, and Will and Charley would try to get around in their hunting course so as to look at the two bear traps, the traps being in the direction in which they hunted. They found the traps undisturbed. I had about made up my mind that I would get no more bear that trip. I was getting a marten, mink or coon now and then, so that I kept a stiff upper lip if the boys did kill a few deer more than I did. Finally one night when I came to camp I found the carcass of a bear, skin and all lying at the shanty door. I thought it was one that either Charley or Will had killed. I found that the boys by chance had met near one of the bear traps, and going to the trap found the bear. As it was a small one they took it out, set the trap and brought the bear to camp.

It was now getting along in December and the snow was getting rather deep and the weather was pretty cold and the game did not move about very much. We all seemed to get a little lazy, and did not get out till after noon. In fact, some days, if the weather was pretty sharp, we did not go out at all but would stay in camp and talk of the hunt and tell where we thought we could find a bunch of deer over in this basin or on that ridge.

The most of the deadfalls set I had not covered so to keep the snow off. A good many of them had snowed under, so I did not care how soon we broke camp and went home. Deer were quite plentiful, and we could find them nearly every day, when we would get a move on, so we continued to stay day after day, and putting in about one-half the time hunting and the other half telling what we would have done if there had not been so many "ifs" in the way.

I would usually shape my course in hunting so as to come around where some of the deadfalls were and spring them. One day I came to one that was pretty well snowed under. I saw that a fox had done a good deal of traveling around the trap and had dug in the snow some about where I thought a marten would be, providing one was there. I kicked the snow away, and to my delight and surprise I found as good a marten as I had caught. I thanked the fox for the favor. I examined all the traps then to make sure that there was nothing in them, but I found no more marten.

We now began to get our venison into camp, taking turns to help each other. I do not just remember how many deer we killed, but I think that Charley and Will killed 15 or 16 apiece, and I killed either 11 or 12.

The boys said I had done pretty well considering the two bear and otter, but when I went to the old elm and brought out the marten, mink and another otter and five or six coon, the boys looked greatly amazed and Will said, "I knew the fool was doing something besides hunting," Charley said he thought he could smell something that smelled like mink around the camp three or four times. I think I got 13 marten, 8 mink, 5 coon, 2 otter and 2 bears. As near as I can remember, I got a little over a hundred dollars for the fur. I do not remember what we got for the venison, but it was war prices. We shipped our venison to George Herbermann, New York.

I tried to have the boys help cut a lot of wood for the next season's hunt, but they said they were not counting chickens as far ahead as that. They hit it right, for neither of them hunted in there. I think Charley hunted on Hunt's Run in Cameron County, and I do not know whether Will hunted at all the next season, but I took a partner and went back on the Kinzua.

This time we were in "swacks," and I will try to tell what luck we had some time, but one thing we did was to put a window in the camp and make the door large enough so that one did not have to get down on all fours to get in or out. Will and I stayed in camp while Charley went out to Kane and sent in the team to take out the venison and the furs and the camp outfit. We got home for Christmas and found all well.

CHAPTER VII.
My Last Hunt on the Kinzua.

As this hunt was about 1868, before there were railroads in this section, we went to Emporium, Cameron County, Pennsylvania, and there took the train to Kane, in McKean County, then by team and bobsled route to camp. This making the journey much farther, we concluded to go by wagon the entire distance, which would shorten the distance nearly one-half.

This time conditions were different than on previous occasion. While there were three in the party before and every one hunted on his own hook, this time I had a partner and we were to share alike in profit and loss. My partner's name was William Earl, and he had recently moved from Vermont, or, as he would jokingly say, from "Varmount." He was somewhat older than myself, and a man who was ever ready to carry his end of the load at all times.

We hired a team and took a full line of grub and the camp outfit, with about sixty small traps and eight bear traps. We went by way of Port Allegheny, Devils Blow and Smithport, taking three days to get to camp, as we had to cut out the road a good part of the distance of the last day's travel. They had just begun to operate in the oil industry in the neighborhood of what is now the city of Bradford, and as they used wood altogether for fuel to drill with, there was a great deal of wood being cut for the purpose. Bill, as my partner was familiarly called, used to say that if we could not get fat on venison and bear meat we would take a wood job, but we found plenty to do without the wood job.

On reaching the camp the first thing noticeable was that the old hollow elm that I had used for a dryhouse to hang up skins in, had met with foul play, for it lay on the ground, having blown down. This made it necessary to build a sort of leanto against one side of the shanty to hang up our furs, as we did not like to have them hung up in the shanty where they would get more or less smoked.

But the first thing we did was to enlarge the door, for it will be remembered that we were obliged to get down on all fours in order to get in or out of the shanty. As we had a good crosscut saw, it did not take long to enlarge the doorway so that one could go in standing up, man fashion. We next cut a window-hole large enough to take a single sash window. Then we replaced the chinkings that the porcupines had gnawed out, calked and mudded all cracks. When this was done, Bill looked it over and said, "By gum, don't it look like living?"

As it was only about the middle of October we went to work at once on a good supply of wood for the camp. We did not quit until we were sure that we had plenty to last the winter, for we intended to stay as long as it was either profitable or a pleasure. After the wood was cut and piled up near the shanty door, we next set the bear traps, as we had brought bait for the purpose.

After the bear traps were set we next looked over the deadfalls that I had built for marten the fall before, putting in a new stake where necessary. We also set crotches and laid poles on them, then covering with hemlock boughs to keep the snow from falling directly on the trap. We fixed up the two deadfalls I had made for bear, as we wished to get all the bear traps out that we could, as we had already seen several signs.

We also built a number more deadfalls for marten on different ridges farther up the stream where I had not set any the fall before. We built a number of deadfalls along the streams for mink and coon. It was now getting well along towards the last days of October, so we put in a couple of days hunting deer, as we had to have bait to set our marten and other traps with.

The first day's hunting we did not get a deer, though we each got a running shot but missed. The second day I did not see any deer but Bill killed a good sized buck before noon. We now began setting the traps that we had built. Bill baiting and setting the deadfalls, while I commenced on the steel traps. We had not baited and set any of the deadfalls that we had built up to this time. The steel traps we set for fox and wildcats, as there was a bounty of two dollars on wildcats at that time.

In setting out the fox traps the knowledge that I had got of the locality was of much benefit to me. I had kept a watch out for warm springs and other good likely places to catch a fox or other animals. After we had all the deadfalls and steel traps out but three or four otter traps, we set one or two at the drift where I caught one the fall before. The others we set where we found otter signs.

While setting the traps we got a marten or two, as well as one or two mink and coon. We had had one or two little flurries of snow, but we did not leave the traps to hunt deer. Now that the traps were all set, we divided up the trap lines as best we could for each one to attend to while hunting deer. In dividing up the lines in this way we saved much time, as we would not both be working the same territory.

Now business began to get quite lively, and we were seldom in camp until after dark, and we were up early and had breakfast over and our lunch packed in our knapsacks. The lunch usually consisted of a good big hunk of boiled venison and a couple of doughnuts and a few crackers, occasionally the breast of a partridge, fried in coon or bear oil. Sometimes the lunch would freeze in the knapsacks and it would be necessary to gather a little paper bark from a yellow birch and a little rosin from a hemlock, black birch or hard maple tree and build a little fire to thaw the lunch. This, however, was quickly done, and was a pleasure rather than a hardship. I have delighted in eating the lunch in this manner for many a winter on the trap line or trail, as have many other hunters and trappers.

Bill and I always had our lunch packed and ready to take up the trail at the first peep of day. Sometimes when we would get in late, tired and wet and our clothes frozen, I would suggest to Bill that we shut up camp and take a wood job, just to see what Bill would have to say. He would say that there would be time to take a wood job in the spring or after he had killed a certain large buck which is usually called "Old Golden." There were but a few days but what we either caught some fur or killed a deer, though sometimes we would have a bad streak of luck by wounding a deer, or having some animal take a foot off and escape, but this would make us all the more eager to follow the trail or trap line.

WOODCOCK ON THE TRAP LINE.

As we had gotten by this time several deer and had caught three bear (one in one of the deadfalls that I had built the fall before, that Will Howard called that "dashed dinged riggin'," when he found the bear in it) we wanted to get them out to Kane, that being the nearest point to a railroad. We started early one morning, Bill taking an axe and I carrying the saw, so that if we found any large trees across the trail that we had cut out the year before we would have the saw to do it with.

After carrying the saw some distance and not finding any trees of much size across the road, we left it and only took the axe. We found but very little in the trail to cut out.

We got to Kane in time to engage a man with team to come to camp the next day and take out the venison and bear and bring in some necessary commissaries that we were getting short of. It was only a few days after this that I found that a bear got in one of the traps. The trap chain having a swivel that was pretty well worn, broke, and the bear went off with the trap. I followed the trail until the middle of the afternoon, when I became satisfied that Bruin was disgusted with that locality, as he had continued his course nearly due east without a stop. I could see no signs that led me to think that Bruin intended to stop for the next fifty miles.

So I gave up the chase and went to camp, getting there long after all good boys should have been in bed. Bill was up and out at the door listening if he could hear a gun shot or anything to indicate what had become of me. We held a council of war before going to bed, and decided to give Bruin another day's rest or travel, as he saw fit to do, before we started on the trail. We would go to all the traps that had not been tended to in the past three or four days and then take up the trail of Bruin and follow him to the end of his trail, no matter how long the trail might be.

There was but little danger of the trail becoming snowed under or lost, as there was nearly a foot of snow on the ground, and the trap would make a broad trail in the snow, which was quite easily followed. The next day, as intended, we put in a full day attending the traps and got some fur, but I do not remember just what. We started out on the trail of Bruin with a three days' ration of the usual lunch, boiled venison, ham, doughnuts and biscuits.

After following the trail about two hours from the place where I had left it, we came onto a man's track that had taken the trail of our bear. This roiled the temper of the Vermonter somewhat, and if I did not say anything, I had a mighty think on. But we had no cause for alarm at this time. The man after following the trail for a mile or two gave up the chase as a bad job, I guess. He stood and stamped about for some time (we judged by the tracks he had made) and then started back nearly in the same course that he had come.

We followed on until dark when we came to a wagon road. Apparently several persons had seen the bear trail, for there was a beaten path for a few yards on either side of the road. We knew nothing about the road or where it went, but finally concluded to take the road leading south for a little ways. If we saw no signs of habitation then we would camp, as that was what we expected to be compelled to do when starting from camp and each had taken a blanket for the purpose.

We had not gone far when a man with a sleigh overtook us, and we learned that we were about one and a half miles from what was called Bunker Hill. The man gave us a ride. We went to a boarding house and stayed over night, rather than camping on Bruin's trail, though we got plenty of camping on the trail of Bruin before this hunt was at an end.

The next morning we were out early and had breakfast at 6 o'clock and started for the trail which we reached before daylight. We had gone a little way when we heard voices coming along the road. We listened a moment and saw that it was a party of three men who had come to take the bear's trail. We waited until they came up to us and one man said, "What in blazes are you fellows doing on this bear's track?" Bill replied rather sharp, "That's our business, but what are you here for?" Then they said that one of the men had seen the track the evening before and as there was no one after it, they had come out to follow up the track and kill the bear. They insisted on going after the bear but after some talk we convinced them that we did not need any help and they turned back.

We took up the trail and followed it pretty lively for a time, as we did not know but those men would cut around and take the trail ahead of us, though they did not do so. We were now on the waters of Potato Creek and there was a good deal of laurel and here we found the first place that Bruin had stopped and made a bed.

It is usually the case that a bear that has a trap on his foot will not travel any great distance before they stop and make a bed and then move a short distance and make another bed. Bruin now began to act more natural, to his family. We began to think that we would soon come to fresh signs at least, but were disappointed for we did not follow the trail far, after we came onto his bed before two men's tracks fell in and took up the trail.

After following for some time on the trail of the men and bear, we came to where the bear had made another stop and we could see that the bear's track was much fresher showing that it had stopped some time. We expected that the men would divide here, one taking the trail while the other worked on the side, but both men continued on the same trail. After following the trail for three or four hundred yards farther, we came onto another bed and this time the bear went out on the jump and Bill said some cuss words about the men. It is possible that I did too.

The trail here turned north. This took us into a section more thickly settled and hunters more numerous. The greater part of the time there was from one to two men on the trail ahead of us and all that was left for us to do was to follow on as fast as we could. The second night we were on the head of Salt Run and we followed the trail till dark. We now had the bear trail to follow instead of the men as all the men had left to go to their camps or homes. Bill said that we would sleep "dash-dang" close to the trail after this, so we soon found a large log to build a fire against. First we would build the fire out a few feet from the log after scraping the snow away. Then we would throw a few hemlock boughs over a pole laid in crotches and then move the fire down against the log, throw a few boughs on the ground where the fire had been moved from and the camp was complete in a very few minutes.

We now began to fear that some one would get in ahead of us and kill the bear and we would lose bear, trap and all. Bill said that we would follow so "dash-darn" close that we would be up in time to attend the funeral. We were so close up that we were no longer bothered only a little while at a time as we would soon overtook any one who hit the trail ahead of us and followed it.

The bear again turned east which took us across the road which runs from Coudersport to Emporium in Cameron County. We were now back in Potter County and only 15 miles from home. Bruin here turned south and true to his nature, led us through all the windfalls and laurel patches to be found and occasionally would break down a few laurel and act as though he intended to camp for a time but apparently would change his mind and go on again.

We were now on the waters of the Conley and night was fast coming on. The trail led across a little bog and we were looking for water and a suitable place to camp, when Bill called my attention to a man standing on the trail watching us. When we came to him it proved to be a neighbor of ours. Mr. Ephraim Reed, who was hunting in there and said that his camp was only a little way down the hollow and asked us to go down and stay over night. We were glad to do so. Mr. Reed said that there were a good many hunters in that locality so we were up and on the trail before it was fairly light.

We were in a section where there was a great deal of laurel and Bruin continued to make camps but as often would change his mind and move on and Bill thought he had concluded to go to the can brake in Virginia. Often when he would go into a wind jam or laurel thicket, we would separate, one taking a circuit on one side of the thicket, the other on the other side, meeting on the opposite side from where the trail had entered but we would always find that Bruin was still on the go. We were in a locality where there were apparently a good many deer and we saw signs of marten quite often.

We were now on the head waters of Hunts Run in Cameron county and we decided to make that section our next hunting ground. While the trail would wind about some, yet bruin's general course was south. Often when bruin would vary considerably from his general course and go into a thicket or wind jam, we would feel sure that this time we would find him napping, but we were disappointed each time. Once when we were circling one of these thickets, I drove a deer out and it ran to Bill who gave him his finish. We were near a lumber camp and sold it for ten dollars and our night's lodging and some grub. We were now getting pretty well down to the railroad near Sterling Run. We were sure that bruin was going to cross the railroad so we left the trail and went down to the railroad and followed along the road until we came to the trail.

The bear had crossed the road during the night and no one had noticed the trail. Here I suggested to Bill that we take a train to Kane and go to camp and go out and take a wood job, but Bill thought that we had about all the job on our hands that we were able to attend to. He was right, for as near as I can remember, the trail led us nearly a half day's tramp before bruin made a stop. The foot that the trap was on began to bleed considerably. We began to fear that the foot would come off and bruin relieved of the trap would escape after all.

We now had some more help, two men took the trail ahead of us following it until nearly dark when they apparently held a council of war, judging from the way they tracked about where they left the trail. We were now in a pine slashing and concluded to camp on the trail, though we knew that we were not far from a lumber camp as we could hear men chopping and driving oxen. We were lucky in finding a good place to camp and water close at hand. As we had a small tin pail with us and coffee, we made a pail of coffee and ate our lunch and fixed our bunk, then we sat down before the fire for a time and talked over what we thought we might do the next day. Then we rolled up in our blankets and it was time to get the coffee boiling again before we were hardly aware that we had been asleep.

Bruin now began to act more like a sensible bear and would zigzag about from one thicket to another. We now got close enough to him so that we heard him in the brush several times. Bill said that he thought that bruin was about to make up his mind to let us take off that handcuff. He proved to be right, for it was not long before bruin's trail led down onto the side of a steep ravine. The sides were not more than one hundred yards apart and were quite clear (only for the piles of pine tree tops) from fallen trees, that had been taken out for logs.

We were standing a little way down the side of the ravine, laying plans as to our next move, as we had come to the conclusion that bruin had either turned down along the side of the ravine or had gone into camp. We had planned that one would go up around the head of the ravine while the other waited on the trail until the one that went around should get on the opposite side. While still laying plans, we saw bruin come out on the opposite side and began to climb the hill.

We had followed the bear for six days and this was the first time that we had seen his lordship. He would go a few steps and stop and look back. We watched our opportunity and when he made a stop, we both fired. Bruin made a jump or two up the hill then tumbled back down again and the fun had ended. We took the entrails out and left him lying across a log and went down the ravine to where there was a lumber camp and there we found that we were on Dent's Run, a branch of Bennet's Branch and in Elk county.

This was the fourth county we had been in since we had taken the bear's trail. They told us at the lumber camp that there would be three or four teams go down to the railroad station at Driftwood the next morning with spars which they were hauling to the river to raft. We got a man with a yoke of oxen and a bobsled to go with us and get the bear and the next morning about 5 o'clock we got the bear strapped onto one of the spars and started down the stream to the railroad and we shipped it, without removing the skin, to New York, where we got either $26 or $28 for it.

We took the train to Kane where we stayed over night. The next morning we went to camp and found all well with one exception, that being, that the shanty was swarming with "deer mice" and a porcupine had tried hard to gnaw his way through the door. The following day we stayed in camp and rested before starting out to see what would turn up the next day.

We first looked at the bear traps, tending what small traps came in on the way. On going the rounds of the bear traps, we found them all undisturbed except one, which might better have been as it only had a porcupine in it and we did not see any signs of bear. We began to think of taking up the bear traps as we thought that bruin had gone into winter quarters. We did not get around to take them up for several days, being busy tending the smaller traps.

It was now getting along into December and the snow was quite deep. We concluded to put in the time hunting deer as we wished to get all we could, to send out with the team, when we had it come in, as it did not cost any more to take out a full load than half a load. The law closed on deer the first of January, although allowing the hunters 15 days to dispose of his venison after it was unlawful to kill deer. We hustled from early morning until long after dark, when we would get to camp and there was hardly a day that we did not kill at least one deer and some days two or three between us.

I will tell of a little scrape I had one day with a yearling buck that I thought to be dead. I was following the trail of three or four deer along the side of a ridge, expecting every moment to catch them feeding, when I heard a noise behind me and looking back, I saw this little buck coming full tilt right towards me. The deer saw me about as soon as I did him and wheeled to run back when I fired and he went down. I set my gun against a tree and started to cut the deer's throat. I took the deer by the ear and straightened his back. About this time that dead deer began to get pretty lively and was trying to get on his feet and as I could not reach my gun, threw myself onto him, thinking to hold him down.

Well I held him about as long as lightning would stay on a limb. When I got through gazing at the hole in the brush where I last saw him, I found that I was sadly in need of a new pair of trousers and vest, as well as a jack knife. I searched a long time in hopes of finding the knife, but did not. I had another knife at camp and after about a two hour's job with needle and thread, I managed to get the trousers so that they were passable in a pinch and all the time that I was repairing the trousers, Bill sat there laughing at me. Now this was the first time that I had supposed dead deer come to life and give me the go-by, though it was not the last time.

I had given him what is called a fine shot, that is I had shot him just across the back and the ball had struck one of the joints or knuckles of the backbone as it proved. I had the satisfaction of killing the same deer two or three days later or at least we thought it was the same one. We had three or four days of mild weather and as we had not been the rounds of the traps for several days, only tending those that came handy while hunting deer, we thought we would reverse the plan and go over all the traps and pay but little attention to deer hunting unless we struck a hot trail. We thought we would take in those traps first in the direction where the bear traps were and go to the traps farthest from camp and bring in some of the traps. We did not expect to get any more bear as it was too late in the season for bear to travel until they had their winter's sleep.

We were in luck this time for as we had usually tended the bear traps, the one that we went to first would have been the last trap to come to. When we came in sight of where the trap was set we saw that there had been a bear dance going on. As the snow was several inches deep, we saw at a glance which way the bear had gone and we only had to step to the brow of the ridge and look down the hillside a little way to see bruin fast among some small saplings. He was rolling and tumbling about trying to release himself.

He looked like a great black ball as he rolled about. We lost no time in putting him out of his trouble. We skinned the fore parts and hung them up in a sapling to use for bait for fox and marten and took the saddles to camp, skinned them out and stretched the skin on the shanty. Later we shipped the saddles to market.

The next day we looked at the balance of the bear traps but found them undisturbed but we concluded to leave them set a few days longer. On going the rounds of the smaller traps, we got a fox or two also a marten or two, but as I remember it, we got no mink or otter at this time. We now had the traps all looked after, so we put in the time hunting deer as the time for deer hunting was soon to close. The weather had turned and frozen so that it had formed a sharp crust and we were compelled to use the driving method of hunting. One of us would stand on the runways, in the beds of basins and in low places on the ridges while the other would follow the trail and drive the deer through to the hunter. I wish to say right here, that I do not like this way of hunting deer but little better than I do of hounding and running deer with dogs. The dog is all right but I want no dogging of deer for me.

We would get a deer nearly every day. It was now the first of January and time to get our venison to camp or out to the road where we could pick them up on the way out to Kane. After we had gathered up the venison and had gone the rounds of the traps that had not been tended while hunting, we went to Kane. Here we engaged a team to come in after the venison and bear and bring in a grub stake to last us until the middle of March when we would break camp and go home. We both went back to Kane with the team to assist in getting over some of the rough places and see that our venison and bear meat was tagged and shipped all right. Then we came back to camp to put our entire time in tending to the traps which we did to good advantage. We had found other good warm springs while hunting, and some that we thought were lasting springs, had gone dry or had frozen up, so we shifted a good many of the traps to the other springs.

Then we took it a little easier only going the rounds of the traps as we considered it necessary and on such days as the weather was favorable. We waited for February when we knew that the old dog coon would begin his rounds of calling on his friends.

We managed to pass the time away fairly well as we would get a fox, mink, marten or something nearly every day so that we busied ourselves. About the middle of February we had several warm days and the time had now come for us to get busy and we were out as soon as it was light. We would follow up all the spring runs until we found the trail of a coon, then follow it up until it went into a tree. Sometimes it bothered us which tree to cut down for the coon would go from one tree to another so that it was hard to tell which was the tree that was the home of the coon (some call it a den). One day we chopped down a great large oak, three or four feet in diameter and nearly sound all the way through and nary a coon to be found. I asked Bill why he did not say cuss words and he said he thought we had spent enough wind in chopping the tree down, without wasting any unnecessarily.

Well, as I said, the coon had been up and down so many trees that we did not know which one was the most likely one. We went to a large basswood tree that had only one track going to it and one away from it but when we pounded on it with the axe, we saw that it was very hollow. I suggested to Bill that we chop it down. Bill thought there were no coon in it and I had but little faith myself but I told him that as he had been wanting a wood job, here was his opportunity and Bill agreed with me, so we laid off our coats and went to chopping. The tree was only a shell. We soon had it down and to our surprise, coon began to run in all directions. Not having had much hopes of finding any coon in the tree we had not prepared ourselves with clubs to kill the coon. We used the axe handle as best we could but one coon got away and went into a hollow stump which we had to cut down. We got five coon. We then took up the trail of the coon that left the tree and after following it about a mile it went into a large hemlock tree that had a hole in it close to the roots. Pounding on it we discovered that it was hollow.

There had been several coon tracks both out and into the tree. We circled around some distance from the tree and found no tracks leading away from the tree farther than a small spring a few rods away. As it was getting well on towards night we did not fell the tree but went back to the old basswood where we had left the coons and took them and went to camp. Bill said that he had a dash-dang sight rather chop wood than to tote those three coons. I carried two and told Bill not to complain and I would let him skin all of them when we got to camp. He said, "Oh, you are a clever jade, aint you?" We skinned the coon that evening but did not stretch the skin until the next afternoon after we had gone out and cut the hemlock and got three more.

We kept up this coon hunt as long as we could find any tracks. It was now getting along into March and we had written home for a team to come in and take our camp outfit and furs out. As we had not been out over the road through the woods, the way we came in, we made a trip out to the main wagon road so that the man who came after us would have no trouble in following the trail to the camp. We now began to spring all the deadfalls that we had set for marten, mink and coon and take up all of the steel traps as we had written to the man to be there about the fifteenth of the month. I think it was a day or two later when the team came and our hunt on the Kinzua was ended.

We got some thirty odd deer and either five or six bear and I think four otter. I do not remember the number of fox, mink, marten and coon, but we did well for there had been but very little trapping done in that locality at that time and furbearing animals were quite plentiful. I have never been back to that camp since. I gave the camp to a man by the name of Ball.

CHAPTER VIII.
Fred and the Old Trapper.

Yes, Fred, you can go with me to attend my traps, come down early as I wish to start at 5 o'clock." Fred was on hand next morning at the appointed hour. We leave the road here and go up this stream; this will take us to several traps and also to camp.

"Are these woods very large?"

"Yes, Fred. It is about fourteen miles either way through them."

"Does any one live in them?"

"No one only the lumberman. Well, Fred, here is the first trap."

"I don't see any trap."

"No, but it is there, just in front of that little stone pen; the bait is in the pen."

"Why don't you take that bush away?"

"Oh! that is part of the knack in trapping; see that is just far enough from the pen to let the animal pass through."

"Oh! I see, and it will step in the trap in going through!"

"That is it, exactly."

"Won't the water take the brush away?"

"Yes, if it gets too high, but you will see that I have put some heavy stones on the limbs that are down in the water; you also see that I turn the water above the trap by throwing up a few stones; this is done to keep the water so that it just covers the traps. You see that bunch of leaves that are a little higher than the rest of the leaves--the pan of the trap is just under those leaves."

"Did that moss grow on the stone pen?"

"No, I put it there to make the pen look old; you see a fox can easily step on that bunch of dry leaves that are on the pan of the trap from the bank. A fox does not like new things. You see this trap is set for mink, coon or fox, whichever may happen along."

"What is the trap fastened to?"

"See that limb that has moss all grown over it. The trap is stapled to it."

"Can't a fox or coon drag it away?"

"Yes, but not far. See the chain is stapled about the middle of the limb, and the animal would not go far before it got fast.

"Fred, you get that rabbit out of the knapsack that we took out of the snare, and we will put some fresh bait in the pen for this is getting too stale; mink and coon do not like rotten meat. Cut it into several pieces so that the animal can not get it all at once. There, that is all right, and let us hurry on to the next trap. Here it is and a mink in it and drowned."

"Where is the pen? I do not see it."

"We do not always have a pen. You see that notch in that log where the water runs over? That is where the trap was set. See this hay wire that is fastened to the trap chain and which is fastened to that stone out in the deep water? The mink could not go toward the bank so it went into the deep water and was drowned."

"Why did you set a double spring trap here?"

"Well, Fred, an otter might happen along and that is just the place to catch it. You see above the log I have fixed to gage the water as at the other trap. I do this so the water will not wash the covering from the trap, or get so deep over the trap that the animal will not spring it when going over it." "I see that you have got those brush on either side of the trap with just enough space for the animal to pass through over the trap." "That is correct, you are catching on, Fred, all right."

"Don't you use bait where you set a trap in this way?"

"Not often; sometimes I fasten a fish with a horse-hair with a hook fast to it so that you can hook it to the lower jaw and fasten it in the water just above the trap; water keeps it moving and attracts the animal. We have got this trap set all right and will now move on to the next. We will take the mink to the next trap before skinning it."

"What is that over yonder on the other side of the creek?"

"That is a coon and it is in a trap. Fred, you take my cane and kill it while I fix up the bait pen, for it has torn things up as bad as a bear would."

"Why did you not use stones to build this pen?"

"Old chunks are just as good and much handier to get, and there was plenty of moss on the old logs near to cover it with."

"Why do you not use old bushy limbs here?"

"You see this trap sets in the mouth of a small spring run; we will cut some little twigs and stick them up in the ground, in place of the brush, to make the runway, as we call it. We will now skin the mink. Rip straight down the hind leg from the heel to the vent. Now lay the knife down and start the skin loose on the legs with the thumb and finger; work the skin down the leg to the root of the tail then take knife and cut the skin loose around the vent working the skin free around the roots of tail until you can get your fingers of the left hand around the tail bone. Now with the right hand near the body of the mink pulling with the right and you will strip the tail clean from the bone. With the knife make a slit on either fore leg about one inch from the heel and around the leg. You are now ready to strip the skin down the body to the fore legs and with the thumb and finger work the leg out. Strip the skin down to the ears and with the knife cut the ears close to the head, continue to strip the skin down to the eyes, cut around the eyes close to the bone and use the knife on down to the end of nose. That was a short job. Now we will put this mink carcass in the back end of the pen and cut the balance of the rabbit up and put it in the pen back about six inches from the trap."

"Don't you use any scent; I have heard people say that you use some kind of scent?"

"I use none, only of the animal itself. It did not take long to take the pelt off that coon; we will strip some of that fat from the carcass and do it up in the skin and put it in the knapsack; hang the carcass up on that sapling. We must be moving now. Our next trap is a bear trap; it sets up in that little sag you see and in a spring that comes out of the side of the hill. I like to set traps in those springs for they never freeze up and the bait keeps much longer. No, there is nothing in it, I can see the clog there all right. Yes, there is something in it; it is a coon and it is dead. Look, there is a fox in a trap."

"Where was the trap set, I do not see any bait pen?"

"Fred, you take this stick and walk up slowly to him; go up close and give him a sharp blow across the back of the neck--that will fix him. You see that big mossy log laying on the bank over there? That was where he was caught. We will now set the trap again. See this little sink in the log? That is where the trap was set; this limb is what the trap was fastened to, one end on the ground and the other comes just up to the log where the trap is set and we will staple the trap to it. We will now cover it with moss, just like on this log, but we will get it from another log. No one could tell that there was a trap there."

"Will not the fox smell it?"

"He might if it was not for this fox carcass. We will skin the fox, just as we did the mink. Look out there Fred, do not disturb the moss or anything on that log where the trap is. Keep away from that. We will put this carcass in the little hollow and will drive a crotched stake straddle of its neck; drive it well down; now take this stick and rake some leaves over it, cover the neck where the stake is quite well, the rest of the carcass only slightly. You have done it very well and the fox will not notice what scent there is on the trap as long as that carcass is there."

"But you had no carcass there when you caught this one and I have heard that a fox was afraid of the scent of iron?"

"That is all bosh. Keep your traps free from all foreign scent and you need not be afraid of the scent of the iron, but if you catch some animal in the trap, then you should have some of the scent of that animal around near the trap, this will overcome what scent there is on the trap. This, however, is only necessary with shy animals like the fox. Coon and skunk are not afraid of what they smell."

"Do you ever wear gloves when setting your traps?"

LOG SET FOR FOX.

"No, that is all nonsense. Get the clamps out of the knapsack and we will set the bear trap. We set the trap this way so that the bear goes in lengthways of the jaws, not crosswise of them. We will now place the trap in this hole that we have dug out, so that the water will be deep enough to cover the trap and be sure that the jaws rest firmly on the ground, so that if the bear should step on the jaws, the trap would not tip up. Some trappers do not do this and then they think that the shy animal turned the trap over. We will now cover the trap with those water soaked leaves after which we will take this piece of moss as large as your hand, and with this forked stick put the moss on it, and place it on the pan of the trap."

"Would the bear smell it, if you put it on with your hands?"

"No, but if the trap should accidentally spring it would be better to catch the stick than your hand. Now we will cut this coon carcass into two or three pieces and put it back in the bait pen about three feet from the trap. There we have it fixed all right. We will now go over the ridge to where there is another bear trap set and will eat our lunch as we go along."

"How did you know that a fox would go on that log where that trap was set?"

"By knowing the nature of the animal. When the fox smelled the bear bait in the pen there, I knew that he would get on the highest point near the pen to investigate and that point was that log."

"Is this the only way you catch foxes?"

"No, that is only one of the many ways. Here we are; the trap is right down in the head of this hollow; that is a dark place down there, yes, that is the kind of a place that bears like to travel through. I can see the pen, but I do not see the clog. Yes, the clog is gone, I guess that Bruin has put his foot in it this time. Now go still and look sharp and see if we can find him anywhere for a bear will try hard and get away when they first see you. He has gone this way, see how he has torn down the brush and has turned up those old logs. He will not do that long and after a little we may be obliged to circle in places to find the trail. Here he has gone up this steep side hill but he will not go far that way. See how he has torn this old tree top up and gnawed those logs and those trees, he has been past here. He has gone straight back down the hill. Now he will keep along this side hill, for he may cross this hollow back and forth three or four times before we find him fast. Here is the trail again, he has gone back up the hill. We will work up the hill so as to keep on the highest ground."

"You have followed these bear trails a good many times, haven't you?"

"Yes, in 1900 I followed one seven days that broke the chain and went up with the trap, and then another party ran across the bear and killed it. I did not even get my trap back. They said they hung the trap up in a tree and some one stole it."

"Hold on Fred, what is that away down there in the hollow?"

"That is the bear, he is trying to climb that tree, I do not think he will make it, for the clog is fast between those two small saplings that stand by the large tree. We will go a little closer, there now! when he turns his head sideways take good aim and put the ball square in the ear. A good job, Fred, he never knew what hurt him. Now make a slit in the skin, right at the point of the breast bone, and then stick him as you would a hog. Do not cut the skin too much. Now Fred get the clamps out of the knapsack and we will see if we can get him out of the trap. Now we will skin him as you would a beef with the exception, we will leave the claws on, for the skins are a much better price where the feet are left. We will be very careful not to cut the hide, for they skin about as mean as a hog does. Well now we will hang the foreparts up in this tree and take the skin and the saddles and pull for camp."

"Are you not going to set the trap?"

"No, it will be dark before we get to camp now and we have got a heavy load to carry, in fact, if it was anything but bear, we would think we could not carry it."

"My, but this is getting heavy."

"Yes, Fred, but this all goes in with trapping and besides it will improve the appetite."

"I guess so, for I am as hungry as a wolf."

"Well, here we are at camp. Fred, you will find the lamp on that shelf close up in the corner. You light it while I start the fire. Now Fred you will find the key to the camp chest behind that ridge post. Open the chest and take the blankets out so that they will be airing. Now in the other part of the chest you will find some tin cups, plates, knives and forks, also some crackers, cheese and ginger snaps. The cheese is done up in waxed paper. You can put those things on the table while I go to the spring and get a pail of water. Now, Fred, you raise that lid and you will find a box sunk down in the ground, where you will find potatoes and bacon. Get some out. You will find the coffee in a sack in the chest and the coffee pot is hanging on that nail. You put the coffee on while I get the potatoes."

"Oh, we cannot wait for potatoes to cook."

"Yes, we can, I will pare three or four and slice them up and put them in the spider with a little water and some bits of pork and by the time the coffee boils, the potatoes will be ready. Fred, just hand me that lid so I can cover these potatoes over. You will find a can of condensed milk and the sugar in the chest. Please set them on the table while I fix the fire."

"You have plenty of good dry wood."

"Yes, I always come over to the camp before the trapping season begins and cut up a good lot of wood. And those old elevated stove ovens make the best kind of a stove for a camp. Fred, you pour the coffee while I take the potatoes up and we will partake of this frugal meal. In the morning for breakfast we will have bear steak, boiled partridge and buck-wheat cakes."

"Well Fred, I feel better, how is it with you?"

"Oh, I feel like a fighting cock now, but I was too hungry for anything. Well Fred, the dish water is hot in that pan on the stove, if you will wash the dishes, I will stretch those skins and dress those partridges. Now if you will spread the blankets on the bunk, I will mix the cakes for breakfast, and then we will be ready for bed."

"How large is this camp?"

"The logs were cut fourteen and sixteen feet long, so that makes it about twelve by fourteen on the inside. The roof is good and steep. Yes, I like a ridge roof and half pitch them, you do not have to make the body so high. Yes, I always chunk well and calk good with moss before I mud it, then you have a good warm camp. Yes, I like to have a 12 x 20, two small sash in each gable."

"Does that roof leak?"

"No, a roof put on with good hemlock bark like that will not leak and will last a long time. Fred we must bunk down for we must be moving early in the morning."

"Come, Fred, turn out, I have breakfast about ready."

"Why it is not morning, is it?"

"Yes, it is six o'clock and we must be moving as soon as we can see, for we have a big day's work before us. Yes, Fred, everything tastes good in the woods. I suppose a keen appetite has something to do with that. Well, it is light, so that we can see to travel, so we will be going. Yes, Fred, you can come over with me again and I will show you how to set traps, many different ways, to catch different animals, and we might have a bear in a pen."

"Do you catch bear in a pen?"

"Yes, and I like a pen for a bear better than a steel trap. No getting away if the pen is properly made."

"Well, here is the bear trap and there has been a wild cat at work at those inwards, so you see I did not bring that trap along for nothing. Fred, you place a few of those bushy limbs around on the upper side of those inwards, while I set the trap. There, that is all right, we will staple to this limb. Yes, he will be quite likely to get into the trap if he comes again, for he can't get at the bait very well from any other way, only over the trap."

"How far is it from where the bear trap was set?"

"About one-half mile. Yes, I suppose he dragged that trap three or four miles to get that distance. Here we are, it will not be a long job to set that trap as he has not torn the bait trap down. Fred, you get the clamps from the knapsack, while I cut that bushy tree for a clog. Yes, we let those limbs stick out about ten inches so that they will catch in the brush and on logs, and that bothers, you see. Yes, those lungs and liver are all right for bait as long as it is fresh. A bear does not like tainted meat. Well, that is all right now, we will go to camp and get a bite to eat, and then pull for home and get the horse and wagon and come out and take the bear meat and the skin in. Yes, we always ship the saddles to New York, they bring a good price.

"Yes, it is more of a knack to stretch a bear skin right than any other skin. Here we are at camp again, we will eat a bite and then pull for home. Good bye, Fred, yes, you shall go again."

CHAPTER IX.
Bears in 1870, To-Day--Other Notes.

One not familiar with the conditions of a wild woods life would naturally think that bears would diminish in proportion to deer and wild animals. However, this does not seem to be the case. Forty years ago, trappers of bear were not as numerous as at the present time. People at that time, hunted more for profit than sport and their forte was the slaughter of deer. In those days it was nothing uncommon to see sleigh loads of deer pass every day on the way to market.

After the first tracking snows of the season, the deer killed in this county (Potter) were hauled by team thirty and forty miles to the nearest railroad station and shipped to New York and Philadelphia but this is not what we wish to write of. We only speak of this to show that the man of forty years ago was of the trail, rather than the trap line.

Forty years ago, the writer was acquainted with nearly every hunter and trapper who made a business of hunting or trapping in this and adjoining counties. Men who made a business of trapping bear as well as hunting deer could be counted on the fingers of your hands, and the grounds on which they operated were the counties of Clinton, McKean, Cameron and Potter.

The names of these men who perhaps were the most interested in bear trapping in the section above mentioned were, Leroy Lyman, Horatio Nelson, Lanson Stephan, Isaac Pollard, Ezery Prichard and one or two others, including the writer.

The traps mostly used were bear pens and deadfalls. It was considered a fairly good day's work for two men to build one good bear pen or two good deadfalls. Most bear trappers, however, had a few steel bear traps for it may be said that nearly every country blacksmith knew how to make a bear trap and how to temper a trap spring. This cannot be said of the average blacksmith of the present day.

Bear forty years ago would migrate then as they do now. We used to think that bear would travel from the Virginias and from Northern New York if not from the New England States to Pennsylvania or from Pennsylvania north or south as the case may be. This was proven from the fact that if there was a good crop of mast in one locality, while a scarcity in another, the bear would all seem to be moved north or south as the case may be as though they had some way of informing one another where plenty of food was to be found. At such times when bear are on a migratory tramp it is not an uncommon thing to find a bear track near your house or barn on going out in the morning when there was snow on, so that the track is plain to be seen. This was no uncommon thing forty years ago, neither is it at the present time (1910) when there is a general scarcity of forage crops such as beech nuts, chestnuts and acorns. I have seen it stated by some writers that at certain times bear will move in a drove and at such times it was not safe for a man to meet a bear for they were very dangerous and would attack any one who chanced to be in their way.

In my upwards of fifty years experience of woods life, I do not call to mind of ever seeing more than three bears on one trail at the same time and these were an old bear and cubs. It has been the writer's observation that when bears were on these migratory trips in search of food or from other cause, they travel singly and not in droves or even in pairs.

During the summer when bears are existing on nettles, wild turnips, berries and other green food, it is not out of the ordinary to find a bear in pretty close proximity to the farm house and close around the fields where he can occasionally get a sheep or lamb.

I have seen and heard much written and said of bear raising from their hind feet to attract people's attention who chanced to come in their way when in the woods. I have never seen a bear raise on his hind feet for battle, in any case, when a hunter or trapper approaches them. I have often seen them sit upon their haunches to listen when they heard a noise and were not sure of its origin.

As to the number of bear at the present time and forty or fifty years ago, through Northern and Central Pennsylvania, there seems to be about as many now as there were then. This I attribute to the fact that much of the country in other localities has been cleared up and thus deprived bruin of his natural haunts.

Forty years ago,--in the early 70's--it was customary then as now, to keep tab on trappers as to what they were doing along the trap line. Trappers of years ago would average from three to twelve bears, according to how plenty they were and to what the condition of the weather was.

It often happens that when bear are plenty on the trapper's trapping grounds, he does not have the best of luck in taking the game. If shack is very plentiful it is sometimes difficult to get the bear to take ordinary bait. The bear will also den up or go into hibernation much quicker if they get fat, than they will if shack is a little scarce so that they do not get quite so fleshy. If the bears get real fleshy early in the season they will den up at the approach of the first cold and freezing weather and sleep until spring. On the other hand, if the bear continues to be a little lean, as he generally is during the summer, he will continue to search for food during quite severe weather. They will leave winter quarters and come out in search of food when there are a few warm days, or a slight thaw, which they will rarely do if they go into the den in good flesh.

The bear is not like the raccoon. Their rutting season in this latitude is in August and not in February and March as with the raccoon and groundhog. Now all of these conditions has much to do with the number of bears that a trapper may get during a season. The number of bear taken in Pennsylvania by the average trapper at the present time and forty years ago may be slightly less now than then but the difference is not great.

There are more bear trappers today than forty years ago. During the months of October and November, 1909, there were nearly one hundred bears caught in traps and killed with dogs in the above counties mentioned. Bears were more plentiful through this section than usual this season, although they did not work north into the beech timber until about the first of November, owing to a heavy crop of chestnuts and acorns farther south.

Comrades of the trap line, if I was in a section of country where large game was as plentiful as it was here fifty years ago, I would not be able to get very far into tall timber, but as it gets monotonous to write of skunk, muskrat and rabbit hunting of to-day, I will tell of some of my experiences of fifty years ago, when it was my custom to hunt deer and bear for profit and pleasure. In those days I made it a point to be in the woods with my bear traps and rifle by the middle of October each year, if health permitted.

In those days all that a trapper and hunter had to do was to get a few miles out into tall timber, build a good log cabin and hit a permanent job for the season. Deer, bear and fur-bearing animals were so plentiful that it only required a small territory to find game sufficiently plenty to keep the trapper on a lively gait all the time. In those days we made it more a specialty of hunting deer for the profit there was in it. We had built our cabin on the divide between the headwaters of the Cross fork of Kettel Creek and the headwaters of the East Fork of the Sinnamahoning. I had built a few deadfalls and bear pens for bear and also had three or four steel bear traps set, but beech-nuts, chestnuts and other nuts were so plentiful that the bear would not take meat bait and I had no other bait at hand. The bear would pass within a few feet of a trap and pay no attention to the bait.

Now at this time, furs were so low that there was but little to be made from the sale of the pelts of the fox, mink, skunk, etc. But it was my custom to carry one or two steel traps in my pack sack and when I killed a deer, I would make a set or two for the fox, marten or fisher, whichever happened along first. As I have stated I spent the greater part of my time in deer hunting. On this particular day I was following a drove of four or five deer, but the wind was so unsteady and whirling about in puffs so that as near as I could get to a deer was to see his white flag, beckoning me to come on as they jumped a log or some other object. Striking the trail of a bear that had gone back and forth several times, nearly in the same place within the past three or four days, since a light snow had fallen, I was satisfied that it was a bear going back and forth from his lodging quarters to his feeding grounds.

So I left the trail of the deer and took up the trail of the bear, taking the track that I thought had been made last. I did not follow the trail far, which led along the brow of the ridge, when I saw that the several different bear tracks were forming into one trail and making in the direction of several large hemlock trees that had been turned out by the roots and lay in a jumbled up mess. I followed the trail carefully until I was certain that the bear had entered the jungle of timber. Here I worked carefully around the jam of timber until sure that the bear was in the jungle and that it would be impossible for me to get near the bear. The density of brush and undergrowth was such that I would drive the bear out before I could get close enough to Bruin to get a shot at him. And this was a time, when I longed for a pard.

Being convinced that I could do nothing alone, I got out on one side of the trail the bear had made in going back and forth and watched until dark, in hopes that Bruin would come out on his way to his feeding grounds. But in this I was mistaken so was obliged to give up the hunt for the time being and make tracks for the shanty. My camp was about five or six miles from Edgcomb Place, this being the nearest point to where anyone lived, where I might get help to rout Bruin. The Edgcomb Place was a sort of a half way house, it being about fourteen miles either way to a settlement. The stage made one trip a week over this road and stopped at Edgcomb Place for dinner and often some one would come out from town in the stage and stop there for a few days' hunt. It was one of these parties that I was in hopes of getting to help me out in this bear hunt.

I started in the morning before daylight as the stage had gone the Kettel Creek way the day before, which was in my favor of catching help at the hotel. As good luck proved to be on my side, I found a man at the hotel by the name of John Howard, who was stopping there for a few days' hunt. He was more than anxious to join me in the bear hunt. We hastened back to camp so as to get onto the job as quickly as possible. We got to the shanty about noon and got a hasty lunch and started out to wake Bruin up if he was still sleeping where I had left him.

When we got to the jam of timber, we found that he had been to his feeding grounds and had returned to his lodging apartments during the night, so we now thought that we would soon make sure of our game. We located the spot the best we could where we thought Bruin was sleeping and began to cautiously work our way in from opposite sides. It only took a short time to work our way into the jam sufficiently to locate a large root, where Bruin's tracks showed plainly that he was sleeping under this root. We continued to work our way up closer to the root with gun in hand for ready action. But still Bruin did not show up, neither could we hear the least bit of a noise from him.

When we were within a few feet of the root, Mr. Howard on one side and the writer on the other side, suddenly, without any warning whatever, Bruin came out of his hole like a shot out of a gun and nearly landed on Mr. Howard, who sprang backwards to escape him. Mr. Howard's feet became tangled in the thick brush, he fell backwards and before he could regain his feet, Bruin had gone over the brow of the ridge, into the laurel out of sight. Mr. Howard was not able to get in a shot at Bruin, as I was on the other side of the root and on higher ground, I managed to empty both barrels of my rifle at him through the thick brush, but Bruin went on down the hill, through the laurel, apparently unhurt.

After following the trail of Bruin for some distance, we began, now and then, to find a little blood, where the bear had crawled over a log or rubbed against the laurel. We followed him until we found one or two places where he had broken down a few laurel and scratched about in trying to make a bed, so we thought the better plan was to let Bruin go for the night and let him make his bed.

But we did not go to camp empty handed for good luck favored Mr. Howard in killing a good, big deer on our way to the shanty. After leaving the trail of the bear, we followed up a spur of the main ridge that led to camp, Mr. Howard going up one side of the spur while I took the other spur. Just before reaching the top of the spur, I heard Mr. Howard shoot and in a few minutes I heard him shouting for help. When I got across the ridge to where he was, I found him dressing a good sized buck. As it was getting dark we lost no time in taking the entrails out of the deer, cutting a withe with a hook, which we hooked into the lower jaw of the deer. We hooked ourselves to the withe and made lively tracks to the shanty, where we could talk and laugh of the day's hunt.

* * *

We were up early the next morning and had our lunch packed in our knapsack, ready for an early start. It had turned warm during the night and the light snow that was on the ground, was fast disappearing. So we lost no time in getting back to where we had left Bruin's track the night before. We could still manage to follow the trail on the snow and we soon found where Bruin had broken down a few laurel and tried to make a bed. But he would not stop long, apparently, when he would move on for a short distance and again break down a few laurels as before to make a nest. We could see a little more blood at each place where he stopped than the one before.

We were working the trail as cautious as we could, when we heard a noise in the thick laurel to our left and got a glimpse of Bruin going through the laurel. We emptied both barrels of our guns in the direction where we could see the brush wiggle, but all of our shots failed to take effect. Bruin now left this laurel patch, crossed a ravine and began to climb another spur of the main ridge. We did not follow the trail long, when we discovered that it was becoming hard work for Bruin to travel far at a time, as he would stop to rest. The snow was now gone so that it was a little more difficult to follow the trail of the bear. We thought that it would be better for one of us to go up the ravine to the top of the ridge and stand about where he thought that the bear would come out at the top of the ridge. Mr. Howard went to the ridge, while I was to follow the bear's trail.

After waiting long enough to give Mr. Howard time to get to the top of the ridge, I took up the trail of the bear. I had not gone far when I came to a bed, where the bear had stopped for a time. I was now sure Mr. Howard would get to his watching place before the bear reached the top of the hill. I was not mistaken, for it was not long until I heard Mr. Howard fire both barrels of his gun in rapid succession. I thought when I heard the two shots that the bear hunt was surely over, but after listening a few moments and hearing nothing from Mr. Howard I was then unable to give a guess what he had done. I worked along on the trail until near the top of the hill when I saw Mr. Howard standing with head down and bearing the expression of a motherless colt.

When I got up to him he said that the bear had stopped near the brow of the ridge and when he came in sight, the bear started across the ridge and he fired both barrels of his rifle at him but the bear was so far away that he could not reach him. The bear now crossed the ridge in the direction of Windfall Run, a branch of the Cross Fork and toward a large windfall. We followed the bear a short distance in to the windfall. Briers and brush were so thick that it was almost impossible to work our way along in the brush and one could scarcely see ten feet ahead. We had followed the trail but a short distance when we could hear Bruin whining like a little puppy and soon we could see him sitting up on his haunches and keeping up the whine. We soon put an end to his troubles. When we removed the bear's entrails, we found that one of the shots that we fired at him at the beginning of the hunt, had passed through the lungs but had not struck any large artery or any vital point. But the wound had weakened him so that he was no longer able to make his way through the thick briars and brush. We had two days of sport but now the real work began.

We were about three miles from camp and any hunter who has toted a three hundred pound bear or a good big deer, lashed to a pole and where the route was up and down steep hills, knows what sort of a job he has on his hands. But comrades, we were not as old at that time as we now are and we could tote a bear or deer as easy then as we could a rabbit now.

WOODCOCK AND HIS CATCH, FALL 1904.

Mr. Howard stayed with me for about two weeks and we had other bear hunts and killed two other bear and we did it almost without knowing that there was a bear within ten miles of us. We also got five or six deer during Mr. Howard's stay with me. Deer were as plentiful in those days as rabbits. Comrades, look over the accompanying picture and note the difference at the camp of a trapper from what you can imagine it was about one's hunting camp at the time we write of.

CHAPTER X.
Incidents Connected with Bear Trapping.

Several years ago, I was trapping for bears on the East Fork of the Sinnemahoning River. I usually went on horse back as far as I could when tending the traps. But boys, don't be bad, as I was, for this was on Sunday that I went to look at the traps. I found the bait-pen of the first one torn down, bait gone and everything showed plainly that Bruin had been there. As I had no bait at hand, I went to the next trap. I found things quite different, for the old bear had surely "put his foot in it" this time, as the trap was gone. On taking the trail I did not follow it far, before I found bruin fast in an old tree-top. I soon dispatched him and taking off his coat, hung up his carcass. Now the bait was gone at this trap also. Let me tell you that this is something that rarely happens, for when the bear puts his foot in a Newhouse trap, he seldom tarries to monkey with bait. I suspected that another bear had been there after this one had got in the trap. As I had no bait I took the lungs and heart of the one I had caught and baited the traps the best I could, then I took the skin and started for home. Well, when I got near the horse you can bet there was some tall prancing and loud snorting. After a long time I managed to get on his back and home with the skin.

The next morning I began to have some doubt whether bears were cannibals or not. I thought I would take some fresh bait and go back and bait the traps up good.

When I got near the trap in which I had caught the bear the day before, I heard a great deal of wrestling going on and it did not take long to see that I had an old he-bear hung up this time. And now was the time that I began to realize what a boy's trick I had cut up, for I had not taken any gun with me; only a small revolver and three cartridges. I found that the bear was dead fast and a big one too. He seemed to be more inclined to quarrel than bears usually are. I took my trapping hatchet in one hand and revolver in the other, and worked my way up close as I dared and awaited the best chance I could get to shoot for he was rolling and tumbling like a ball. I fired at his head but missed it. I fired the two remaining cartridges just back of the fore-shoulders. He paid about as much attention to it as I imagine he would if it had been a flea that bit him. After waiting some time to see what effect the shots would have and noticing no change in Bruin's countenance, I concluded I would see what I could do with a club. I soon found that I and the club were not "in it," so I gave it up as a bad job and went home after the team and a gun. On my way home I had to pass the house of an old trapper by the name of Stevens. Of course, he was out to see what luck I had, and when I told him my story, he gave a great laugh and said he would go and let the bear out of the trap. When we got back to the trap the next day we found the fight all gone out of Bruin, for the two shots had penetrated the lungs and he was nearly dead.

* * *

Pard, whom I call Co, and I went camping many years ago on a branch of the Susquehanna River in Lycoming County, Pennsylvania. At that time all that part of the country was an unbroken wilderness and we were several miles from the nearest town. Now Co was a good hunter but despised trapping, saying it was no gentleman's sport, yet he was always ready to do his share in camp life.

One evening in December Co did not turn up at dark, the usual hour for his return, still I did not worry much until eight o'clock, but from that time until about nine I kept going to the door and giving an occasional "Kho-Hoop," just to let him know the direction of the camp if he was within ear shot. As Co did not return, about nine o'clock I shouldered my rifle and started out in the direction that he had gone, shooting off my gun, and occasionally letting out a shout that echoed from hill to hill, but no answer came back in reply. The weather was growing extremely cold and I began to feel very much worried about Co for although I knew he was a good woodsman, I imagined all sorts of calamities had befallen him. At every high point I would fire my gun but never an answer could I hear. I kept this up till midnight, and then retraced my steps to camp intending to take an early start in the morning, when I could see to track my wandering partner.

Judge of my delight, when about half a mile from camp the sharp report of a rifle rang out on the clear night air, and I knew Pard had returned alive. I hastened to the shanty where I found Co all right but as mad as a hornet. As he raved around he exclaimed: "No one but a--fool would catch anything in a--steel trap. If you must trap things, get them in something that will stay put." When Co cooled off a little, I said: "Come old man, tell us what has happened." "What has happened," said he, "enough has happened, I should think. I went where you set that tarnal old bear trap and some critter has got into it and broken the chain and carried it off, and he makes a track bigger than an elephant. He's making for the big windfall and I followed him more than forty miles, and he was farther ahead of me than when I started, and I hope he will get into the old windfall and stay there till doomsday." Well, Pard felt better when he had eaten the hot supper I had left for him and we turned in for a few hours' sleep.

The next day we went to town and got a number of men and dogs and the following morning started out early on the track of old bruin. We soon struck the trail and located the beast in a big ravine. Stationing the men around where the bear was likely to break cover, I went in with the dogs to drive him out.

Now there was one young chap among the crowd called Dan, who proved to be of rather a timid nature. The battle which soon followed proved very short owing to the number of guns opened on the bear the moment he broke cover and he was soon dispatched and nearly as soon skinned and cut up. But when I looked for Dan he was nowhere to be found. A searching party was organized and after beating the bush for some time, poor, frightened Dan was finally located in the top of a small beech tree and came tumbling down inquiring if the bear was "sure dead."

***

I have often thought I would like to relate some of my experiences in the woods while deer hunting. Many a time while following a herd of deer or a wounded one over ridge after ridge, has the sun set and the stars come out and I found myself many miles from my cabin or any habitation. Then I would find a large fallen tree, that laid close to the ground, gather a pile of dry limbs and bark, scrape away the snow from the log, often the snow being a foot deep, build a fire where I scraped the snow away. When the ground became thoroughly warm, I would rake the coals and brands down against the log, put on more wood, and then I would place hemlock boughs on the ground, where I had previously had the fire. Soon they would begin to steam and after frizzling some venison (if I chanced to have it) before the fire I would take off my coat, lie down on my stomach, pull the coat over my head and shoulders and sleep for hours before waking. Sometimes I would have the skin of a bear to put over me, and for doing these things my friends would scold me, but the reader will know, if he has the blood of a hunter in him, that I enjoyed it.

But this is not what I started to write about, it was of a day's hunt after a bear on the 16th day of December, 1903. On the day previous, the afternoon sun sinking to rest in the west, casts its rays for a moment upon a solitary hunter's cabin in the hills of old Potter, then the bright glows faded away, the sun disappeared behind the mountains and it was a soft beautiful twilight, while I stood just outside the cabin door meditating. Mart (that is an old liner who had come to my cabin to have a few days' hunt) came out of the cabin and I said, "old man, what are you thinking about?" The reply was, "just watching the sun set." "Don't you think the coon will be out tonight if it holds warm?" "I don't know what the coon will do, but I know we went around a bear over in that jam in Dead Man's Hollow. (This hollow is so called because a fisherman a few years ago, found the body of a man who had gotten lost and died in the snow the winter before).

Well what do you think you will do about it? I think we had better turn in early so as to get an early start in the morning and see if we can find where the bear is sleeping. "Agreed," said Mart, and we were soon in bed, but it was a long time before I closed my eyes in sleep for I was familiar with the woods in the neighborhood where the bear was supposed to be and I mapped out and laid every plan that was to be carried out the next day before I went to sleep.

At four o'clock in the morning we were astir and soon breakfast was ready and eaten, lunch put up and at the break of day we were on our way to where bruin was supposed to be, a distance of about five miles, which is no small job for an old cripple like myself. After about three hours we were on the ground where we were in hopes of finding bruin. Mart was to circle several points outside of where we thought the bear was snoozing; this was done to make sure that the bear was in there. I took a position where the bear was most likely to come out if he was there and should be started by Mart. My position was in an open piece of timber on the point of a hill and near a very thick jam of trees that had been broken down two years before by a heavy ice storm and near the bear track where he had gone in several days before. Mart was to make another circle somewhat smaller than the one he had previously made for we now knew that the bear was in the jam of timber.

After completing the second circle Mart was to drop below the jam where we were quite sure bruin was napping and work his way through the fallen timber. This worked all right, for soon I heard Mart cry out: "Look out, he is coming." Soon I heard the crashing of the brush and could tell that bruin was coming directly toward me, and in another minute he broke into the open timber. My rifle was already pointed in that direction and bruin had scarcely made two jumps in the open timber when I fired. The bear made a loud noise like that of a hog and I knew that he was hit hard and could already see a crimson streak in the snow. But bruin steadily held his course, in a few yards further he made an attempt to jump a large fallen tree and I fired again. This shot was more fatal than the first, and he fell to the ground and could not rise. I hurried up and fired a shot through his head which soon quieted him. Mart was soon on the scene and after a little rejoicing we soon had his hide off, and cutting the fore parts off and hanging them in a tree to be brought out the next day. Mart took the saddles and I the skin and started for camp, which we reached shortly before dark, and as we had prepared things for supper before leaving in the morning, supper was soon ready which consisted of buckwheat cakes, wild honey, baked potatoes, bacon, bear steak and tea. Dear readers, do not tell Mart, but I think that he took a hot toddy after talking the hunt over and over. Again, we laid down to rest our weary selves and dream of the hunt which may never come.

CHAPTER XI
Pacific Coast Trip.

As I am always looking for taller timber to plant my traps in and as the drift of the trapper seems to be to the west, the Rockies and the Pacific Coast, and as I have had some experience in the Rockies, and along the Pacific Coast region, I will speak of some of the advantages and disadvantages that the trapper will meet with in that section.

The trapper will find the fur bearers more plentiful and many more kinds of animals to take, than is found in the East, which is a great advantage to the trapper. The hunter will find deer quite plentiful in many places in the Rocky Mountains and on the Pacific Coast. In 1904 I was in Humboldt and Trinity Counties, California and I found deer so plentiful and tame that it was no sport to shoot them. While the law limited the hunter to two deer in a season, the people in the mountains made their own laws, as to the number of deer that they should kill. Black and brown bear are plentiful all through the Rocky Mountains and in the Coast ranges. You see much written of the grizzly bear in this region, but it is doubtful if a hunter or trapper would see one or even the track of one during a whole season's trapping. The trapper will find marten, fisher and lynx in many places in the Rockies and in the Coast Range but nothing to what there was a few years ago.

Now one who is contemplating trapping in the Rockies or on the Pacific Coast, must bear in mind that the conditions that a trapper meets with in this region are far different from what they are in the East. The trapper who is planning a trip in that section before starting out should examine his feet close to see that there are no tender spots on them. The man who makes a success of trapping in this region must be a man who can stand grief and hardships a plenty, for he will run up against it often. He will find the mountain streams hard to get along; he will have but little use for a boat as the streams are rapid and full of boulders. In most cases the trapper will be compelled to take his outfit into the mountains by pack horses, and in many cases it will be necessary for the trapper to be the horse.

The trapper to succeed in a financial way must take in a supply of provisions to last at least until the first of June, for it is during April, May and even June that he must do his bear trapping; for the bear holes up or goes into hibernation down in the lower land and does not show up much in the mountains until spring.

The trapper must provide himself with a good number of traps of different sizes from the No. 1 for marten to the No. 5 for bear; and that means a whole lot of packing and hard work. He must have at least one pair of snow shoes, and should have an extra pair in case of a mishap, in the way of breakage. One good gun is all that is likely to be needed, and don't load yourself down with a lot of revolvers, hunting knives, etc. A good strong pocket knife is all that I have found necessary, though one should have more than one knife no matter what kind he may use.

Here I will say a word as to a gun especially for the trap line. The manufacturers of guns have as yet failed to make it. The Marble Game-Getter comes the nearest to it of any now made, but that is not just to my liking. We would do away with one of the barrels, and have a single barrel, 44 caliber straight cut, with cartridges for both ball and shot with 15 inch barrel, skeleton stock, similar to the Stevens Pocket shot gun. Mind, I am speaking of an arm on purpose for the trap line, and this kind of a gun would do the work and be light to carry.

Now the expense for an outfit to go into the mountains for a season's campaign is necessarily a considerable item. It is quite necessary that the trapper has a number of camps on his line at advantageous points, for the trapper cannot cover sufficient territory from one camp to make it pay; besides, a number of camps on the line will relieve the trapper of much hardship. I mention this matter thinking it might be of some interest to some one whose feet are itching to get into a big game country, and are thinking of only the game, and not of the hardships they are sure to meet with. Another thing that is well for the trapper who is looking for a happy hunting and trapping ground to remember is, that he will no longer find game as plentiful as it once was, in any place that is in any way easily accessible. If the trapper will take into consideration the expense and hardship that one must put up with in going on one of these outings, it might be that he can find quite as much pleasure and profit in looking up a trapping ground nearer home.

I will mention one or two places where one can find some sport where it will not require the hardship nor expense, and at the same time will find deer and some other game quite plentiful, with a fair sprinkling of the fur bearers.

In Humboldt County, in California, on Redwood River, deer and bear can be found quite plentiful, and there are some marten, fisher and a few lynx, coon, mink, skunk and fox. The fox are mostly grey and you may by chance meet occasionally with a mountain lion. To reach this section the best way is from San Francisco by boat to Eureka, then by rail and wagon.

Another section where game and fur bearers are fairly plentiful and of easy access, is in the vicinity of Thompson's Falls, in Northern Montana.

But if only a good outing is wanted, that can be had in Pecos Valley, New Mexico. You will not find much to trap other than muskrats and coon on the river and lakes, but they are quite plentiful, especially the latter. You will find coyotes and some grey wolves, and some antelope, which are protected. Duck shooting is good, the climate is mild, only freezing ice the thickness of window glass in the coldest weather, which is all thawed out and gone by ten o'clock. This section is easily reached by rail.

* * *

In July, 1902, I was spending a few days at Spokane, Wash. Nearly every day I would take an old cane fish pole and go to the river just above the falls and fish for bass. I would shift my post from one point along the bank of the river to another and sometimes I would go out on the boom timbers and fish among the logs. Some days I would get a bass or two, but oftener I got nothing further than the pleasure of drowning a few minnows.

Nearly every morning I noticed a man would come down along the bank of the river and go in the direction of the mill. Sometimes he would stop and watch me for a few minutes, and then pass on without saying anything. But one morning he came along when I happened to be sitting close to his path. I looked up and gave the usual morning nod. The gentleman, for such he proved to be, inquired what luck I was having. I replied that I guessed it must be fisherman's luck, for I got but few fish. He replied that he thought that there were very few bass in the dam, as there was so much fishing done there.

I was quite sure that he was right from the number of fish I caught, and I could see a number of others scattered about the pond, and some on the logs, some on the boom timbers and some in boats. The next morning I was back at my old post, and this man came along as usual. He stopped, laughed and said that I seemed to have plenty of faith. I replied that the occasion demanded great faith. He inquired if I lived in the city. I told him that I lived in Pennsylvania and was only out in that country to see the sights and get a few fish and a little venison and later might try to get a little fur.

He informed me that his name was Nettel (Charles Nettel) that he was a lumber inspector and that he was going to have a vacation the next week. He intended going to the North Fork of the Clearwater on Elk Creek, where he had a camp, and that if I wished to fill up on trout and venison, I had better join him, as he had no one selected to accompany him yet. I said, "Thank you, I would be pleased to do so," as quick as I could, for fear he would change his mind. I now dropped my bass fishing and would drop into the mill where Mr. Nettel was at work and catch a few minutes chat with my new-found friend, as an opportunity would occur, until the time came to go to Mr. Nettel's camp. As I had a complete outfit, including blankets, tin plates, cups, knives, and forks, a takedown or folding stove with the necessary cooking utensils, which I had not yet unpacked, we concluded to take the whole kit along so that if anything had happened at Mr. Nettel's camp we would have a tent as well as the other camp outfit, but we found Mr. Nettel's shack all right. We took a train to near a place called Orofino on the Clearwater River in Idaho where we repacked our outfit, putting it into sacks.

We engaged a man with two pack horses to take our plunder to camp which we found to be all right, and I wish to say that this was the farthest up the gulch in the Rockies that I had been at that time.

I found my friend all right on the trout question, for trout were so plenty it was no sport to catch them. The next morning after we were in camp we climbed to what Mr. Nettel called the bench, but I thought it was the moon. We had hardly got to the level, or bench, when we say plenty of elk tracks so we followed in the direction in which the fresh trails seemed to lead.

We had not gone far when I noticed something moving in the underbrush, which might have been taken for a rocking chair for all that I could tell. We stood still a few moments when three elk came out in sight. We watched them feed for a few minutes, then made a noise like a deer blowing, and the elk stopped feeding, stood and listened and looked about for danger; Mr. Nettel again snorted and the elk trotted off.

We now separated a little and began walking across the bench. We had not gone far when I saw two buck deer feeding and shot one of them. Mr. Nettel soon came to me and we took the entrails out of the deer and drew the carcass down to camp where we sure had venison as well as trout.

The man who packed our outfit up the gulch for us had a little whiffet dog with him, and in some manner he neglected to take the dog back with him. We were a little worried at first because the man had left the dog with us, but later I at least was pleased that the dog was with us.

We had dressed the deer and hung the meat up on trees near the shack. The second night after we had the deer hanging up, along in the night the dog kept growling so that after a time, as the moon was shining, I thought I would get up and see what was worrying the pup. When I opened the shack door the pup lit out like shot from a shovel, and I could see the outline of some animal taking up a tree. I could hear the bark from the tree falling to the ground like hail.

Mr. Nettel was still sound asleep, so I said nothing but took my gun and stepped outside the shack. I could see the outlines of something standing on a limb of the tree. I took the best aim I could owing to the dim light and fired. The tree stood on the side of the gulch, which was very steep, and when the gun cracked the object in the tree apparently flew right up the side of the gulch from the tree.

The pup gave chase and within fifty yards I could again hear the bark from the tree and soon again I could see the outline of the animal on the tree. I was working along out towards the pup, when Mr. Nettel, close to my side said, "It is a lion; be careful and take good aim this time and kill him, if you can." I got up to the tree where I could see the cat fairly fell, and with all the care possible, I fired. The cat lit out from the tree, but this time he went down the hill instead of up, and when he struck the ground it was broadside instead of on all fours. As good luck would have it, I had hit him square through the shoulders.

The cat was a little over seven feet long, and Mr. Nettel said that it was not a large lion, but as it was the first one that I had seen then I thought it was longer than a twelve-foot rail. We pulled the cat up to the shack and turned in again. It was only eleven o'clock and Mr. Nettel was soon sound asleep, but I had too much cat excitement for me to do any more sleeping that night.

In the morning we skinned the cat, gathered dry leaves and stuffed the skin and had a stuffed cat in camp. Later, we sold the skin to a party for three dollars. We stayed in camp two weeks, feasting on venison, trout, grouse, and other game. Some of the time we spent prospecting for gold, but we failed to strike it rich.

At the end of the two weeks allotted Mr. Nettel, he was obliged to return to his work, and I can say that I never spent two weeks' time with more pleasure than I did with the friend I found while fishing for bass.

CHAPTER XII.
Some Michigan Trips.

Owing to the recent fires (1905) in the northern portion of Michigan, which have undoubtedly killed many of the smaller fur bearing animals in that section, has called to mind experiences I had trapping and hunting in both the Lower and Upper Peninsulas of that state. In the fall of 1868 on the first of October, a party of four of us took a boat at Buffalo, New York, and went to Alpena on Thunder Bay, Michigan, where we purchased provisions for a winter's campaign hunting and trapping.

We engaged a team to take our outfit up the Thunder Bay River, a distance of about twenty miles, where the road ended. The road was an old lumber road and rather rough over those long stretches of corduroy. We camped at the end of the lumber road the first night and the team returned home the next morning. We took our knapsacks with some blankets and grub and went up the river to find a camping ground to suit our notion.

Mr. Jones and myself took the one axe that we carried with us and began clearing a site to build the camp on. Mr. Goodsil and Mr. Vanater went back after more of the supplies, which included another good axe and a crosscut saw. They cut out a road as they returned so that we could drive to camp when it became necessary. At the end of a week we had up a good log cabin, and all was ready to begin to slay the deer and skin the fur bearers. Two of the boys now went down to Alpena to get the mail and send letters home. On the boys' return next day they brought word that we would not be allowed to ship any deer out of the state. This put a wry face on Goodsil and Jones, for deer hunting was their delight. It was not so bad with Vanater and myself, for we could find plenty of sport with the traps and tanning a few deer skins. Vanater was an expert at it, graining the skins in the water and using the brains of the deer and coon oil for tanning and then smoking the skins.

We did not kill many deer though they were plentiful, but venison was so cheap in Detroit and other Michigan cities that it did not pay one for the trouble. By the last of October there was quite a fall of snow and Mr. Goodsil, who was a gunsmith, suddenly came to the conclusion that he was neglecting his business at home and we could not persuade him to stay any longer. It was only a few days later when Mr. Jones also concluded that he was neglecting his business and left us. Now I began to wonder if Mr. Vanater or myself would be the next to get the home fever, but knowing the metal Charley was made of, I expected that I would be attacked first.

Charley and I being now left alone began building deadfalls for mink, marten, fisher and lowdowns for bear. I will explain that a lowdown is one of those affairs, half pen, half deadfall, which are built by first making a bed of small poles, then placing on this bed notched together the same as for a log house. The logs should be about twelve inches in diameter, and two tiers will make the pen high enough. The space inside the pen is usually made about seven feet long, two feet high and twenty inches wide. The roof is made of poles or small logs pinned to cross logs, the one at the back end of the pen forming a roller hinge. The cover is raised up and fastened with the usual lever and hook trigger, which the bait is fastened to. The bear in order to get the bait goes over the logs into the pen. I wish to say that while this sort of a trap is quickly made, I do not like them, as the bear will rub the fur madly in its struggles, and they are an inhuman sort of an affair at best.

BUILDING A BEAR "LOWDOWN".

To get back to my story, Charley and I did fairly well in catching mink and marten, but the bear had either migrated or gone into winter quarters. The coon had also gone into winter quarters. The snow was getting quite deep as it was now past the middle of November, and it now proved to be my luck to be left alone in camp. One night when we were coming to camp, we had to cross a stream on a small tree which had fallen across the creek. There were several inches of snow on the log and Charley was carrying a small deer on his back. I was behind him carrying the guns. Charley worked his way carefully across the log but just as he was about to step off the log on the opposite bank he slipped and fell striking his left leg across the log, breaking the bone just above the ankle joint. Fortunately we were only a short distance from camp so that Charley hobbled to camp, using his gun for a crutch.

When we got in camp it did not take long to see that the bone was broken. I fixed wood, water and food as convenient as possible for Charley and took a lantern, a lunch in my pocket and started for Alpena, reaching there shortly after daylight the next morning. Engaging a team without any delay we started back to camp. Reaching camp about three o'clock in the afternoon, we found Charley quite comfortable and feeling quite chipper under the circumstances. While the team was eating we fixed both blankets on the straw and a mattress which we had brought for the purpose from town, and fixed things as comfortable as we could. We were soon on our way back to town, which we reached about midnight. The next morning the doctor set the broken limb with but little difficulty.

After staying two or three days and making arrangements with a young man to come to camp every Saturday and bring mail and word from Charley, I returned to camp, where I found things all right. While out to town I bought a pair of snow shoes. I had never used them, and for the first few days it was who and who to know which would be on top, myself or the snow shoes. I finally mastered them and found them a great help in getting about in the deep snow. It kept me pretty busy attending to the traps.

One night after Charley had been gone about three weeks, on nearing camp, I saw a big smoke coming out of the chimney. I first thought the cabin was on fire, but I soon saw that that was not the case, and knew some one had started a fire. When I got there I saw some one had been there with a team. When I rapped on the door Charley called out, "Come in, I am running this camp now." Well, I tell you I was pleased to hear that voice call out, "Come in." It was some time before we thought it best for Charley to go out very much, but he could keep camp and I had company. We stayed in camp until the middle of May, thinking that we would have a big catch of bear in the spring, but were disappointed for we only caught three; but we caught quite a lot of coon. We did not trap any for muskrat.

My next trip to Michigan was to Kalkaska County, and I had two partners, Moshier and Funk by name, and both were residents of the state. Our camp was on the Manistee River near the Crawford and Kalkaska County line. This trip was some ten or twelve years later than the one previously mentioned, probably 1878. We killed some thirty odd deer, and Mr. Moshier having some friends living down close to the Indiana line, he shipped our venison down to his friend and he sold it for us. I do not know where he sold it but the checks came from a man by the name of Suttell, N. Y. We caught 11 bear during the fall and spring. We caught a good number of mink, coon and fox, also a few marten.

I should have said that on my trip on Thunder Bay River we caught several beaver, but on the Manistee we saw no fresh beaver signs but plenty of old beaver dams. We would make an occasional trip on to the Boardman and Rapid Rivers for mink. On Rapid River two or three miles above Rickers Mill was a colony or family of three or four beaver, but we did not try to catch them.

My third trip to Michigan was to the Upper Peninsula, in Schoolcraft County. A pard of mine by the name of Ross and myself had a boat made at Manistique, and started the first of September. We poled and rowed the boat up the Manistique River for a distance of about a hundred miles, according to our estimate. The boat was heavily loaded with our outfit, and we were nearly a month making the trip up the river to where we built our camp on a small lake about one-half mile from the main river. We found mink, marten, beaver and coon quite plentiful, but from what I read bear and wolves are more plentiful there now than they were about 1879. At that time there was not a railroad in that section, nor scarcely a tree cut in the northern part of the Upper Peninsula, with the exception of up about the Iron Works where they were cutting timber and burning coke and charcoal. In fact, I found bear more plentiful in Lower Michigan.

About the fifteenth of October we had the camp in shape and a big pile of wood cut and piled close to the door. We now began to explore the country for the best sites to set our traps, mostly Nos. 2, 3 and 4, besides seven bear traps, all Newhouse. We would build deadfalls along the line, for we would not set a steel trap only where we were quite sure that we would make a catch. We used the water set mostly for wolves and fox, and of course, for mink and coon.

Good springs were not so common where water sets could be made as in Pennsylvania. We could find occasionally a good log crossing where we could get in a set for wolf, but suitable places of this kind were not plentiful. We worked for beaver all we could. We would break a notch in their dams and then set a trap just on the edge of break in water just deep enough so the beaver would spring the trap. It was while trapping here that I learned to make the bait set for beaver. This is to use the kind of wood beaver were feeding on for bait.

We caught three or four wolves on the ice close to the bank. Sometimes the ice would settle along the banks and the water would run over the ice too close to the shore and then freeze. This made a good path, or rather place for the wolf to travel. Now, where a spruce or cedar tree would fall into the lake so as to leave a narrow space between the boughs on the tree and the bank, was a good place to set. We would watch the weather and when it began snowing we would go to one of these trees from the ice or water side, cut a notch in the ice, put in some ashes or dry pulverized rotten wood. The notch cut in the ice must be just deep enough to let the trap down level with the surface. The clog was concealed under a bough of the tree.

Now, I wish to say that I was never able to catch a timber wolf unless I was able to outwit him, and in order to do this the conditions and surroundings must be perfect for making the set. Where we found good places to make a set of this kind we would place the carcass of a deer several yards from shore out on the ice. This would entice the wolves to come around, and of course increase our chances of making a catch.

We were bothered some by having a wolverine follow a line of deadfalls, tear down the bait pen and take the bait, but we did not allow him to do his cussedness long before we would put a trap in the way.

We would sometimes have the parts of a deer taken down by a lynx where we had hung up venison so that it would be convenient to use for bear bait. We never objected much about it for we were willing to trade venison for a cat almost any time, for deer were very plentiful.

In April, when we were taking up our traps and getting ready to start down the river as soon as the water dropped so that we dare start, we were going onto a stream one day to take up three or four traps that we had set for beaver, our route led us across the point of the ridge. The point faced to the southeast, and the snow was off in spots on this point. When we went over this point in the morning we saw many deer run from these bare spots, so when we came back along in the afternoon we were as careful as possible and kept the highest ground so as to get a good view on this bare point to see how many deer we could count. There were upwards of forty in sight at one time. How I wish I could have had that picture.

We did not dare to start down the river until the first of June, on account of the high water. We had been told that there was a camp on the head of the river where they were cutting wood to be burned into charcoal. While we were waiting for the water to drop we took a knapsack of grub and some fishing tackle and started to find the wood choppers' camp, which we did on the second day after leaving camp. We stayed ten or twelve days at this camp, and while there a Frenchman invited me out to a lake two or three miles from their camp and fish for bass. He said he would take along a couple of traps and we would have some rats for breakfast, as we were going to camp at the lake over night. I did not say much about rats for breakfast, as I thought the man was joking. But sure enough, we had rats for breakfast, also plenty of fish.

Well, after the man had argued and plead the case of the rats from all points of view, and I had done a good deal of snuffing and smelling, I tasted, yes, I ate a piece of muskrat and I must confess it was of a fine flavor and would be splendid eating if it was not a rat. However, I have not tried any more from that day to this. I prefer partridge, and I have never been in a place where there were as many partridges as there were in Upper Michigan.

It is remarkable how long and well one can live on one hundred pounds of flour, twenty-five pounds lard, ten pounds salt and some bacon, (tea and coffee if one thinks he can't get along without it), in a good game and fish country with a good gun and fishing tackle.

We started on our return trip down the river on the second day of June. There had not been a man to our camp during this time. We were well satisfied with our catch with one exception, that being bear, as we only got four and they were all rather small. We had a splendid journey on our return trip down the river. We would see deer at almost every turn and once we saw a bear swimming the river. We caught lots of fish, all we could use, with hardly an effort.

CHAPTER XIII.
Hunting and Trapping in Cameron County, Pa., in 1869.

In my last letter on hunting and trapping in Cameron County, I promised to give Bill Earl's and my own experience in hunting in that county the next season. Well the story is not long, as we had our camp already built, we concluded not to go out into the woods until it was time to begin hunting and to put out bear traps. Accordingly on the last day of October we took a man with a team to take our traps, camp outfit and the grub stake to camp.

Going by the way of Emporium in that county, we were compelled to stay there over night, the distance being too far to reach camp the first day. At Emporium we purchased what more necessaries we needed, that we had not brought from home. We reached camp the second day about 10 o'clock. When we came in sight of the camp, Bill was walking ahead of the team with an axe cutting out brush here and there as needed. All of a sudden Bill stopped, set down the axe and looked in the direction of the shanty. When I was close enough so Bill could speak to me, he said, "I be-dog-on if the wicky is not occupied." I asked, "What with, porcupines?" Bill's reply was that he had known porkies to do some dog-on mean work, but he had never known them to build fires.

I could now see the shack, and sure enough there was a little smoke curling up from the chimney. Bill said that he hoped that there was no one there that wanted to tarry long, for he was dog-on sorry if that wicky was large enough for two families.

We found the shanty occupied alright. There was a sack of crackers set on the table and a pot of tea set in the chimney and a couple of blankets lay on the bunk. After Bill had sized up the contents of the camp, he concluded that the occupants did not intend to stay long, judging from their outfit, but Bill was mistaken. Bill said that he would proceed to clean house at any rate.

We had taken in new straw for the bunk, so we threw the old boughs and the other litter outside and burned it and went in for a general house cleaning. Just before dark, two men came in great haste. One rushed into the shack and demanded to know what in h--- does this mean. Bill said, "nothing, just moving in is all."

Then the spokesman said, "Do you fellows pretend to own this camp?" Bill replied that we did, as we did some dog-on hard work building it at least. The one man continued to go on with a great deal of telling what he would do and what he would not, until we had supper ready, when we asked the men to eat with us. The man that had done very little talking readily consented but the other man was still inclined to bully matters, but he finally took a stool and sat up and ate his supper. After supper we learned that they were from near Wellsville, N. Y. We made arrangements for the men to sleep on the floor, or rather on the ground at the side of the bunk.

The next morning after breakfast was over, the man who proposed to run things to his own liking said that he did not see any other way but what we would all have to get along together the best way we could in the shanty. This was more than Bill could stand so he opened on the man and said, "See here, stranger, I am dog-on if a aint willing to do almost anything to be neighborly, but I am dog-on if it don't take a large house for two families to live in, and this shack is altogether too small."

It now began to look as though we were not going to be good neighbors very long, when the man that had but very little to say, up to this time, said, "See here, Hank, you know that this is not our shanty. I told you that some one would be here and want it," and he took his blankets, gun and sack of crackers and started off down the run. After the other man had done some more loud talking, he gathered up the rest of their plunder and started on after his partner with the remark that he would see us again. Bill replied that he would be dog-on pleased to have him come when we were at home.

We were a little afraid that they might return and do us some dirt, but they did not. They went farther down the run and built a sort of a shelter out of boughs and pieces of bark where they stayed about two weeks, when they went home, leaving the field to Bill and myself.

We put in two days cutting wood and calking and mudding the shanty wherever the chinking and mud had been worked out by squirrels and other small animals. As soon as we had this work done we put in our time setting our bear traps. We also built two bear pens. After we had the bear traps all set, we then began putting out small traps, setting the most of the small steel traps for fox and building more deadfalls and repairing those that we had made the year before for marten on the ridges, and along the creek for mink and coon.

After this work was done we gave more time to bear hunting. We had a good deal of freezing weather without much snow for tracking. Being very noisy under foot, we were compelled to hunt for several days by driving the deer, that is, one of us would stand on the runways in the heads of basins or hollows and in the low places on the ridges where it was natural for deer to pass through when jumped up. In going from one ridge to another, we would get a deer in this way nearly every day, and one day we had the good luck to get three bears while driving, an old bear and two cubs. We were also having fairly good luck with the traps.

The first snow that fell to make good tracking was a damp one, and hung on the underbrush so much that it was impossible to see but a few yards unless in very open timber. Here I wish to relate an incident that nearly caused my hair to turn white in a very short time. I am not given very much to superstitions or alarmed at unnatural causes, but in this case I will confess that I felt like showing the white feather.

I was working my way very cautiously along the side of a ridge and down near the base of the hill in low timber, as that is the most natural place to find deer in a storm of this kind. I had just stepped out of the thicket into the edge of a strip of open timber where I could see for several rods along the side of the hill. I had barely stepped into the open when I caught sight of some object jumping from a knoll to a log where it was partly concealed behind some trees, so that I was unable to make out what it was. I was sure that I had never seen anything like it before, either in the woods or out in civilization. I could get a glimpse of the thing as it would pass between the trees, then it would disappear behind brush or a large tree for a moment, then I would get a glimpse of it as it would move.

Sometimes it would appear white and then a fire red. I could see that it was coming in my direction. As I always wore steel gray, or what was commonly known as sheep gray clothing, which is nearly the same color of most large timber, I stepped to a large hemlock tree, leaned close against the tree, set my gun down close to my side and stood waiting to see whether the thing was natural or otherwise.

It was not long before I could see that I had been frightened without any real cause, for it was a hunter who had dressed in fantastic array to put a spell on or charm the deer. He had on a long snow white overshirt and had tied a fire red cloth over his hat and a black sash was tied about his waist. I stood perfectly quiet against the tree until the man was within a few feet of me, I could no longer keep from laughing, and I burst out with laughter. The man jerked his gun from his shoulder as he turned in the direction in which I was standing and gazed at me for a moment and then said, "You frightened me." I replied that I guessed that he was no more frightened than I was when I first caught sight of him.

Well the man explained that he always dressed in that manner when the underbrush was loaded with snow, as the deer would stand and watch him with curiosity until he was within gun shot. When in New Mexico many years after I had tied a red handkerchief to a bush to attract the curiosity of the antelope, and it reminded me of the hunter that I had seen working the curiosity dodge on the deer.

That night when I got into camp, Bill had not got in but came soon after, and he had hardly got the shack door open when he began roaring with laughter. I inquired what it was that pleased him so. "Pleased me so?" "I guess I was pleased, and had you seen the dog-on nondescript that I did, you would have laughed your boots up." I asked if he had seen the man dressed in red, white and black. Bill asked, "Did you see it too?" I told him of the hunter that I had met and talked with. Bill said that he had not been close enough to speak to it, and he was dog-on if he knew whether it was safe to get too close to the dog-on thing or not.

We had good tracking snow from this time on during the remainder of the hunting season. We now each hunted by himself, working as usual over the ground that would bring us in the locality of our traps, which we would look after and relieve any fur bearers that we chanced to get.

We met with one mishap during the season. Well along toward December I went to one of the bear traps that we had not been to in a number of days. The trap was a blacksmith made one with high jaws. I found the trap a short distance from where it had been set, tangled in an old tree top with a bear's foot in it. The bear had been caught just above the foot. As the trap jaws closed tight together the trap clog had got fast solid in the brush soon after the bear had been caught. The animal twisted and pulled until he had unjointed the foot, worn and twisted off the skin and cords of the leg and was gone. He had escaped some time during the night before I came to the trap.

I reset the trap and then took the trail of the bear, which had taken a northeasterly course. I followed the trail until nearly night, when I became satisfied that he was making for a large windfall on a stream known as the South Fork, some fifteen miles away. I gave up the trail and returned to camp, which I reached about 10 o'clock at night. Bill was still keeping supper warm for me well knowing that something was out of the ordinary and wondering what it was.

The next morning we held a council and concluded to look after a few traps near camp and put in a day of partial rest and prepare to take the bear's trail early the next morning. As planned the next morning, we had our blankets and a grub stake strapped to our backs and were off for the trail some time before daylight. Striking the bear's trail where I had left it about 9 o'clock in the forenoon, we followed the trail good and hard all day through wind jams and laurel patches, coming to the big windfall just before dark, very tired.

We put up a rude shelter and camped for the night at the edge of the windfall. In the morning as soon as it was light enough to travel without danger of passing over the trail we were on the move. There were several hundred acres in the windfall so we concluded to go around and make sure that the bear was still there. Bill skirted the jam to the left while I went to the right. Not long after daylight it began to snow. We met on the east side of the jam about 11 o'clock without seeing anything of the crippled bear track, though I had crossed the trail of two bears that had gone into the jam two or three days before.

We now concluded to go back to where the two bears had gone into the jam and one of us stand near the trail while the other one would drop below the trail and work around on the opposite side and drive them out if he could. The wind was blowing strong from the northeast, which would make it next to impossible for the bears to wind the watches. Bill said that he would watch as he could stand the cold weather better than I could. It was now snowing very hard, and we knew that the bears were aware of the approaching storm and had gone to the windfall to go into winter quarters. Chances were that they would not come out unless driven by getting close on to them. We were in hopes that the three bears might be all in one nest, and that the one that did the driving would stand a fair chance to get a shot at them as they left.

I made my calculations from what I knew of the jam about where the bear would lay. Good luck was on my side this time and I hit it just right, coming on to them from the opposite side from where they had gone in, but I did not see or hear them when they went out. The first thing I knew of their whereabouts was when I came on to where the bears had been breaking laurel brush for their bunk. Will I did some fine looking and listening, but all to no purpose, as they had got the wind of me and had gone out. Undoubtedly they would not have done this had they been in their nest a few days longer and had got well to sleep.

They had gone in under two large trees that had been blown out by the roots. They had taken dry rotten wood torn from the two old trees that formed the root to their winter quarters, and with laurel brush and other matter they had made very good quarters for the winter. I soon discovered that the lame bear was not with the two other bears. I did not follow the trail very far when I came onto the trail of the lame bear going on still further into the jam, but I did not follow it but continued on after the two bears to learn what luck Bill had had. I heard no gun shot and was afraid that the bear had not come within gun shot of Bill, although the bears were following nearly back on their trail that they went in on.

When I came to the edge of the wind jam, I saw that the bear had of a sudden made some big jumps down the side of the hill. One of them had turned back into the jam while the other had followed down the hill, and Bill's track was following the trail. I did not go far when I saw Bill tugging away at the bear trying to draw it down to the hollow and near where we had camped the night before.

It was still snowing very hard, and after getting the bear down to the hollow and near to what was called in those days a wagon road--a near trail cut out through the woods--we went to the camp where we had stayed over night and rebuilt the fire and ate a lunch. We had not eaten anything since morning, not wishing to spare the time. It was snowing so hard, and as we knew that we would not be able to reach camp until well along in the night, we concluded to again use the camp of the night before. We gathered a few more hemlock boughs and made the shelter a little more comfortable and went to roasting bear meat on a stick to help out the grub we had brought with us, so that we could look further for the lame bear the next morning.

When morning came, it had snowed more than twelve inches, and as we were satisfied that the lame bear would not leave the jam, we concluded to go down the run about five miles to where a man lived by the name of Reese. Arrangements were made with him to get the bear down to his place where we could get it later. From Mr. Reese's we went to camp and waited a few days for the snow to settle a little. On the way back to camp we looked at two or three bear traps and found a small bear in one of the traps, and the last bear that we got during the season.

We now began to take in the bear traps as we came near one on the way to camp. The snow was so deep we were obliged to reset the most of the small traps, although we had when setting out the traps taken every precaution to set in such places as would afford them all the shelter possible. After tending all the traps again, we went once more to see if we could route the lame bear. We spent two days searching the windfall in every quarter, but were unable to find a trace of the track. We were quite positive that she was still somewhere in the jam, but the snow had fallen so deep that it had completely obliterated all signs.

Two years later I was one of a party that killed a bear and captured her two cubs. The old bear had one foot gone. I am quite sure that it was the one that had escaped from our traps.

We now put in the time hunting deer and looking after the small traps until about the first of January, when we pulled all of our traps and went home. This ended my hunting with William Earl, one of the best pards that I ever hit the trail with, or followed a trap line. Bill left these parts and went back east to his native state, and after a time I lost all trace of him.

CHAPTER XIV.
Hunting and Trapping in Cameron County.

It will be remembered that when Mr. Earl (or Bill, as I preferred to call him,) and the writer followed the bear from the Kinzua in McKene County, through Cameron County, that we saw signs of bear, deer, marten and other game quite plentiful in the region of Baley Run, Salt Run and Hunt's Run, and that we concluded to pitch our camp in that quarter. As there were no huckleberries in the vicinity of our homes, we decided to kill two birds with one stone, that was to pick some huckleberries and build our camp for the next season's hunt.

Accordingly about the last days of July, we took a team and our outfit for camp building and started for Hunt's Run by way of the Sinnamahoning and Baley Run. At this time the country in that section was an unbroken forest of pine, oak and hemlock with a goon sprinkling of chestnut. As the saying was in those days, "God owned the land in that section," so all we had to do was to go into the woods, select our camp site and proceed to build. (Boys, let me stop long enough to say it is different nowadays; you must go through a whole lot of red tape and get a permit to camp and the permit only lasts two weeks, when you must get a renewal.)

The site we selected for our camp was on the left-hand branch of Hunt's Run. We rolled up the usual box log body, about 10 x 14 feet. We put up a bridge roof, putting up about four pairs of rafters and then using three or four small cross poles for roof boards. We then peeled hemlock bark, making the pieces about four feet long, which we used for shingles to cover the roof with. After the roof was completed, we felled a chestnut tree which we split into spaults about four feet long. With these we chinked all the cracks between the logs, striking the axe into the logs, close to the edge of the chinking and then driving a small wedge in the slot made by the axe to hold the chinking in place.

Next we gathered moss from old fallen trees and stuffed all the cracks, using a blunt wedge to press the moss good and tight. We then begun on the mason work. We found a bank of clay that was rather free of stones and made a mortar by using water, making the mortar about as stiff as mortar usually used in house plastering. The chinking and mossing had been done from the inside, while we now filled the space between the logs good and full of mortar, or rather mud.

The next work was to take the team and haul stones, which we found along the run and put up the fireplace. Considerable pains was taken and we done a pretty good job, as we hoped to use this camp for a number of seasons. After the fireplace was completed, we hung a door, using hinges made of blocks of wood and boring auger holes through one end. Shaping the other end on two of these eyes to drive in two holes boring into the logs close to the door jams. The other two eyes were flattened off and made long enough for door cleats as well as to form a part of the door hinge. Now a rod was run through these eyes or holes in these pieces. This formed a good, solid door hinge. Then a door latch was made from a slat of wood, which worked on a pin in a hole bored in one end of the slat and a hole bored through the door. A small hole in the slat and a string tied to latch and run through a hole in the door furnished the means of raising the latch. A loop for the latch to work in and a catch on the door jam and the door was complete.

We next put in the window and made a bunk or bedstead from small poles and the hut was completed. I think we were about four days doing the work including an hour or so each day spent in picking huckleberries enough for our special need. Now as the camp was completed, we began to search for a place where we could find berries more plentiful than we had found them near camp. On the hillsides facing the river, where there were barrens, we found more.

While searching for huckleberries we found a deerlick or salt log, which the deer were working good. Bill said he guessed we had better appropriate the loan of the lick for one night to our own use, and see if we could not get some venison to take home with us as well as huckleberries.

When the sun was about an hour high, we took our guns and went to the salt log. There was no blind made to get in to watch them. We selected two jack pines that stood near together and we each climbed into a tree, breaking some of the boughs out that obstructed our view in the direction of the lick and laid the boughs across some limbs to sit on. We had scarcely got our seats fixed when I heard the crack of a limb off to our left. I whispered to Bill and pointed in the direction I had heard the breaking of the limb. Bill shook his head, to indicate that he had not heard anything, but had hardly done so when I saw Bill begin to cautiously shift his gun from the way it was pointed and slowly move it so as to shoot to his left. When he had the gun worked around so it pointed in the direction in which he wanted it, he began to raise it slowly to his shoulder. I thought to myself, that means venison for breakfast. I thought right, for when Bill touched the trigger and his gun spoke, I saw two yearling deer jump into sight and my gun came to my shoulder from habit, but there was no need to shoot.

The second jump that the deer made one of them fell dead, the other one ran a few rods, stopped and looked back to see what had become of his mate. Bill's gun came to his shoulder like a flash, but I hollowed, "Don't shoot." Bill dropped his gun and said, I came dog-on-nigh making a fool of myself. We got down from our perches and dragged the deer (a yearling buck) out away from the lick, removed the entrails and Bill made a knapsack of the carcass and started for camp.

The sun could still be seen shining on the highest peaks of the hills. Bill said, "That fun was over with too quick; I had one of the most comfortable seats I ever had. I had no time to enjoy it, when you called my attention to those little bucks and spoiled all my comfort." We got to camp before dark and stripped the skin from the deer, spread it out, cut all the meat from the bones, layed it on the skin, sprinkled some salt over it, then wrapped the meat up in the skin, saving out a few choice pieces to frizzle over the coals and eat with our lunch before bunking in for the night.

We had seen some parties, while picking berries during the day. They told us that there was a man by the name of Sage living down on the river near Emporium, who had a large clearing on the hill only about a mile from where we were, or about two miles from our camp. He told us in which direction we would find the field, and said that we would find Mr. Sage there, as he was up there cutting oats. As the grub stake for the horses was getting rather low, and as we were not yet ready to go home, Bill said that if I would stay and jerk the venison (for here we cannot keep venison by hanging it up in a tree, or on a pole, as you can on the Pacific Coast or in the Rockies), he would go and see Mr. Sage.

In the morning I began preparation to jerk the venison, while Bill went in search of grub for the horses. There was no road, but there was but very little down timber in the woods in those days, only occasionally a wind jam, which you had to work your way around. Bill found the clearing all right, and got oats in the bundle for the horses. Bill also made arrangements with Mr. Sage to bury eight bushels of potatoes and leave them on the hill where we could get them as we wished. Bill also killed a large rattlesnake on his way to the field, which he brought to camp, where we skinned and took out the oil. When we were skinning the snake Bill remarked, "that he thought the fur rather light on the varmint, but it was a pretty cuss." Let me say that at our place on the head waters of the Allegheny we had no eels, rattlesnakes or wartelberries, so we concluded that we would stop one night on the Sinnamahoning and get some eels to take home with us.

While Bill was gone for horse feed I was busy jerking the venison. I gathered a good hill of dry hemlock bark from the logs, burned it to a good pile of live coals. I now made a rack or gridiron by driving four crotched stakes in the ground about the embers and then laid small poles across in the crotches to form a rack to spread the venison on over the coals. I stood hemlock bark up about the rack, freshly peeled from the tree and covering the top over also with bark, which forms an oven. It is necessary to remove the top or cover occasionally and turn the meat, and say, boys, next June when you are out camping just kill a small deer and prepare the meat as described. Is it good? I guess yes.

Having our work completed at the camp, the next morning after we had got the horses fed and the venison prepared, we drove back onto Baleys Run. Here we camped near the mouth of the run, and that night we set fifty eel hooks, some in the run and some in the main Sinnamahoning. I think that we caught twenty-two eels and some trout. As we were now in a section where there were some barrens, which contained good huckleberry picking, we put in the next day picking berries until near night, and drove home at night, a distance of about twenty miles. All the time while picking berries, setting eel hooks and trout fishing, of which we did enough to supply our needs, we kept a close watch for signs of animals that we intended to take in later on.

We saw signs of mink, coon and where an otter had been at play on a steep bank of the run. We saw signs of bear in several places where they had torn old logs to pieces in search of grub and ants. We saw at one place where a bear had dug out a woodchuck, and I should judge by the amount of digging he had done that he earned his chuck. We saw considerable signs of bear in the huckleberries, and of them will have more to say later on.

* * *

About October first, Bill and your humble servant again started for camp, which we found all right. From all appearances it had been occupied for several days by someone, probably berry pickers, and as usual they had burned up what wood we had cut. Bill made a little kick, and said they were welcome to the camp, but he would be "dog-on" pleased if they would cut what wood they burned. Our first week in camp was spent in cutting a good supply of wood and mudding the shack a little in places where we failed to do good work the first time.

Being located well up at the head of the streams, it made it necessary for us to do a good deal of traveling to get from one stream to another where the water was of sufficient size to afford good trapping ground. Steel traps being none too plenty with us now, we started in to build deadfalls. The territory so far as trapping was concerned was left to Bill and I, and we took in the waters of Baley Run, the Portage, Conley Run and Hunt's Run, as well as several lesser streams. As the Baley was the farthest from our camp, Bill said we would put up the traps on that stream first. Bill said that we would go at it man fashion, for we would be compelled to get our grub from the trap line, for there was no chance to take a wood job in that section of the country. I suggested that we might get a job at the lumber camp, where we sold the deer the year before, and get a few beans and a little pork. I guess that Bill did not like the idea, for I remember he only gave me a grunt for an answer.

Say, boys, the question of pork and beans leads me to ask how many of you who have a fireplace in your camp have a bean hole? Now, Bill and I had one in our camp, and I tell you we thought it fine and we did it in this way. We dug a hole in one corner of the fireplace about two and a half feet deep and about eighteen inches in diameter, using the regular old style of bake kettle. This is merely an iron pot, with a close fitting flange lid so as to seclude all dust and ashes, and we used it in this way. We would first rake a good lot of live coals from the fireplace into the bean hole, having the beans already in the kettle. Then we would put the kettle down in the hole and rake the hole full of live embers, being careful to cover the hole over with plenty of ashes.

We prepared the beans about in this fashion: After washing we soaked them for about twelve hours. The water was drained off and the beans were then put into the kettle with the necessary trimmings, which consisted of a good chunk of pork put in the center of the beans, and two or three smaller pieces laid on top, a pinch of salt providing that the pork was not sufficiently salty. A spoonful of brown sugar or rather a little baking molasses and a little pepper. Now this kettle was allowed to remain three or four days in the hole without disturbing farther than to cover over occasionally with hot embers. You ask if beans are good baked this way--we guess yes. We have heard a great deal about the famous Boston baked beans, but we wish to say that they are not in it compared to beans baked in a bean hole.

Well, to get back to the trap line. We took the Baley waters first. This was about six miles from camp, and as it was still a little earlier in the season than we cared to begin to take fur, we would build the deadfalls and have them ready to set when we thought that fur was ripe enough to begin to gather. Bill used a good heavy axe, and would cut the dead pole and bed pieces and the stakes and fit them all ready to put up. He would then go on and select a place to build another trap and get the material all ready as before and then move on to the next place. I would follow him up and build the trap, make the bait pen and have the trap all ready to set when the right time came. The triggers we would make evenings in camp. We always used the three-stick trigger, for then we could adjust the trigger so that we were sure that the front legs of the animal were over the bed piece, when the trap was sprung. In that condition there was not get-away for the animal that tried to snip the bait. We would build traps on one stream until we had a plenty for that stream. We would take up another and put in a supply on that stream, and so on until we had gone over as much ground as we could work to good advantage.

All the time we were putting up these deadfalls we were keeping a watch out for likely places to set our steel traps for fox and other animals. After we had gone over the streams we built the necessary deadfalls in the dark, heavy timbered sections where we thought likely that there might be marten. As it was now well along toward the last of October, we set our bear traps on the different ridges in the sections where the chestnut timber was the most plenty. The chestnut crop was good and we knew that the first hard freeze would open the burs. Bill said we got to get a move on us from early in the morning until after dark when we would get into camp. We wished to get all the traps out now that we could. Later we were going to put in some time gathering chestnuts, as soon as they began to fall, as there was good money in gathering them. At this business there was lively competition with the squirrels, coons, bears and other animals to see which could gather the most, so naturally there is but a few days good picking after the chestnuts fall.

Bill said that we would be in a deal while the nuts lasted and we did, for we gathered several bushels. I do not just remember how many now, but that wasn't all we got while we were gathering chestnuts. One day we came to where a bear had been raking for nuts and as it was only about a mile from camp I said to Bill that it might be possible that if we would stay out and watch for Bruin as long as we could see to shoot, we might get a shot at the bear. Bill said that he preferred to let the traps do the watching. There was a little mist of rain falling, and just the right kind of weather for Bruin to be prowling around. Some way it seemed to me if we stayed and watched we would get a shot at a bear, but Bill had no faith and said that I would get good and wet for my trouble. I told him that if he would take what nuts I had gathered along to the shanty, I would stay and watch awhile at least. Bill agreed, and said that he would have a hot supper ready for me when I came to camp. I suggested to Bill that he have the frying pan hot when I got there, for I would bring in some bear meat for supper. Bill said that I need not bother to skin his, as he would eat his hair and all.

As soon as Bill was gone I selected a point where I could see down the hill, as well as over a good stretch of the top of the ridge. I had only fairly picked my ground to watch when I heard the brush crack close to me from behind. My gun came to my shoulder as I turned in the direction of the noise, and there stood Bill a-grinning. I asked him what had changed his mind. He said that if I could stand it he could, so he stepped along the ridge a few yards and I leaned up against a large hemlock tree. He had scarcely taken his stand when all of a sudden I saw him begin to slowly raise his gun to his shoulder. I knew that he was about to shoot at something, but thought it must be a deer. I thought that I ought to shout and scare it away, for I thought that Bill had come back on purpose to beat me out of the sport, and I guessed right. Bill said after he had started to camp it seemed to him that he had done wrong in leaving me to watch alone, and that I would kill a bear. So he turned back and got there just in time so as not to frighten the bear away, as well as to shoot it, which was a yearling and weighed about 125 pounds, with a fine pelt.

Bill apologized for the little trick. Said he would never do anything of the kind again. He never did. A good reason being that another opportunity never occurred. But later I will tell how I got the laugh on Bill. The next morning Bill took the saddles of the bear to Emporium and sold the meat, but he said that bear meat was not at a premium in Emporium. I think he got about $6.00 out of the saddles. While Bill was gone to Emporium I took two bear traps and went on to a ridge where I thought would be the most likely place to catch a bear, as there was considerable beach timber on that ridge in places. Beach nuts last long after chestnuts are gone, and bear would be likely to work in this timber. As we had not got all of our small traps out yet, Bill said that if I would finish setting the rest of the small traps, he would put in the most of his time hunting deer, as the leaves were now pretty well off from the undergrowth, so that the woods were now quite open. This I agreed to, as I knew Bill to be a good deer hunter, while I was a little skeptical as to some of his trapping methods.

Well, as the busy season was with us now, it was an early breakfast and a late supper day after day. Yet we were able to keep up the pace from the natural stimulating desire for sport, being anxious to know what the results of the next day would be. We were having the usual success of the average hunter and trapper who, as Bill said, if willing to get a move on, our supply of meat and game was never lacking, for I always shot at small game when hunting deer. Bill said that he did not like to come into camp empty handed, so he would shoot a grouse or a squirrel whenever a chance occurred. We had no snow up to this time, so that deer hunting was a little dull, and Bill said that he would take a line of traps, either on Baley Run or on the Conley, as I liked. I said, take your choice, Bill, so he said he would go to Conley Run, which was a little farther from camp than the Baley Run, and one or two more bear traps than on Baley Run.

I found a coon or two, and I think I got a fox and one marten, but no mink or other furs. I found that a bear had been to one trap and torn down the bait pen and taken the bait, but left the trap unsprung. I knew that he would cut the same trick again, if I set the trap there, so I bent over a small sapling and hung the carcass of a coon on it for a bait. The carcass hung four or five feet from the ground.

RESULTS OF A FEW WEEKS' TRAPPING.

I set the trap under the carcass and said to myself, "Old fellow, when you take that coon, there will be a bear dance." I got to camp long after dark, but when I came in sight of camp and looked for a light, there was no light to be seen, or any Bill to be found in camp. I lit a light and looked at my watch. It was only a few minutes of eight o'clock. I got supper and waited until nine o'clock, but no Bill came, so I laid down on the bunk to rest, expecting Bill to turn up every minute.

I dropped to sleep and when I awoke, the fire had burned out and Bill had not returned. I looked at my watch. It was after three o'clock, and I knew that there would be no more sleep for me. I went outside and listened, but no sound could be heard. I got my breakfast, put an extra lunch in my knapsack, and sat down and waited for the break of day. As soon as the first streaks of light appeared in the east, I strapped on my knapsack, took my gun and started in the direction in which I had known Bill to take. I followed the ridge to the Conley Run waters, over which Bill would likely come if he had been detained in that region.

When I came to the head of a run that led to the main Conley waters, I stopped at the brow of the hill. I could look down into the hollow. Here I knew that I could be heard for some distance. I listened for some time to see if I could hear a gun shot or any other noise that would lead me to the whereabouts of Bill. Not a sound to be heard, not even the hoot of an owl. I gave a long whoop and then listened, but still no answering sound. I again gave a long continued "co-hoop" and Bill burst out laughing, and asked what was the matter with me. Bill had sat down on a fallen tree that lay close to a large pine tree to rest before making the last pull to the top of the ridge. He had caught a glimpse of me just before I came to the brow of the hill where I stopped to send a wireless message. Bill skulked behind a pine tree to see what I would do and give me a scare, when I came along.

When I inquired what had kept him out all night, he said that he got so big a job on his hands that he could not get to camp. Bill said that he had got about half way down the side of the hill from the ridge leading down into the Conley River, when he jumped a buck, which Bill said slid down the hill like a greased rag. He fired at the pile and happened to catch him well back to the hips. The deer being wounded through the small intestines made it very sick, but it was still able to lead Bill a merry chase. Bill had been working from the middle of the forenoon until about three o'clock in the afternoon before he was able to get in a finishing shot on the buck. While following the deer, he had come near one of the places where we had a bear trap set and found that a bear had been caught. He followed the trail a little ways, and as it led in an opposite direction from that taken by the deer, Bill said he thought he would finish one job at a time, so he continued after the deer.

Before Bill was able to get in the finishing shot on the deer, it had swung around in the direction of the trail of the bear, so that when Bill finally got the buck, he knew that he could not be far from the trail of the bear. He hung up the saddles of the deer, which he had started to take to camp, and let the bear rest until the next morning. After hanging up the saddles he didn't search long until he found the trail of the bear, and followed the trail only a little ways, when he found Bruin fast in a clump of brush. Bill then killed the bear, and taking out the entrails, rolled the carcass up over a log and again started for camp with the deer saddles. He did not go far when it was so dark that it was difficult to travel and carry the deer saddles and gun, so Bill said he thought he would build a little shelter and camp for the night.

Bill had started for camp with the saddles of the buck as soon as he could see to travel. He was near the top of the ridge on his way to camp and had sat down to rest when I came to the brow of the hill and began to "co-hoop" to see if I could get any word from him, which I did and much closer than expected. Bill brought his load up to where I was, and threw it down with the remark "I suppose that you did not think to bring along an extra lunch, did you?" When I told him I had the extra lunch, and also a bottle of tea (Bill being a great hand for tea). Well, said Bill, "then we are all right, once more." We now hung the deer saddles up, and went back after the bear. After setting the bear trap again, as Bill did not have time after he had killed the bear, we started to carry the bear to camp whole. We soon found it too heavy to carry that way, so skinned it and hung up the foreparts and took the skin and hindquarters.

The next morning, we went back after the deer. We went to where Bill had left the fore parts of the deer; then we went to where the fore parts of the bear were left, intending to take them as far as where the deer saddles were and leave them there, and take the deer saddles to camp. When we got to where the bear meat had been left, we found that a cat had been there, and filled his shirt on bear meat. It was not far to where we had a steel trap setting. I told Bill to go on slowly with the deer meat, and I would go and get the trap and set it for the cat. Bill said that he thought that would be the right thing to do, as there was a two dollar bounty on wild cats. He said we could carry the pelt of the cat a great deal easier than we could tote the bear meat; he thought that the cat skin and the bounty would even things up for the bear meat.

I soon had the trap set for the cat, and then hurried on to catch Bill. We went to camp with the deer and the next morning we took the bear and deer saddles to Emporium and shipped them to New York. The distance that we toted those saddles must have been ten or twelve miles. Say boys, won't a man do more hard work to get thirty cents out of a coon skin, or a saddle of venison, or bear, than he would to get thirty dollars in some other way? As it had been three or four days since we had been over a good part of the trap line, we now got back to regular business, each one taking up his line of traps. Each night when he came to camp, we would have some kind of pelts to stretch, either two or three coon, a mink or two, as many more fox, with now and then a marten. It would take the evening to stretch the pelts and tell our day's experience just what particular trap we got that or this fox in, or that mink or coon; just how clever some shy old fox has worked to get the bait at a certain trap; on what particular ridge or point we had seen Old Golden's track (you know all large buck deer have the name of "Old Golden".)

Every man of the woods or trap line knows what pleasure there is in relating the experience of the day's hunt or of the trap line to his pard during the evening in camp. Yet, I will tell of one occurrence though I have told the story many times, and I cannot say that I relate it with any great amount of pleasure. Still since many years have passed, I have often laughed over the circumstance. I can still see that sympathetic grin of Bill's, when he would ask "if it hurt me much."

It was a lowery morning, and Bill proposed that we go together and look after a line of traps on Salt Run, and then put in the balance of the day still-hunting deer. We went down to the lower end of the line, worked up the run so as to be near the top of the ridge and in a locality where we expected deer to be. We had not looked at more than three or four traps, when we came to one that was set under the bank. The trap chain was stapled to a root, and was stationary (and let me say here that I believe it bad policy to fasten a trap to anything, stationary) and it certainly was in this case for me. The water was quite deep right at the point where the trap was set and came close up to the bank. In order to see the trap, it was necessary to lie down on my stomach, and lean my head over the bank.

When I looked down under the bank, I saw that there was some animal in the trap. The trap chain was drawn tight and when I drew gently on the chain I could tell that some kind of an animal was in the trap. I little suspected that it was loaded, as it proved to be. I could not see what sort of an animal it was, but supposed it was a mink. It did not like to be drawn out in sight, and I was afraid to pull too hard on the chain for fear I would draw his foot out of the trap. I let up and straightened up to consult Bill, as to the best thing to do. Bill said, pull him out and if he gets away, we will get him at another trap, and I now suspect that Bill knew what was coming. I leaned down over the bank and stuck my head down to see where the chain was. All of a sudden I was struck with something more terrible than lightning if not quite so fatal, and for the next half hour I was rolling on the ground and washing my eyes. Bill said that I danced the Bear dance and a Pot Full of Catfish all at the same time. When I recovered enough to see what "hit me", I found that I had been terribly shot by a measly skunk square in both eyes. Bill was grinning and asking "if it hurt much" and telling me that I could see better after a little and lots of other sympathetic nothings. I hope that none of you may ever have the experience that I met with by the treatment of that infernal skunk.

After the atmosphere and my eyes had cleared somewhat, we went on and looked after the balance of the traps on the run. We then started out to hunt deer, Bill taking one side of the ridge and I the other. I saw nothing more of Bill until I reached camp long after dark. I worked along the different spires of the main ridge and through the heads of the different basins, and only got a glimpse of an old buck's tail, making over the ridge and beckoning me to come on. He had come over from the opposite side of the ridge and had got wind of me before he was fairly in sight. I kept on working the different points and basins, shaping my course as best I could in the direction of the camp.

A drizzling rain kept up all day, and deer had not moved very much. I felt confident that towards evening the deer would come out in the open to feed in spite of the rain, and pretty well toward night I had the satisfaction of seeing three deer feeding along the hillside and coming in my direction.

The wind was in my favor, and as the deer were rather too far to shoot, I stood quiet, only occasionally moving from one tree to another as a favorable opportunity occurred. The deer finally worked up in gun shot, and they proved to be an old doe, a yearling and the doe's fawn. The yearling was undoubtedly the doe's fawn of the year before. I was very careful to make a sure shot on the doe. The yearling and the fawn only took a few jumps when the gun cracked and the doe went down, and stood looking at the old lady to see what had happened to her. I gave the yearling the contents of the other barrel. He made a jump or two and went down, the fawn still standing and wondering what was taking place, but before I could get a load into my gun, the little fellow thought it best to move on.

I took the entrails out of the two I had shot, hung them up and took a lively pace to camp. Bill was already in and had supper waiting. Bill asked me if I had seen any deer, and when I told him what I had done, he said that he had seen a deer. I told him that if he had used a little skunk eye-opener, he probably would have seen some deer.

As it had now been three or four days since we had made the rounds of the bear traps, we concluded that we would not spend any particular time in deer hunting until we had looked all of the bear traps over. We were quite sure that some of the traps would be likely to be in a mixup with bruin as the weather had been favorable for bruin to be prowling around. Further we had seen several fresh tracks in the past few days. Early in the morning with an extra lunch in our knapsack we started out to see what luck with bruin, each taking a different route.

Bill went to Baley Run, while I went to Conley Run. I had not gone far out on my road, when I came across a man that had been out as he said, hunting deer. But from the story he told, I judged that he had put in the greater part of his time hunting himself, and he was still lost.

The man informed me that he was from Lockhaven, Pa., and that his name was Henry Jacobs; and that he was boarding at a farmhouse on the Portage but had gotten a little mixed and was unable to find his way out to his boarding place. I told him that I was on my way to the Conley waters to look after some bear traps, and if he wished he could go with me to the main branch of the Conley. Then he could follow the stream down until it emptied into the Portage, and to the road which would take him to his boarding house, which Mr. Jacobs seemed pleased to do. But it proved that Mr. Jacobs' destiny was in other directions.

The first bear trap that we came to, we found a "porky" in it. I could see that Mr. Jacobs was very much excited and began to ask many questions as to bears and bear trapping. When we came to where the second trap was setting, we found things generally torn up and the trap gone, and it was plain to be seen that it was no cub that had taken the trap this time. The bear had gone only a few yards, when he had gotten fast in some saplings, and he had gnawed the brush and raked the trees and "raised Ned" generally; but had finally released the clog and had gone on down the hillside.

By this time I had discovered that Mr. Jacobs had become pretty nervous and was shaking rather too much to do good shooting. At every rod we advanced along the trail, it was plain to be seen that Mr. Jacobs was becoming more and more excited. We did not follow the trail far when we discovered Bruin fast again. We went up within a few yards of the bear, who did not seem to like our company and would chank his jaws and snort similar to an angry hog.

I told Mr. Jacobs to shoot the bear, and he did shoot somewhere, but I could not say that he shot in the direction of the bear. As my attention had been on the bear, I had not noticed Mr. Jacobs in particular, but when I saw that he had entirely missed the bear, I looked at him and he was shaking so from excitement, that he could not have hit a barn, and drops of sweat stood all over his forehead. He had a double barrel rifle, and as soon as he fired the first shot, he advanced a few steps toward the bear and fired again, and at once began to reload his gun, all the time going nearer to the bear until I was afraid that he would get so close that the bear could reach him. I had to caution him and tell him to step back, that he was getting too close.

When Mr. Jacobs had one barrel of his gun loaded, he immediately fired again, with the same results of the other two shots. I told him to take my gun and try it, which he did with no better results. Mr. Jacobs was all the time becoming more and more excited, and the sweat was running off him like a man in the harvest field. I loaded my gun, while Mr. Jacobs was loading his, and after Mr. Jacobs fired another shot with no better results, I though that the fun had gone far enough, and shot the bear.

After the bear was dead, Mr. Jacobs wondered why it was so hard to hit a bear's head. "Just look at it," he said, "it is as large as a dry goods box". As soon as the bear was dead, Mr. Jacobs wanted to know if I would sell the bear. When I told him that I expected to sell it, he asked what it was worth. I told him that I thought the hide and meat would bring thirty or thirty-five dollars. He drew out his purse and said, "I will take it." I told him that if he wanted the bear, that we would call it twenty-five dollars, as he should have something for his part in the game. He declared that the hunt had been worth a hundred dollars to him.

We made a sort of a litter or drag rack with which we managed to haul the bear down the hill to an old lumber road where it could be reached with a team.

Not long after this I received a copy of the Williamsport Sun containing the report of a monstrous bear captured by Mr. Jacobs in the wilds of Cameron County. It was a bear story equal to the one the prophet relates when the children called him Baldy.

When I got to camp I found Bill stretching a couple of mink skins. He had also got a fox or two, and said that a bear had been in one of the bear traps, but had escaped, leaving two toes in the trap. Bill was considerably down at the heel over the escape of the bear, and said that if he had attended to the trap the day before, that the bear was then in the trap; that he had put up a hard fight before he had made his escape.

When Bill called for my report I took out a marten skin and the money that I got for the bear and layed them on the table and told Bill there was my count. Bill said that I got the marten from one of the deadfalls, but he was dog-on sorry if he could tell where I caught the money. When I told him about Mr. Jacobs and the capture of the bear, Bill said he would have given a summer's work to have been there and seen the man sweat.

I said that I would relate how it happened that I got even with Bill for the bear that he killed on my watching grounds.

Well, after we had gone the rounds of the traps, we again put in our time still-hunting. Bill had gone south of camp, while I went east. I had traveled until the middle of the afternoon without having any luck or seeing any deer. So I shifted my course to the west and worked my way in the direction of a "burn-down" that was in the head of a hollow. As soon as I came to the brow of the ridge and looked down into the basin I saw four deer feeding and working towards me. The wind was blowing directly from the deer towards me, so I stood quiet and in a few minutes the deer fed up within easy range. I pulled the gun onto an old doe in the lead, and broke her down almost in her tracks. The three remaining deer made a few jumps in my direction and stopped and looked back, which gave me a good shot at a yearling buck, which also went down in my sight. The other two deer ran close by me and over the ridge into the green timber. I had hardly cut the deers' throats when Bill called out, "This is a dog-on pretty trick that you have played me."

Bill had been following these deer all day and had followed to the "burn-down" and had seen the deer on the opposite hill, but too far away to shoot. As the wind was against him he had dropped down the hollow a ways, crossed and worked up around on the opposite side to get the wind in his favor, and was just about ready to fire on the deer when I began shooting. After Bill had explained how he had been working the deer all day and then have me slip in just as he had the game bagged and swipe it, Bill claimed was dog-on mean. I cautioned Bill to hold his temper and I would call it even on the bear he swiped from me, and told him I was pleased to have him on hand to help hang up the deer.

We had worked along now up to about the middle of December with the various ups and downs that one on the trap line and trail always meet with. We had killed twelve or fourteen deer, and I think we had caught six bears and had made a fair catch of fox, mink, marten and some other furs. There had not been much snow up to this time, when a fall of 12 or 14 inches came all in one night. Bears had not denned up to this time, but we were quite sure that bruin would now go into winter quarters. We concluded to gather up the bear traps and all the small traps that were not setting in springs that did not freeze, or those setting in other likely places to make a catch. In nearly the last bear trap that we went to get, we found a bear, and when we began to skin it we found that it had lost two toes on one forefoot. We concluded that it was the same bear that had escaped from Bill's trap some time before, although it was eight or ten miles from where the trap was that had held Bruin's toes.

A day or two after the heavy fall of snow we got a letter from a man by the name of Comstock, living at Pittsburgh, Pennsylvania, asking the privilege to come and camp with us and hunt deer until the season closed, the first of January. He stated that he had never killed a deer, and that he was very anxious to kill one. We wrote him to come on, and that one of us would be at Emporium on the following Friday to guide him to our camp. Friday morning I went to Emporium and found Mr. Comstock there as agreed. He had paraphernalia enough to equip a fair-sized army, so we hired a team to take the outfit to camp and also bring out the saddles of a bear and what venison we had on hand.

For three or four days Mr. Comstock hunted all by himself but had no luck in the way of killing deer, as he said it took more time to hunt the shanty than he had to hunt deer, and suggested that we all hunt in company. We had now been on the ground long enough so that we had learned all the runways. Bill said that if I would take Mr. Comstock down to a certain runway, which he had given the name of Fork Point, and place him on it, he would drive the ridge and see if he could not drive a deer to Mr. Comstock.

Bill started a bunch of five deer and succeeded in getting a shot and breaking a foreleg of a large doe. As the doe with the broken leg soon dropped out from the other deer, he was sure that the deer had start enough so that they would come through to where Comstock and I were watching, he decided to take the trail of the broken legged doe, and as good luck, the deer did come through to Mr. Comstock, and as he had an Osgood gun with four shots, he succeeded in killing a very large buck. After firing the four shots, the fun began.

Mr. Comstock was determined to take the buck to camp, as he wanted to take the deer home whole. We had a very steep point to climb for a distance of five hundred yards to reach the top of the ridge. The deer weighed about two hundred pounds. Any hunter will tell you what an awkward job it is to carry a deer of that weight lashed to a pole. Mr. Comstock would not consent to drawing the deer for fear it would rake the hair off. Well, we could not carry it up the steep point on the pole, as the swaying of the deer would throw us off our feet. Mr. Comstock said that he would carry it alone if I would help him get it on his shoulder. Mr. Comstock was a large man, weighing over two hundred pounds, but nevertheless I did not think he would be able to carry the deer and told him so. After some hard tugging we got the deer on his shoulder and he started up the hill. I started to get out of the way, and I was none too soon in doing so. Mr. Comstock had not taken a half dozen steps when back he came, deer and all, like ten thousand bricks. But as he did not break any limbs or his neck, he was bound to try it again, which he did with the same result. But this time he was quite badly bruised, and he was now satisfied to leave the deer until morning, when Bill went with us and we made a sort of a litter and carried it to camp whole; and he was a proud and happy man. When Mr. Comstock and I left the deer and decided to await reinforcements, we struck the trail of Bill, drawing a deer in the direction of camp, so we now knew why Bill had not followed the trail of the deer through to where Comstock and I were watching.

It was now about the closing time for deer hunting, so after Mr. Comstock had left for home, Bill and I put in the time until the first of March tending the small traps with the usual success of the average trapper, getting a fox, or mink or marten or some piece of fur nearly every day.

When the team which we had written home for came and got our camp outfit and our furs, we broke camp and went home to await another trapping season.

CHAPTER XV.
Trapping and Bee Hunting.

Comrades of the trap line and trail, as every trapper and hunter likes to know what other trappers and hunters are doing, I will tell of some of my last season's (1908) doings. Having been somewhat relieved from my old enemy--rheumatism--I concluded to take a trip south and see if I could not find a place suitable to my liking where I might escape some of the rigorous cold of the Northern Pennsylvania winters.

I went first into Southeastern Missouri. Here I found land cheap, unimproved lands ranging from $3.00 to $15.00 per acre; also plenty of timber for fuel and building purposes; plenty of fish of various kinds, some deer, a few wild turkeys, no bear, some mink, plenty of raccoon, a few otter and fox; with minor other fur-bearers, which was all quite satisfactory to me, but I did not like the water.

From Poplar Bluff, Missouri, I went to Kenset, Arkansas, where I found the conditions as to the price of lands satisfactory, although the country was much less broken than Southern Missouri. As to water, well, there was water almost anywhere; in fact, you could hardly cross the streets without wading in water. The people who were natives of that country informed me that the water in the streets was not always so plenty, as they said that there had been very heavy rains of late. Here I found game of all kinds quite scarce, although I was told that southeast of Kenset game was quite plenty, including bear, deer, turkeys, quail, etc., and that mink, otter, coon, opossum, also a few wolves, were to be found. The water gave me the chills in three days, so I concluded to move to other parts of the lower St. Francis River, in Lee County. There appeared to be quite a plenty of mink, otter, coon and some bear, but the cane brakes were pretty thick in the bottoms.

I think that if one was well prepared for trapping, they could do fairly well in either St. Francis or Lee County. I went from Hanes in Lee County, Arkansas, to Memphis, Tennessee. From Memphis I went to a town by the name of Shepard, on the Hatchie River, in Haywood County, Tennessee. Along the Hatchie River there were signs of otter, mink and coon quite plenty, and in some places the cane brakes were quite open. I liked the lay of the land here very well. It was just rolling enough to suit my fancy, but again I failed to find our cold, Pennsylvania spring water. From Shepard I went to Pickens, in Pickens County, South Carolina. Here I found fairly good water, but other conditions were not entirely to my liking.

While I did not have time to look up the game or rather the fur-bearers as thoroughly as I would have liked to, yet I saw considerable signs of mink and coon and was told that there were quite a number of otter in that section on some of the streams. From Pickens I bought a ticket to Columbus, Ohio, where I intended to stop over a day and call on the editor of the greatest of sporting magazines, *Hunter-Trader-Trapper*, but when I got to Columbus my courage failed. I was afraid that the editor would be too busy pushing the quill to bother with a lone trapper, so concluded to hasten back to old Potter, where chills, jiggers, ticks, fleas and poisonous snakes are unknown, and where the cold, sparkling spring water flows from the mountain side to your very door. Say, boys, you may think that I am stuck on the water question. Well, I am, and I have good cause to me. Only for spring water, I should not have been able to have made the journey which I am writing of.

For the past two years, barring the time I was south, I have drank from four to six quarts of cold spring water every twenty-four hours. I have got more relief from rheumatism than I ever did from all the rheumatism remedies that I ever knew of, and I have tried the most of them. I used all the salt in my food that I could to aid the desire for water, and took six drops of oil of wintergreen three times a day. Now, if any of the old trappers have rheumatism and the good spring water, I ask you to try it.

Well, after getting back home and resting a few days and the frost began to hit the pumpkin vine, I began to feel as I imagined that the wild goose does about their migratory time. At least I felt as though I should fly if I did not get into the woods. We were having splendid weather for camping, and the warm, dry, sunny days afforded splendid weather for bee hunting, and after the trap and gun then my delight is to trail the honey bee to his den tree.

One day when a young man called on me and said that he would give me an interest in a "goose pasture" to go out in the woods and camp, I was interested. Smoky Jim (that is his nickname) although his name is Charles Earl, and there is nothing smoky about Charley except his pipe, which he is very fond of, too much so, I think, for so young a man. Well, when Charley said that he would like to go and camp out in the woods, I was practically as good as gone. I knew Smoky to be a lively kid and all right, although he had never put in any time as a trapper or a bee hunter. I said, "Smoky, can you see a bee fly?" Smoky said that he thought he could, for he knew that he could tell when one stung him, but he had never watched to see how far he could see one fly.

I found that Smoky was given to making comical remarks as well as to smoking. I said, "Smoky, what day can you go?" He replied, "Any day."

This was on Tuesday, so I said, "Alright, Smoky, be here Thursday and we will start early Friday morning."

Smoky said, "Alright, but we will not get a darn thing while we are gone if we go on Friday unless we get drowned, and there will have to be more water in the creek than there is now or we won't get that much."

I had already made application to the State Tourist Commissioner for a permit to camp on state lands. It may be well to state here for the benefit of those who wish to so camp in this state (Pennsylvania) that the authorities will not give a permit to camp for a longer time than 14 days. In my case they were very obliging and made out the papers for several applicants of 14 days each, so that it would only have been necessary to have signed one of the applications and send it on a few days before the previous application had expired.

WOODCOCK FISHING ON THE SINNAMAHONING.

We were all ready to start Friday morning. Our route lay over the mountains a distance of about 20 miles from the head waters of the Allegheny to the head water of the west branch of the Susquehana waters, known as the East Fork of the Sinnamahoning. We pitched our tent just at the point where the Buffalo and Susquehana Railroad begins to cross the divide, known as the Hogback, by means of several switch backs. It is a splendid sight to see two or three trains working their way up the mountain's side on a clear, frosty morning, when the steam and smoke show so plain.

We did not get the tent in good shape for the first night, nor did we get our bunk up, owing to its being so late when we got to our camping ground. The first night in camp we had a sharp frost and in the morning

Smoky Jim's fever for camping had dropped fully one-half. He complained that any one that would go into such a country to camp should be reported for trespassing on the rights of the porcupine.

It took until the third day to get our camp in good shape. We built a skeleton frame of small poles all over the tent, leaving a space of about 18 inches between tent and frame, and thatched it good with hemlock boughs. While we were working at the camp we had our bee bait out, and the second day after we put out the bait no bees came to it. Smoky laughed at me and said that a honey bee was too intelligent to stop in a place like that, but Smoky was wrong. The next morning after the sun had got well above the top of the hills, so as to warm up things down in the valley, I heated a large stone quite hot and burned some honey comb on it. It was not long before Smoky called out to me and said that there was one fool of a bee. It was not long before we had bees a-plenty. We paid no attention to them farther than to keep plenty of bait out for them. Every bee hunter knows how much steadier a bee flies after they have the bait well located.

After the camp was well completed and a good pile of wood cut we gave our attention to the bees. We soon located two lines, one going nearly east while the other went nearly south. I told Smoky to take his hatchet and go across the creek some 50 rods and make an opening or a stand about half way between the two lines, or about southeast from the stand, and when he had it ready, to call to me and I would bring the bees over and we could get a cross line and locate nearly the tree that the bees were in.

We soon got the direction in which the bees flew. I then told Smoky to take the line that now flew in a westerly course from the stand and in the direction of two or three large maple trees. The other line now flew nearly north from the stand and back toward the creek where there was considerable large timber still standing.

Leaving the bait on the stand, I took the course of the bees that were now flying north and went to a large birch tree that was standing on the bank of the creek. I was still several rods from the tree when the bees began coming to me and I knew that the tree was close by. I was looking the different trees over to see which tree the bees were in when Smoky began to halloo as though something terrible had happened him.

Guessing at the cause of Smoky's shouting, I continued on in the direction in which the line led and soon saw the bees going into the large birch tree. I took my knife and cut the letters B T on the tree and then went to Smoky, who was still making the woods ring with his shouts.

Smoky began guying me, saying that I was an old bee hunter but it took Smoky to find the first bee tree. I did not tell him that I had found the tree that the other line of bees went to, but agreed with him. I told him to mark the tree that he had located and then he could go and locate the other tree if he wished while I would go to camp and be getting grub ready.

In about three-quarters of an hour Smoky came to camp and began washing for dinner and said not a word. When I saw that Smoky would not talk, I said, "Well, Smoky, did you find the other bee tree?" He said, "Oh! you keep right on baking flapjacks." Well, after Smoky regained his speech and told how blamed bright I was, he was going to go right to work and take out the honey from one of the trees at once. I told him that as we had no screen to put over his face, the bees would sting him to death, and that he had better wait until early the next morning when it was frosty.

Smoky said that he would not go without honey for the flapjacks when we had two bee trees so close to the camp. So he took an old burlap and removed every other thread in a space of about ten inches square, making a sort of an open-work to cover his face, then pulling the sack over his head and buttoning his coat close up about his throat Smoky was ready for the fray.

He cut the birch tree, the one that I had located, that tree being a little closer to camp. There was over a hundred pounds of honey in the tree and we had only one large pail in the camp, and that we had to have to use as a water pail. The tree did not break in falling so as to break up the honey and waste it. While we cut a large beech tree and took a block of about four feet long and split it in half and dug out two large troughs to hold the honey, which was very nice, being nearly all white honey, and Smoky said, "Old Golden, won't we live high now, rabbit, partridge, baked potatoes, buckwheat flapjacks and honey to swim in."

It was now the 20th of October. I told Smoky that we would go up the creek a mile above camp and put out the bee bait, burn more honey comb, and leave the bee box on the stand and await results. In the meantime we would take a couple of bear traps and go on to a ridge and set them. It might be possible that we would get a bear, although we had not seen any bear signs on what ground we had been over. We took the traps, Smoky carrying them, while I carried the bait. The hill was high and rough and I found it about all that I was able to do to climb although I went very slow and rested often. I did not complain, for Smoky was doing all the complaining necessary for both of us. He said that we would not catch a darn thing unless it was a cold, and he didn't think that we would get that much. It proved later that Smoky was wrong in his reckonings.

We set the two bear traps in as likely places as we could find for bear to travel, and put in the balance of the day traveling through the woods in search of bear signs. Not a track or sign could we find, and when we reached camp at night I was seemingly more dead than alive.

The next morning after we had left the bee bait on the old road bed and then climbed the hill to set the two bear traps, Smoky said that we would go down to Hull's, a distance of about three miles, and see if he could get cans to put the extracted honey in. We had made a sack from two towels and had begun to strain or extract the honey from the comb and had the water pail nearly full of strained honey, and were sorely in need of the pail to carry water in.

When I got to where we had left the bee bait, on the old road bed, I found plenty of bees at work. I soon got the line which went up the stream and a little to the left of the road and directly toward two large soft maple trees, the only trees of any size in that direction for a long distance. I said to myself, a quick job for you must be in one or the other of those maples. I left the bait and went to look for the bees in one of the two trees.

When I came to the trees, bees came to me in great numbers, but I could not see a bee going in or out in either. I was satisfied that the bees were in one of the trees, but after looking for a long time I thought that I must be mistaken, that the bees were farther on and up on the side of the hill. I gave it up and moved the bait up the road to a point about opposite where the line would strike the hillside and where several trees were left standing, making a good opening by cutting away the brush. I then released the bees from the box. After they had done much circling I was quite sure I saw two or three of them swing back in the direction of the soft maple trees.

I left the box and went along the creek in search of mink or coon signs, so as to give the bees time to get the bait well located, as they will then fly so much steadier and without doing so much circling. When I returned to the bait, the bees were flying steadily in the direction of the two soft maples and there could be no mistake this time. I took the bait down and placed it in the road opposite the two soft maples and began the second time to search the trees. After looking a long time without seeing bees going to or from the trees, I was again compelled to give it up. I began searching among the old timber, old stumps and stubs, as it was in the midst of an old bark slashing. I would search among the old down trees a while and then look over the two soft maples.

I had kept up this search from 9 o'clock in the morning until 2 o'clock in the afternoon. When I was approaching the two maple trees from the southwest side I readily discovered bees going into the tree close to and just above a large branch or prong of the tree which made it impossible to see them until the sun was just in the right position to shine square on the place where the bees entered the tree.

In my younger days I always carried a pair of climbers and a rope, so that when I found it difficult to locate the particular tree that the bees were in, when they were in thick timber, I could climb any tree no difference how large and locate the bees. This would often save much time in finding a bee tree. I would often climb a tree that stood in a favorable place on the bee line and cut off the top of the tree and make the bee stand up 30 or 40 feet from the ground. This I found a great advantage in lining bees in a thick, bushy section. That day is past with me for I am too clumsy to climb any more.

When I got to camp, I found Smoky at work putting the honey that was strained into cans and he said that he had concluded to change his name from Smoky Jim to Sticky Jim. We concluded to let bee hunting go for a day or two and set two more bear traps south of camp, although we had seen no signs of bear. Hear I will mention one of Smoky's dry remarks.

We took two bear traps and bait for them following up a hollow south from camp to the top of a ridge where there was quite a large clump of green timber still standing. When we came to the head of the hollow and near the top of the ridge where we thought would be a good place to set a bear trap, I pointed to a small scraggly beech sapling and told Smoky to cut it. Then to cut off a piece six or eight feet long for a clog. Also to measure the size of the ring in the trap chain and cut the clog off so that when the ring was put down over the end of the clog, sixteen or eighteen inches to a prong, it would fit the ring fairly close. This would make the ring or chain secure to the clog, as it would give the ring no chance to work about, while I would make a bed to set the trap in and have the trap set by the time that he got the clog ready.

It was now that I found that Smoky had brought a small hatchet weighing less than one-half pound instead of the larger belt axe, but there was nothing to do only to cut the clog with the little hatchet. So Smoky went to work cutting the clog while I went to setting the traps. After a while Smoky came with the clog and he had cut it off where it was considerably too large for the ring in the chain. I said, "Smoky, I guess you did not size that ring or the clog very much for you have got it much too large." Smoky replied readily, "Yes I did too, the tree has grown that much since I began to chop it."

After a time we managed to get the two traps set and got back to camp. That night about 10 o'clock, Smoky woke me with a punch in the ribs and at the same time saying, "Get your gun, the whole Siwash tribe of Indians are on us." On the impulse of the moment I though Smoky was right for I could hear many voices and the barking and snarling of dogs. In a moment all that had ever happened to me and many things that never did, nor can happen, passed through my mind but it was only for a moment when some one called out at the tent door saying, "Get up, you have visitors."

We asked who was there and the reply was, "Oh get up, two sleeps is better than one any time." I got up and put on my pants and unbuckled the tent door and there stood a half dozen men and as many more dogs. Two of the men had a large demijohn strung on a pole and they were carrying it on their shoulders, two more of the men had coons slung over their shoulders. The boys said that they were out coon hunting and by chance ran into our camp and thought that they would call on us and learn what we were doing. The demijohn contained cider, and the barking of the dogs was caused by getting into trouble over scraps that had been thrown about camp.

We invited the boy in and asked them to tell what luck they had had hunting coon. They said that they had only got the two coons on their way up, but thought that they would do better on their way back down the creek. The boys lived about six miles down the stream. The creek ran close along the wagon road nearly all the way so the boys would follow along the road allowing the dogs to hunt along the creek for coon. The boys concluded to stay and eat their lunch before starting back. We made them a cup of hot coffee and set out a plate of honey and the boys ate their lunch, drank cider, and told stories until nearly 1 o'clock.

They said that they had had a dandy time hunting coon along the last of September while coon were working on the corn and they said that they had killed about 30 and one wildcat. I asked if they did not think September rather early in the season to kill coon? They said that they thought that there was as much sport in it in September as at any other time of the year. I asked if there was any more sport in coon hunting in September than there was later in the season? They said that they did not know that there was. I replied that then they were out at least one-half or more on the price of the skins. They replied that it would be a queer jay that would put off a coon hunt a month for the difference that there might be in the price of a coon skin. I saw that I was up against it and that my argument had no weight in the matter, so I dropped it.

When told that we were putting in our time mostly hunting bees, the boys said that we were losing the best time of our lives by not having some good coon dogs along with us, and Smoky quite agreed with them. However, I could not see it in that light. After the boys left, Smoky and I had to laugh over the boys' jolly time until near daybreak before we could get to sleep again and we quite agreed with the boys that the second sleep was better than the first.

It was now the first of November and we had not put out any small traps, as the weather was still very warm and dry for the season of the year. Each day we could see away off to the southwest by the black heavy smoke that the forest fires that had been burning in that direction were coming nearer and nearer to us. Smoky said that he thought that a coon skin in October was worth as much as in November. He said by the time that we could get our traps out the forest fires would have the whole country burned over and all the game driven out. Smoky was not far from the mark in his prophesying.

We now began to put out the small traps at as good a "jag" as I was able to stand the travel. We had, while bee hunting at odd times, selected and prepared many of the sets so that we were now able to set out many more traps in a day than we could have done had we not fixed and selected many places for sets. The fourth day of November was a very warm day in Potter County, and as we had not tried to get any bees west of camp, I told Smoky that we had better let the balance of the traps go for a day and try the bees in that direction as it was not likely that we would have many more days that bees would fly during the season.

We went about one-half mile west of camp and put out the bee bait and burned more comb. It was not long before a bee came to the bait and then another and another, until we had several at work. As soon as the first bee that came was loaded up and began to make preparations to go, I told Smoky to keep a good eye on him to see which way he went, as the quicker we got a line the quicker we could move on.

When the bee first started from the bait, he jagged off east, then he circled so that neither Smoky nor I could tell which way he went. I told Smoky that I was afraid that the bee went back up the creek toward a tree we had already found. Smoky said that he did not know what made me think so, for no one could tell which direction that bee went. I told Smoky that I had always noticed that the way that the bee first started when leaving the bait was pretty sure to be in the direction of the tree and to get in position so that he could see well if the bee should fly back up the creek as we had no time to spare on bees flying in that direction.

It was not long before we had bees a-plenty and they came from a tree that we had already found. I told Smoky that we would leave some bait there so that those bees would not follow us, and we would move down the creek some distance before we would try for more. We moved nearly a mile, and while I was fixing a stand--there was no stump or good place to set the box--so I cut a stick about four feet long, an inch in diameter and split the top end into four parts, or in other words quartered the stick, then with two small sticks the size of a lead pencil, pressed down in between these quarters. It spread them so as to form plenty of space to set the box on. The other end of the stick is sharpened to drive firmly into the ground. As I was about to say, while I was fixing the stand, Smoky discovered a bee working on a witch-hazel bush close by the stand. Smoky said that he thought that the bee must have the rheumatism and was gathering Pond's Extract to bathe his joints in (it is with this shrub that Pond's Extract is made) and this was the cause of Smoky making the remark, I suppose.

It was necessary to burn comb here as we soon had three or four bees at work on the bait and in a short time we had bees a-plenty. They flew just to the right of the wagon road in a westerly direction and on to the side of a very steep hill where there was considerable standing timber. We soon got the course of the bees' flight, but there seemed to be two lines, as some of the bees would fly to the left of a large tree that stood Just on the bank of the road, while others would fly to the right of the tree. This caused Smoky to remark that we had another sticky job on our hands, saying that there was two different lines. I told Smoky that I thought not. It was all the same bees and that the bees would soon all be flying to the left or lower side of the tree.

Smoky wished to know how I made that out. I explained that I thought the bees were around the point of the hill and up a side draft that came into the main hollow some sixty rods below where we were and that the bees that were flying to the right of the tree flew in a direct line to the tree by flying up over the point of the hill then down into the hollow; those that flew to the left of the tree flew around the point of the hill and up the hollow to their tree. Smoky laughed at my idea and said that bees always flew in a straight line--does not everybody say as straight as a bee-line?

I told Smoky that was all very well in a level and open country. That a bee knew that it was no farther around the rim of a kettle than up over the bail; that a bee was far too wise to carry a load up over a hill when he could get there in the same distance on a level; that bees in their flight would often vary their course and fly along the side of a hill to keep out of a strong wind until they were nearly opposite the tree, when they would make nearly a square turn to the tree. That they would also vary their flight from a straight line to follow an opening as a road cut out through the thick woods.

The flight of the bees, as I suspected, was soon all to the left of the tree standing on the bank of the road. We moved the bait down to the mouth of the side draft and soon had a line flying nearly up the hollow. I told Smoky to take the bees some forty rods up the hollow and make a stand while I would follow and inspect the trees that looked favorable. Soon Smoky halloed to me and said that the bees had nearly all left him. I told him to make the stand where he was. As he had passed the tree that was the cause of the bees dropping off all at once.

Just below where Smoky was and a little up on the bank from the hollow stood a large maple tree. I started to inspect the tree. Bees were flying all about me and as soon as I was near enough to the tree to see, I could see bees flying all about the tree, some forty feet from the ground. I called to Smoky and told him that the bees were treed in a large maple.

This was on the fourth day of November and was a very rare thing for bees to be working at that time of the year in this section of the country. This tree made the sixth bee tree that we had found while in camp.

This ended our bee hunting and we now put in the balance of the time, while in camp, with the traps. It will now be necessary to go back to the 20th of October to a time that Smoky said was the biggest day of his life.

On the 20th of October we started out to look at the bear traps with little hopes of getting anything more than a porcupine. Up to this time we had not seen any signs of bear, only what had been made during the summer, where the bear had dug out woodchucks and torn old logs to pieces in search of grubs, and where they had dug wild turnips. These signs were so old that we had but little hopes of getting a bear while in camp and Smoky was continually condemning the country.

We went up along a hollow that led to the top of a high ridge where we had a bear trap setting and where I thought was the most likely place to catch a bear, but found the trap undisturbed.

We next crossed a narrow ridge where we had another trap. The trap was set in a spring run and the banks on either side of the run were quite thickly grown up with low brush. Smoky was in advance a few steps so that when he came to the edge of the thick brush that grew on the bank of the run, parted the brush and looked through at the trap, he caught a glimpse of some black object moving in the run. He quickly stepped back and held up his hand, his eyes sparkling with excitement and he whispered to me, "By Moses, we have got him." Smoky being given to much joking, I asked, "What have we got?" for I had not heard any noise of any kind. Smoky said, "A bear, by long horn spoon-handle." I stepped past Smoky and looked through the brush and there was a large black porcupine moving about a little in the trap.

I stepped back and said to Smoky, "Well, shoot him." Smoky said, "No, I will miss him. You shoot him," at the same time handing me the gun. I now saw that Smoky was in earnest and surely thought we had a bear and I burst out with laughter. Smoky was amazed and said, "You blooming simpleton, what is the matter with you?" The look of anxiety and the manner in which Smoky spoke still caused me to laugh the harder.

When I could cease laughing long enough to tell Smoky what was in the trap, Smoky's change of looks of excitement and anxiety to one of disgust was pitiful. Smoky began to condemn the country and tell how foolish we were to come to such a forsaken place as that was to trap where there was nothing but porcupines.

After resetting the trap we went on to the third trap, which was setting about a mile farther north. It was necessary to cross two narrow ridges in order to reach the trap. Smoky was in a moody state of mind and lagged along behind, hunting partridges, killing two or three.

When we reached the top of the second ridge and the trap was in the hollow beyond, I heard some sort of a noise where the trap was setting, but I was unable to tell what it was. Smoky was behind somewhere on the line, but while I stood listening he came on in great haste. He had heard the same noise and was hurrying up to inquire what it was.

I told him that I was unable to tell just what it was, but was afraid that some dog had got caught in the trap as the sound came from the direction in which the trap was. Smoky said that it was a different noise than he had ever heard a dog make.

I told Smoky that I feared that it was some hound that was in the trap and was making the pitiful sort of a howl and that we must hurry on and get him out of the trap. When we were half way down the side of the hill, the noise ceased, but I could now see that the noise came from some distance farther down the run than where the trap had been set and I knew that no dog could move the trap and clog. We now went a little more quietly. I soon got sight of Bruin rolling and tumbling in a bunch of small birch saplings where the trap clog was fast, good and stout.

Smoky had not got his eye onto the bear yet, when I stopped and pointed in the direction of the bear and said, "Smoky, there is the gentleman that you have been so anxious to see." Smoky had not yet got his eye onto the bear and he said, "That's no darned dog that makes that noise. What is it? I don't see anything." "No, Smoky, it is no dog; neither is it a porky; it is a bear this time all right."

I pointed at the clump of yellow birches and said, "Don't you see him down in the gulch there?" When Smoky got his eye on the bear, you should have seen them sparkle. This was the first bear that Smoky had ever seen outside of captivity. When I told Smoky that we would go up close to the bear and he (Smoky) should shoot it, he again reached the gun to me and again insisted that I should shoot it, saying that he would surely miss it, the same as he declared in the case of the porcupine. I told Smoky that he had plenty of cartridges and that it would be some time before it would be too dark to see to shoot and that he must shoot the bear. It took a great deal of urging to get Smoky to shoot, he declaring all the time that he knew he would miss it.

I said, "Smoky, you must not shoot at the bear but at the base of the bear's ear," which he finally did and Bruin was out of his trouble almost before the smoke from the rifle had cleared away.

The bear was a large one, measuring seven feet two inches from end to end. We were unable to get it out of the woods whole. Smoky insisted that he would carry it if it was as large as a mountain. He soon gave up that idea and we cut the carcass into pieces and took part to camp and returned the next day after the balance. That night after we got to camp with the bear we had for supper bear steak, partridge, rabbit and bacon with warm biscuits and honey, baked potatoes, butter and coffee, with the necessary trimmings, which caused Smoky to remark that the country was all right for a living, but thought that society was rather limited.

The day after we had brought in the remainder of the bear, we could see the smoke from the forest fires that were burning away to the southwest, loom up thick and black. It was plainly to be seen that the fire was steadily working in the direction of our camp and was getting in close proximity to where we had a bear trap setting. I was afraid that the fire would burn sufficiently hard to spoil the trap unless it was taken up, so Smoky said that if I would "mix the muligan" (get supper) that he would go and get the trap, which I readily consented to do, telling Smoky to bring the trap down to a small creek and put the trap in the water.

Smoky got back about the time I had supper ready. He came in and put his gun up and washed ready for supper without saying a word. I saw that Smoky was looking down-hearted but thought that he was a little tired and homesick, so I did not say much to him, but after a little I said, "Charley, did you get anything in the trap?" He answered very short, saying, "If I had you would be likely to see something of it, wouldn't you?" so I said no more.

After supper was over and the dishes washed, Smoky took a piece of paper from his pocket and handed it to me with the remark, "What do you know about that?" I unfolded the paper and found that it contained a lock of bear's hair. I said, "Smoky, what is it? Another one of your jokes?" I thought that Smoky had taken the hair from the bear that we had caught two days before. Smoky remarked that he thought that the joke was on him as much as anyone, and then explained that a bear had been in the trap and he got out.

He described the circumstances, and it was plain to be seen that the guide or stepping stick had been placed a little too close to the trap which had caused the bear to step his foot partly over on to the jaw of the trap and had only been caught by the heel, which was not sufficient to hold him, although Smoky said that the bear had put up quite a fight before it had got out. Smoky said that when he came to where the trap was set and found it gone, he thought he would have the biggest time of his life. A bear all by himself, and when he found that the bear had got away, he felt like throwing himself into the creek along with the trap. I told Charley not to take the matter to heart so, for if he followed the trap line and the trail very long that he would have many a slip just at the time that he thought he had the game bagged.

The next morning the fire was sweeping over the whole country so we hustled around and pulled all of the traps that were not setting in the water or that were not out of reach of the fire. The fire put an end to trapping for everything but a few mink along the stream.

I wish to speak of one of Smoky's dry remarks. Smoky is a strong Republican. A few days after the Presidential election we were going up a small draft to look after three or four traps that I had set for fox. The first trap that we came to was undisturbed. The second one was lying at the side of the brook all in a bunch, chain and all. Plain to be seen that it had been dropped there by human hands. As soon as I saw the trap I said, "Smoky, some one has dropped that trap there." "There has been some animal in it and it has gotten out, see, there is blood on the jaws." "Very true, Smoky, there has been some animal in the trap, but human hands took it out, for no animal leaves a trap, clog and all, lying free in that way, with the trap chain slack in that way." It only required a glance about to see that there had been a coon in the trap and had been fast. Just up on the bank there lay the club that they had used to kill the coon with. After giving my opinion of the gentleman that had taken the coon, I began to reset the trap again where it was before.

Smoky objected to again setting the trap there only for some one else to get the game again, but I told Smoky that lightning rarely struck twice in the same place so we would set the trap again. We started up the hollow and were soon discussing politics again until we came to where the next trap was setting. Just before we came to the trap, Smoky picked up an empty cartridge shell. A few yards farther on lay the second trap which had had a fox in it, as was plain to be seen by the tooth marks on the small brush and by the fur on the trap. That the fox had been shot was evident by the amount of fur that was lying on the ground where the animal had been caught.

This was more than I could stand without giving vent to my feelings. After trying for some time to find words to give the case justice, and failing, Smoky remarked with all the coolness imaginable, that there was one thing certain about it, that it was a Democrat that took the fox and coon. I was astonished at the remark and asked what he meant. "Well, if it had been a Republican that had taken them, he would have taken the traps, too."

We were now getting our trap line down to a few traps along the main creek, and we now worked those traps to the best of our skill, as we wished to get our share of the mink. We had not put out any mink traps until the first of November. The weather had been very dry and warm but as it had now turned cold and I found that I could not stand the cold as I once could, I told Smoky that we would take what mink pelts we could get in a few days and pull stakes. Smoky replied that that sort of "chin music" suited him. So after ten or twelve days of mink trapping we pulled the rest of the traps and went home, having to my idea a pleasant time.

Smoky agreed that the time was all right but he thought that the society was a little slow for him, saying that if it had not been for the boys on the coon hunt we would not have seen a half dozen persons since we had been in camp. We had not made a large catch of furs but I thought that we had done fairly well, all things considered (one old played-out trapper and a kid who had never set a trap for anything greater than a muskrat or a ground hog).

WOODCOCK AND SOME OF HIS CATCH.

We had caught while in camp one bear, ten mink, eight coon and some other furs as shown in the accompanying picture. After we left I set a few traps about home, catching three fox and a few skunk and four more mink, making fourteen mink in all. We got $4 and $4.50 for the fox, and $4 to $6 for the mink, and from 80 cents to $2.25 for skunk, and about the same for coon. We got 30 to 40 cents each for muskrats.

This will about complete the story of my trapping for the season of 1908. I am sorry that I am no artist, as I could have sent some fine pictures, consisting of the bear in trap, as well as many other animals in traps, and other pictures that would have been interesting had I been able to take them at the right time and place.

CHAPTER XVI.
Hits and Misses on the Trail.

Many years ago when deer were plenty in this section of the country (North Central Pennsylvania) and dogs were allowed to run deer at their will, there being no restriction by way of law against hounding deer, I started from the house about 10 o'clock in the morning to go to some traps that I had set for mink along the creek in a swamp not far from our place. There was an old road or path that led from the wagon road down through the swamp to the creek. Along this path it was thickly grown up with laurel and other underbrush that nearly shut out the path.

I was accustomed to follow this path to the creek when going to look after my traps. On my way up to the road I heard dogs barking as though they were on the trail of something, but thought nothing of it as it was a common occurrence to hear hounds running nearly every day. I was following this path and had got within a few rods of the creek and was just about ready to climb over a fallen tree that lay across the path.

The tree lay up from the ground about a foot or so and it was perhaps three feet from the ground up to the top of the log. I was just in the act of climbing this log when a good-sized buck deer went to jump the log also and we met, head on. I had no gun and if I had would have had no time to use it. I seized the deer by the horns and forced him back from the log with a startled cry at the same time. The deer, instead of trying to get away, seemed bound to come over the log to where I was, so I held to the deer's horns, not daring to let loose.

I could keep him from raising over the log and after he tried several times to jump the log, he then tried to break loose from me, but I had the advantage of the deer owing to the log being so high that the deer could not pull me over, neither could the deer get in shape to strike me with his feet under the log. I think that I was so badly frightened at the sudden meeting with the deer, that I did not know what to do so I hung tight to the buck's horns and called as loud as I could for help, thinking that some one might possibly be passing along the road, which was not so far away, hear my call and come to my assistance, but no one came. A man by the name of Nelson lived about a fourth of a mile away, who had a large bulldog. The dog's name was Turk. This dog would follow me at every chance that he could get. As no assistance came, I had about made up my mind to release my hold on the deer as my strength was fast leaving me, when I thought to call for Turk. I began calling as loud as I could and it seemed that the dog had heard my calling before I began, for almost before I was aware of his presence the dog sprang over the log and seized the deer by the hind leg, but the dog had barely grabbed the deer when the deer kicked him away from the path into the laurel.

In an instant the dog, with an angry yelp, jumped and seized the deer by the throat and in a moment the deer ceased to struggle and began to settle to the ground. As soon as I dared to release my hold on the deer's horns I got my pocket knife out and sprang over the log and ran the knife blade into the deer's throat. The deer did not seem to notice the knife. I think that the dog had choked the life out of him. The battle was over and it was only a few minutes but it was the hardest battle that I ever had and the dog came to my assistance none too soon for I could not have held on much longer.

This did not end the fight, for I had hardly begun to dress the deer before two dogs that were in pursuit of the deer came up. I was compelled to use sticks, stones and clubs to break up a fight between the bulldog and the hounds, though I finally got the row broke up and drove the hounds off in order to keep peace.

Boys, I am not sure whether the incident just related would be called a hit or a miss. I will tell of an incident that I call a hit. A man by the name of Wells and a brother of mine were camping near the old Jersey Shore turnpike and were trapping, also hunting deer. One day they had been off on the west side of the turnpike setting marten traps and had built a number of deadfalls and had also set several steel traps for foxes. On their way home to camp they had to cross several low ridges which were good sections for deer. It was nearly sundown and just the right time for deer to be on their feet feeding so we spread out along one of the ridges in hopes that some of us might get a shot. There was a good tracking snow and deer tracks were plenty. We were on the last ridge before we dropped off into the hollow to where the camp was and it was beginning to get dark in the heavy timber. I had come out onto a short spur of the ridge and was standing looking over the ground very carefully to see if I could not see a deer feeding, when I heard a shot fired by one of the boys. In a few moments a bunch of five or six deer came in sight, making their way around the point at breakneck speed.

I opened fire on the bunch without taking aim at any particular deer, as it was too dark to get down to real business and the deer were in too much of a hurry to change their feeding grounds to give me very much of a show. I was not stingy of my ammunition and pumped lead at the bunch as long as I could guess where the deer were. As soon as I had ceased to waste ammunition I heard my brother calling for me. When I got to him he was at work taking the entrails out of a good sized buck. We dragged the deer down to where the deer were when I began shooting to see if I had chanced to hit one of the bunch. It was too dark to see much but we found a little blood on the snow in one place but concluded that I had not done much damage.

We dragged the buck that my brother had killed to camp, got our supper and made plans for the next day's work. It was agreed that I should look after the bunch of deer and see what effect my shots had on the deer that we had found that had bled some. I was to work this bunch of deer while the other boys went to look after the marten traps, being quite sure that there would be a marten or two in the traps, for we had built some deadfalls where we saw fresh marten signs quite plenty.

The next morning I was up early and had breakfast before daylight and ready to start out and carry out the work as already planned. It was about one-fourth of a mile from camp to the turnpike and as the deer which I was going to look for were making their course, the last I had seen them, in the direction of the road, I was going to go to the road and then go north along the road to see if they had crossed. The boys would take the same path to the road that I did when they would go south of camp to look after the marten traps.

I had my gun and stood in the cabin door waiting for my brother and Wells to get ready as I would accompany them as far as the road. The boys were having some trouble belting their leggins and creepers on to their satisfaction. I became tired of waiting and made the remark that I could go and kill a deer before they could get their feet dressed. My brother said that I had better be going then, so I started on up the path to the road. It was thawing a little, just enough to make the snow pack. I had gone about a hundred yards from camp when I saw a track of a deer where it had stepped into the path, then had turned back about forty yards to the left of the path. A large birch tree had blown down, knocking one or two smaller trees down so that it made a little jam. Seeing that the tracks were so fresh I knew that the deer was close by and as the woods were open I was quite positive that the deer must be about the jam of trees, when a large doe stepped out in sight and it was only the work of a moment to let her down in her tracks. When the gun cracked out jumped a yearling buck that was lying down just in the edge of the jam and bounded over the trunk of a large birch and stopped broadside to me and I let him down. Thinking of what I had said on leaving the cabin and what my brother had said to me I ran back to camp as quick as I could go without even stopping to cut the deer's throat. As I came around the corner of the cabin I heard my brother say to Wells, "I bet a gander that he has killed a deer all right, for he would not shoot twice so quick at anything else."

Well, the boys had not got their feet dressed yet, but chance had allowed me to make my word good only I had killed two deer instead of one. The boys helped me to hang up the deer and then went to the marten traps while I went in search of the deer I had started after. Soon I struck the trail of the deer and shortly saw that one of them had a broken leg and I did not follow the trail far when the wounded deer dropped out and left the others. I began doing the creeping act and soon found the deer lying on his trail. I hung the deer up and went back to camp thinking that I had enough sport for one day and would let well enough alone.

When the boys came in at night they brought in two marten skins.

CHAPTER XVII.
Lost in the Woods.

One writer contends that the pocket compass is but very little use to a man in a dense forest. This, I think, depends largely upon circumstances. While the writer has spent a good portion of fifty years almost continuously in the woods, he has seldom found it necessary to use a compass to guide him out. Now this is due partly to the natural faculty of locating any particular place. This faculty of locating any certain place or point by giving or knowing the proper direction to take after one has traveled all day or for several days in the woods, I am inclined to credit to a sort of natural instinct.

I have often thought of the story of the Indian who was met by a man in the woods who asked the Indian if he was lost. The reply was, "No, me ain't lost, wigwam lost, me here." Now I can say without boasting that it is seldom that the camp or a given point gets lost with me, while it is not an uncommon occurrence for the writer to get lost or rather bothered himself in a strange locality. But after a moment's thought, I say the camp or the point I wish to reach is in that direction, and it is not often that I miss my calculation.

As I have had several occasions to search for parties lost in the woods, I wish to relate a particular instance of one man who was lost. It was an uncle of mine by the name of Nelson, and the writer went in search of him. To illustrate that those who are lost lose their heads as soon as they find that they do not know where they are.

Now I wish to say that if you lost your course or get bothered in your bearings, do not lose your head, for if you do you are lost, but keep cool and keep your head. Sit down and fill your pipe, and while you smoke draw a map of the country carefully in your mind, and almost invariably you will locate yourself and in so doing will locate the camp.

To get back to the lost man in question whose name was Amos Fish, and at the time, was the proprietor of the Cherry Springs Hotel, in this county. This hotel was located in the heart of the largest forest in Pennsylvania, and originally was a great resort for hunters from all over the state as well as southern and western New York. (The time of which I write was somewhere in the 60's--have forgotten exact date.) There were several men boarding at this hotel and my uncle and myself were among the number boarding with Mr. Fish, hunting, as were other boarders. This hotel stood in the center of a field containing perhaps eighty acres of cleared land, and there was not another clearing or a building within a distance of seven miles.

One morning after there had been a fall of four or five inches of snow, which made fine tracking, Mr. Fish thought that he would go out that morning and try and kill a deer. He left the house going through the field in nearly a due east course. After going about one mile he crossed a stream which ran in a north and south direction. Mr. Fish had fished this stream for trout many a time. After crossing this stream Mr. Fish crossed a broad ridge and went on to a small stream known as the Sunken Branch, and a tributary of the stream Mr. Fish had previously crossed. Now Mr. Fish was fairly well acquainted with the location which he was in, but in his search for deer he had got a little mixed in his whereabout and at once lost his head.

My uncle when coming in from hunting that evening crossed Mr. Fish's track on the ridge near the head of the Sunken Branch, and had heard him shoot several times but supposed that he was shooting at deer. When the hunters all got in that night and Mr. Fish failed to appear, the matter was discussed by the hunters from all points of view. It was generally thought that Mr. Fish had had good luck killing deer and had been detained in dressing and hanging them up, or that he had wounded a deer and had been led a long way from home in getting it.

When it got well along in the evening and Mr. Fish failed to come then it was feared that he had met with some misfortune. No one would believe that he was lost, as it was known that he was pretty well acquainted with the woods in the direction that he had been known to take. But as the time went on and still Mr. Fish did not come, we all began to fear for his safety, as the night was very cold, so every few minutes some one would go out and fire a gun. This was continued all night, though there was no answer.

My uncle and myself had an early breakfast and started some time before daybreak for the locality in which uncle had seen Mr. Fish's tracks and heard gun shots which were thought to have been fired by him. Shortly after daybreak we found the track of a man which we could readily see had been made during the night. After following the track some distance we were convinced that we were following the track of Mr. Fish and he was lost, for his tracks would go in a zigzag sort of a circle and crossing his tracks previously made.

After we had followed Mr. Fish's track for an hour or longer we saw him coming nearly towards us with his hat in his hand. We stood still and he came close to us before he seemed to notice us. He had no gun, and when he stopped he stared at us and did not seem to know us. Uncle then spoke to him and said, "Amos, what is the matter, are you lost?" Mr. Fish replied that he wanted to go to the Cherry Springs Hotel. In a few minutes after eating a good lunch which we had carried with us for that purpose, he seemed to know us.

When questioned as to what he had done with his gun, he apparently had forgotten that he ever had a gun. But after a time seemed to remember the gun in a vague sort of way, and said that he must have left it by a tree but could not tell in what direction the tree was. After a search of a half hour we found the gun standing by a tree where apparently Mr. Fish had traveled around for some time.

When we came to the creek on our way to the house and at the place where Mr. Fish had crossed it in the morning before, he asked what stream it was. When told that it was the place where he had crossed the creek the morning before and asked if he did not remember the creek as he had fished there many a time, he said that he had no recollection of ever seeing the stream before. Shortly we came out into the field and Mr. Fish did not know his own house. Asked who lived there and did not seem to recognize his own home until he had been inside the house for several minutes with his family.

I have related this instance of Mr. Fish to show how necessary it is for one who has got slightly mixed in his course to keep cool and not allow himself to become excited. If he does he immediately loses his head and is at once lost, as in the case of Mr. Fish. He was at no time more than four miles from his house, and was quite familiar with the ground he was on during the whole time. He was lost while following the deer that he was in pursuit of. They led him into a windfall perhaps containing one hundred acres, and it was while in this that he became bothered as to the right course to go to his house. He at once lost his head, or more proper, his reasoning faculties, and at once became lost.

Mr. Fish was east of the ridge and road and as he had a compass, all there was for him to do was to consult the compass and go west to the road, but Mr. Fish declared that his compass would not work, and it might have been possible that he held the compass so close to the gun barred that the compass did not work properly.

In my more than fifty years' life in the woods as a trapper and hunter, it has been my lot to search for several persons lost in the woods. Once in these same woods I searched for three weeks for a little child four years old. At first the search for days was carried on by more than a hundred men, then another man and myself continued, then my companion gave it up. I continued alone for days, but there has never been a trace of the child seen or heard of, since its grandmother last saw the little fellow sitting on the door step eating a piece of bread and butter on the morning of its disappearance, along in the early 80's.

To speak of the use of the pocket compass, I would say to the trapper or hunter that where he can it is best to locate his camp when in a section of a country where the woods are very large, and the trapper or hunter is not well acquainted with the locality, on a stream or in a valley of considerable size, or near a public highway or some landmark that is readily recognized by the trapper. Even thought it may be after nightfall, for the thrifty trapper or hunter will oftener find himself on the trail after the stars are shining than he will in camp before dark. Now it is quite necessary that the camper should first acquaint himself with these land marks for some distance either side of his camp (when I say some distance I mean miles) and especially get the general course or direction that the stream runs or other landmarks, for this is where the real use of the pocket compass comes in play.

Now when you start out place out a line of traps or on the trail of a deer or other animal, all that there is to be done is to know whether you are on the south, north or other direction, as the case may be, from this valley or other landmarks. Now the trapper or hunter soon becomes so accustomed to traveling in the woods that when he makes up his mind to strike for camp, he can tell about how long it will take him to reach this valley that the camp is located in. When the time comes to go to camp consult the compass, and as it is known what direction to take to hit the camp, or at least the stream or other landmark on which the camp is located.

Yes, boys, if any one is in the habit of getting lost the pocket compass is a very useful instrument in finding the way, providing it is properly used. Let me say, however, that no matter how often "the shanty gets lost," don't lose your head, for if you do, the compass or the landmarks will do you no good.

CHAPTER XVIII.
Traps and Other Hints for Trappers.

All trappers have their favorite traps--the writer has his. Every boy knows that the Newhouse trap is at the top of the ladder, as to quality, but as to convenience, well, I prefer the No. 1 1/2 Oneida Jump trap, which is superior to all others on the market for small game. This trap is now made with jaws much thicker than the original "Jump" (Blake & Lamb), and the way the chain is now fastened gives the animal a straight draw instead of a twist, as was the case with the Blake & Lamb style. The Oneida Jump however, is lacking in strength of the springs, being much weaker than the Blake & Lamb of the same size but in all other ways I consider it far better than the original Blake & Lamb. The spring being so much weaker than the Blake & Lamb springs were, is a serious drawback, as the Oneida Jump trap of this size will not hold a large raccoon or a large fox.

Now, while many trappers might not seriously object to the trap on these grounds as they use many different sizes of traps or a different size of trap for each animal. This I never do in trapper the smaller animals, for when I make a dry or ground set, I set the trap for any animal from the fox to the coon or wildcat, although I may be more particular making the set for mink.

It makes a trapper feel sore to go to a trap and find that a fox or coon has been in his trap and escaped. This rarely if ever occurs when using the Blake & Lamb No. 1 1/2 trap, or as the original was called No. 2, though it had the same spread of jaws as the No. 1 1/2 Oneida Jump. Now the advantages that the Oneida Jump trap has over the long spring trap are many. The most desirable are perhaps the easy manner in which the "jump" trap can be concealed. In fact, a practical set can be made in certain places where it is entirely impracticable to make the set with a long spring trap. Another advantage that the "jump" trap has over the bow or long spring trap is its comparison to the long spring trap in shipping by express. This, if going on a long journey, to your trapping grounds, is not safe by freight, as the trapping season may be over before your traps reach you. Still another advantage is the amount of room saved in packing, for you can pack two of the "jump" traps in the same space required to pack one long spring trap. The writer has had a good deal of experience in this matter and knows the difference in handling the two makes of traps.

Now I do not like to use the double spring "jump" trap where I am trapping, for I might possibly catch a dog or other domestic animal and it is a hard trap to get a live animal out of.

Many, perhaps most trappers use the No. 1 trap for trapping mink, muskrat, marten, etc. The No. 1 Newhouse or Victor is sufficiently strong for these animals but as I have stated, I do not think this the best plan if the trapper is operating on grounds where there are larger animals to be taken, as most frequently the one set can be made to catch several kinds of animals. I have found also that one is more liable to catch the animal by the end of the toes in a No. 1 trap than in the No. 1 1/2, but where one is trapping for the purposes of saving the fox, skunk or other animal alive, then the No. 1 trap should be used, as the animal is not so liable to break a leg or to hurt the foot so badly.

For otter I prefer the single spring Newhouse trap, owing to the fact that it is more easily concealed than the double spring trap. I see that a number of writers think that the No. 5 bear trap should have a larger spread of jaw so as to catch higher on the bear's foot. Now I do not intend to dictate to others as to what kind of a trap they should use, not in the least, for I have my own ideas as to traps and guns as well as the manner of using them. Now as for myself, I think the Newhouse No. 5 bear trap could not be improved, as to spread of jaws. The grasp is just right to catch the bear through the thick of the foot where there is no danger of the bear twisting the foot off. In case where the trap has a spread of jaws sufficient to grasp above the foot and for more space for the bear to place his foot well between the jaws, will say there is plenty of room in the Newhouse No. 5 trap, if the trap is properly set. I also see that some trappers want the swivel in the trap chain 8 or ten inches from the bed piece, or the point of fastening. Now I am somewhat puzzled as to an explanation in this matter, as it seems to me that the swivel will be far less liable to become useless by being twisted or wound around saplings, etc., where the swivel is close to the bed piece than it would be if placed eight or ten inches out in the chain. I prefer to have the swivel in my trap chain placed as close to the trap as possible.

WOODCOCK AND HIS STEEL TRAPS.

Another thing that I have but little use for is a trap from which the animal must take the bait in order to spring it, for often the animal will go up close enough to a trap to inspect the bait but will not touch it.

I do not think that there should be a latch on any trap, as I think that often the animal's foot is thrown free from the trap, or at least causes many catches by the tips of the toes and the animal escapes, becoming a hard animal to catch thereafter. The animal having a part of the foot resting on the latch and the toes striking the treadle sufficient to unlatch the treadle, the released jaw will throw the latch with the portion of the animal's foot resting on the latch, free from the trap, or at least may often cause a slight catch of the toes or other part of the foot. All that is necessary is to leave an extension to the arm or heel of the treadle to catch over the jaw of the trap. The trap may be made to spring hard or easy by simply raising the pan slightly higher or lowering it to catch farther on to the jaw of the trap more or less as desired.

Now boys, I have given a few of my ideas as to traps, and if any of you have any suggestions to make as to improvements on the animal steel traps, let us hear from you through the columns of the H-T-T. I believe that manufacturers of animal or game traps would be glad to make any improvements on their traps could they be convinced that the suggested improvements were really of any value.

* * *

As I get many letters from trappers who are beginners in the business making inquiries about camping and the necessary traps, guns, etc., I will try to give a few practical hints to those who have had but limited experience of trapper's life. While, like the setting of a trap, there is no single code of rules that will answer for all localities and conditions, I will give a few general rules.

The trapper should first try and inform himself of the nature and conditions of the locality where he intends to trap. If the waters are of such a size that a boat can be used to advantage, then the boat becomes a necessity. Now in regard to traps. If the section where you intend to trap has the larger animals like bear, otter, beaver, etc., then the trapper should provide himself with a sufficient number of traps of different sizes as he may be able to tend and do it well.

I would advise to start with, that the trapper has about one-half dozen No. 5 bear traps, one dozen No. 4 wolf and about the same of No. 3. But the greater number of traps will be Numbers 1 1/2 and 2, if of the Jump or Blake & Lamb pattern. If of other patterns would say use the Hawley & Norton Nos. 1 1/2 and 2, say 75 No. 1 1/2 and 25 No. 2. The genuine Newhouse is of course the best long spring trap made, but a little more expensive, and we find that the H. & N. fills the bill. We prefer the B. & L. on account of its lightness and convenience in setting.

Now, if the trapper is trapping where the animals are no larger than fox, raccoon, wildcat, etc., then I want no traps larger than the No. 2 1/2, nor smaller than the No. 1 1/2 Blake & Lamb.

Now about the gun. If you are in a large game country it is quite necessary that you carry a good rifle. I like the Winchester and not of too large a caliber, but if there is no large game in the locality then I think one should have a Stevens pistol, ten-inch barrel, or a Stevens Pocket Shotgun, 15-inch barrel, and in either case have a good holster to carry it in. As for myself I prefer a Pocket Shotgun. It might be well to have a large shotgun in camp. You will also want your belt axe or hatchet and a good heavy sharp axe at the camp.

As for bedding, this will largely depend on what kind of a cabin or camp you have. If you are in a tent, two persons should have not less than six good blankets. If your camp is so situated that you can drive to it with a team or pack horses, then you should have a straw mattress. But if you are in a locality where you can get cedar or hemlock boughs, you should use only the finer boughs. Begin at the foot of the berth and push the larger or butt end of the bough into the ground and then begin the next row so as to lap or shingle onto the first row, and so on until the head of the berth is reached.

If you use a tent, I find that it is a good idea to make a skeleton frame of good heavy poles over the tent and about twelve inches above and around the tent and shingle it well with boughs, so that the snow will not fall directly on the tent. It will be a great help in keeping out the cold. But I think it is best to have at least one good log cabin well chinked, mudded and banked. Always select a spot where it is easy to drain away the surface water on all sides of the camp, and if possible have the main camp close to good pure water which is a great protection against malaria.

If you are doing a stroke of business so that you will need more than one camp, the others need not be quite so tidy as the main camp, for it is not likely that you will occupy them more than a night or two at a time. Your temporary camps need not be larger than 6 x 8 and quite low, as this will save both fuel and bedding. Do not forget to get up a good supply of wood at all the camps before the trapping season is open, for you will find plenty to do after the trapping season opens without cutting wood.

The main camp should be at least 10 x 12 feet inside. A place should be provided for curing furs outside. Furs should never be cured by a fire or in a warm place, for this will have a tendency to curl the ends of the fur and give it a woolly appearance. There can usually be a place fixed either on the outer gable or under the eaves of the cabin to cure the furs.

Now, as to the commissary part. You will, of course, to a great extent select the kind and quantity according to the distance and convenience in getting the grub to camp. The camper will find that the most convenient as well as better satisfaction, as a rule, will be found in taking provisions to camp in a crude state, i.e., wheat flour, corn meal, beans, bacon, with the necessary supply of tea, coffee, sugar, good baking powder, salt, pepper and a quantity of rice. If, as I have before stated, the camp is so located as to be of easy access by wagon, then choose a bill-of-fare to your own liking.

The medicine box should contain a box of good cathartic pills and a quantity of 2-grain quinine tablets, with any other medicine you may wish. Other necessities about the camp are a good supply of strong cord, a few feet of small rope, a yard or two of muslin, a yard of oilcloth.

It may be well to give a few suggestions about a temporary camp for a night, if by chance you should get caught out and unable to reach camp. You should select a place before dark. If a large fallen tree can be found that lies close to the ground where you wish to build the fire it is best. If the log cannot be readily found then select a bank or knoll to build the fire against. First, build the fire out from the log five or six feet where you will make your bed so as to warm the ground. Now set two crotches about four feet high and place a pole in these crotches. Then from this pole place three or four poles, one end on the ground, the other resting on the pole that rests in the crotches. Then place boughs, bark, or anything to break the wind. This shelter will, of course, be placed over the spot where you will make your bed. Now rake the coals and live embers down against the log where you will have the fire for the night. Now place some boughs over the spot where the fire has been and where your bed will be.

With this kind of a camp you can get along through a rather chilly night. You should always carry matches wrapped in waxed paper in three or four different places about your person. You may lose your match safe.

If convenient, when going into camp, you should take several stretching boards for different kinds of fur with you. If not, you can usually find a tree that will split good and you can split some out. It is usually hard to find withes that are long and straight enough to bend so as to form a good shaped stretcher. You should always aim to stretch and cure the furs you catch in the best manner. In skinning you should rip the animal straight from one heel across to the other and close to the roots of the tail on the under side. Work the skin loose around the bone at the base until you can grasp the bone of the tail with the first two fingers of the right hand while you place the bone between the first two fingers of the left hand. Then by pulling you will draw the entire bone from the tail which you should always do.

Sometimes when the animal has been dead some time the bone will not readily draw from the tail. In this case you should cut a stick the size of your finger about eight inches long. Cut it away in the center until it will readily bend so that the two ends will come together. Then cut a notch in each part of the stick just large enough to let the bone of the tail in and squeeze it out. It is necessary to whittle one side of the stick at the notch so as to form a square shoulder.

You should have about three sizes of stretching boards for mink and fox. For mink they should be from 4 1/2 inches down to 3 inches and for fox from 6 1/4 inches down to 5 inches wide, and in length the fox boards may be four feet and the mink boards three feet long. The boards should taper slightly down to within 8 inches of the end for fox and then rounded up to a point. The mink boards should be rounded at 4 or 5 inches from this point. You will vary the shape of the board in proportion to the width. Stretching boards should not be more than 3/8 inch thick. A belly strip the length, or nearly the length, of the boards 1 1/4 inches at the wide end, tapering to a point at the other end and about 1/4 to 3/8 inch thick. Have the boards smooth and even on the edges. Other stretching boards should be made in proportion to the size and shape of the animal whose skin is to be stretched.

You should not fail to remove all the fat and flesh from the skin immediately after the skin is on the board. If a skin is quite wet when taken from the animal it should be drawn lightly on the board until the fur is quite dry. Then turn the skin flesh side out and stretch.

It is always best if you can go into the country where you intend to trap. This is especially important if the ground is a new field to you. During the summer or early fall, acquaint yourself with the streams and the general surroundings, and prepare some of your best sets for the mink and the fox.

If you have a dog of good intelligence take him along, though he may not be broken to the business of trapping. It is many a fox and coon that my dog has saved for me when they have escaped from footing or a broken chain. If the dog is of much intelligence, and you use care in training him, you will soon find that a dog will learn more about trapping than you supposed possible. If you have long lines of traps your dog will inform you more than once that you have passed a trap that chanced to be a little off the main line.

* * *

Brother bear trappers, how do you like this style of bear trap (see frontispiece) for toting through the woods three or four miles from camp and at the same time tote a couple of sheep heads or the head of a beef for bait? In times gone by I have carried two or three Newhouse bear traps and bait to bait them with from one to five miles in the woods to pinch old Bruin's toes. Such is a pleasure to any red blooded man, who was born a real lover of the open and the stimulating effect of obtaining that $30 or $40, which the hide and meat of the bear brought, had on the trapper, was nearly equal to the desire to be out in the tall timber.

Now brother bear trappers, these traps that you see on my shoulder are of my own make and are made with a half circle bed piece instead of a straight bed piece, as the ordinary trap is made. I wish to call your attention to how this trap fits the shoulders and how much easier it is to carry than the trap with the straight bed piece and note how much more readily you can get your gun into shape for action. Many a deer has given me the slip before I could drop the bear traps and get my gun ready for action when I have been toting bear traps in the woods. But with this style of trap your gun can be put in operation at once, regardless of the traps.

Boys, another thing that I have learned in the last five years' experience in trapping in the south, (this was written Spring of 1913) is that it requires a trap a size larger to trap small fur bearers in the south than it does in the north, owing to the difference in conditions of the streams and the soil. Well friend Bachelder, there is no use of you and I talking or worrying any more over our bear traps or bear trapping. The gentleman sportsman and his dog has ordered you and I and all other trappers of Pennsylvania for that matter to cast our traps on to the scrap pile and we must submit.

CHAPTER XIX.
Camps and Camping.

I will say that the conditions and location in which one is to camp makes a great difference in the preparations. If one is just going outside of town to camp for a few days outing, commodities may be to your liking as to quality and quantity. In these days, should the larder run low, it is only necessary for the camper to step out a short distance to a farm house where he is almost sure to find a telephone. In such cases all that the camper has to do is to 'phone to town, ordering his favorite brands delivered to camp, and soon an automobile is on the road laden with supplies, hastening to the campers' relief.

Conditions are different when the camper is far from town; or perhaps miles from a dwelling or perhaps even a public road and the camper is compelled to pack his camp outfit, grub stake and all over miles of rough trail, or it may be no trail at all; then the camper must curtail his desires to their utmost limit.

If the camper is on strange ground, and the camp is to be permanent or for some weeks, it is best for the camper not to be in too big a hurry to select the camping ground, and take up with any sort of a place. It is even better to make a temporary camp and look the locality over and select a place where good water can be had, and wood for fuel is plentiful and near camp. If possible, select a spot in a thicket of evergreen timber of a second growth and out of the way of any large trees that might blow onto the camp.

If the ground is sloping, place your camp parallel with the slope, whether tent or log cabin, as the surface water can more readily be drained off, and not allowed to soak into the ground and cause dampness inside of the tent. A ditch should be dug around the tent to drain all surface water, and eaves so the water will not soak inside. If a log cabin, the dirt from the drain can be thrown up against the logs of the cabin.

If the camper expects to camp through cold and snowy weather, it will pay him to place a ridge pole in crotches placed firmly in the ground. The pole should be a foot above the ridge of the tent, then place poles from the ground, the ends resting on this ridge pole as rafters to a building, then nail a few poles to these rafters sufficient to keep boughs from dropping down onto the tent. The boughs should be of an evergreen variety. This outer covering should be well thatched or covered with these boughs. This extra covering adds greatly to the warmth and comfort of the camp, as it protects from the wind blowing directly on the tent, also keeps the snow from falling onto the tent.

It is also a great convenience if this ridge pole is allowed to extend out three or four feet, and a strip of canvas run over the pole and down to side poles, so as to form a sort of an awning so one can step outside to wash when it is raining without getting wet. It also makes a convenient place to pile a small amount of wood, and will be found useful in many ways such as hanging furs, clothing, etc., out to air.

Do not make your bed on the ground. Build a box bedstead by driving four posts into the ground, then nail pieces across, up about twelve inches from the ground. Lay small poles on these cross pieces, then nail one or two small poles entirely around on the posts above the bottom pieces forming a sort of crib. This crib may be filled first with boughs, then on top of the boughs put a quantity of leaves or grass, when the mattress is lacking. There will also be store room under the bed, which would be wasted if the bed is made on the ground.

Brother camper, when you are going well back into the tall timber where you are obliged to pack your outfit over a rough trail or perhaps no trail at all, do not waste any energy packing canned "air" in the shape of canned fruits. Take your grub in a crude state in the way of flour, beans, lard, bacon or pork, and if fruit is taken, take it in a dried form. Take the necessary supply of tea, coffee, sugar, salt and pepper, also that unavoidable baking powder.

WOODCOCK FISHING ON PINE CREEK.

As to preparing an emergency camp for a night, if the weather is cold, and there is snow on the ground, the camper should pick a place where he will be as much sheltered from the cold winds as circumstances will allow and where he can get wood as conveniently as possible.

Select a log (if one can be had) that lays close to the ground. Now, scrape away the snow about six or eight feet back from this log, and where you will have your bed, build a fire, on this space the first thing you do. Then build a cover over this space or fire, by first setting two crotched stakes about four feet apart and five or six feet high, back three feet from the log. Cut a pole, and place it in these crotches and then from this pole lay poles long enough to come back so as to give room for your bed, covering the space where the fire is built; one end of the poles resting on the ground. With evergreen boughs, cover this entire framework, top and two sides--toward the log open.

Now scrape the fire down against the log and proceed to build your fire for the night. Cover the space where the fire was with fine boughs; this is your bed. Take off your coat, and spread it over your shoulders, rather than wear it on you as usual.

When the camper has plenty of time, and a good axe, in building an open campfire the thing to do is to cut two logs six or eight inches in diameter and three feet long and place them at right angles with the back log, and three or four feet apart; then lay the wood across these logs. This will give a draft underneath the wood and cause the fire to burn much better than where the wood lays close to the ground.

CHAPTER XX.
Deer Hunt Turned Into a Bear Hunt.

A friend by the name of Dingman invited me to come to his camp on More's Run, a tributary of the Sinnamahoning. This was something like forty years ago, when deer were plentiful and several men in this section made it a business to hunt for the money that there was in it, and Nathan Dingman was one of those men. It was about eight miles from my place to Mr. Dingman's camp.

One morning after we had a fall of snow, I packed my knapsack with as much grub stake as I was able to carry, with my gun and blanket, and started over the hill to Mr. Dingman's camp. After I had crossed the divide, I did not go far before I began to see deer tracks. There was no road or trail down the run, and the run was pretty well filled with timber. I had about all that I could handle without deer tracks, but when I was within about a mile of Mr. Dingman's camp, I came onto the trail of several deer that had only been gone a few minutes. I could not stand it longer, so I hung my pack and blanket up in a tree and took my track back up the stream until I was quite sure that I was well out of range of the deer, and then climbed the ridge until I was near the top of the hill and on advantageous ground.

The direction of the trail of the deer where it crossed the stream led me to think that the deer were going south, or down the ridge but on the contrary they had turned to the right and up the ridge. I had not gone far along the ridge before I began a sharp lookout. I suddenly found the deer lying in a thicket of low laurel. They broke from cover at a breakneck speed. I fired both barrels at them with the best aim that I was able to get, and had the satisfaction of seeing one of the deer, a good sized doe, stumble and partly fall, then hobble on in the direction that the other had gone.

It was nearly sundown and I only followed the trail a short distance when I could plainly see that the deer had a foreleg broken, and she soon left the trail of the others, and went down the hill all alone. Knowing that the wounded deer would soon lay down if not disturbed. I left the trail, went back, got my pack, blanket and went on down the creek to Mr. Dingman's camp. I found Mr. Dingman about to sit down to a supper of roast potatoes, venison and other good things to be found in abundance in the woods in those days.

The next morning we were out at daybreak after the wounded doe. Mr. Dingman said that when the doe was started up that she would come to water, and that she would stop on the creek below where I had left the trail, which led down the hill until in sight of the creek, when it turned to the right, then went back up the hill only a few yards to the right of her trail where she had gone down.

When I saw what the doe had done, I thought to myself, old lady, you are well onto the game, and we will have lots of sport before we get you. I was well aware that she had seen me when I passed by on her trail where she had gone down the hill, and thinking that she would go to the creek below where Mr. Dingman was and told him the game the doe was playing. He said that she would come to water at the point just below the camp, and that he would go down there and watch, while I should follow the track through. I told Mr. Dingman that I was afraid that we were too late, and that the doe had already gone out, that she had made her bed so that she could watch her trail where she went down the hill, and had slipped out after I had gone down the hill on her trail.

Mr. Dingman thought that he could get the runway before she would get through, even if she had gone out when I came through on her trail down the hill. In hopes that the deer had not taken the trail and lit out when I came through the hill, I worked my way cautiously back up the hill, only occasionally going in sight of the trail so as to keep her course, but as I feared, when I was about halfway up the hill, I found her bed, but the doe was gone. I took the trail and followed it up the hill until she struck the trail of the deer that she was with when I first started them, and instead of going down the ridge, she took the back trail of the other deer. I followed it back until near where I had wounded her, when she again broke down the hill and crossed the creek near where I first found their trail, and had gone back onto the same ridge that she had come from.

Now the only thing for me to do was to leave the trail and go after Mr. Dingman again. When I found him and we got back to camp, it was about noon, so we got a warm dinner before continuing the chase. When we got up to where I had left the trail, we held council and made our plans for the next move, and decided that as the old lady was continually doing the unexpected, we would follow her track, one going on each side of the trail a few yards from it.

We had only gone a short distance up the hill when we found the old lady's bed, where she had laid down, so that she could watch back on her trail, where she had come down on the opposite hillside. We did not go far when the trail turned to the left and went up the side of the ridge toward the head of the creek. We continued along the trail one on either side and soon we came to where a large hemlock tree had fallen parallel with the side of the hill. Mr. Dingman was on the upper side and above the fallen tree, while the deer tracks led away below the tree. All of a sudden I heard the report of Mr. Dingman's rifle, so I stood still for a minute, and hearing nothing more I went to see the cause of the shooting. The doe had gone beyond the fallen tree, then turned back and went about midway of the tree, on the upper side and lay down. Mr. Dingman caught a glimpse of the old lady as she went out, but did not catch her.

We did not follow the doe far from where she lay behind the fallen tree, for we crossed the trail of a bear going west, and partly in the direction of that of the wounded deer, which continued to work her cards on us all afternoon without our getting sight of her. At dusk we trailed her into a small thicket at the edge of the farm owned by a man by the name of Foster, at the extreme head of the run.

As it was too late in the day to do any more with the old doe, we concluded to go to Mr. Foster's and stay over night, and take the trail early in the morning. It was snowing a little and we thought that the thicket would be an easy place to find our game, should it snow enough to cover the tracks. In the morning when we got up, we found six or eight inches of snow on the ground, that had fallen during the night. We had an early breakfast, and started out to again play the game with the broken legged doe.

Before we got to the edge of the woods, we struck the trail of some animal, that had gone across the field in the early part of the night before it had snowed much. We were not positive what sort of an animal it was, whether man or beast. The trail was leading straight across the field without a curve in it, and was making straight to a laurel patch that was one and a half miles away on the Taggart farm, less than a mile below Coudersport.

Mr. Dingman said that it was a bear. I admitted that it was a bear all right, but replied that I would say it was making for the Adirondack Mountains in New York, rather than the laurel patch on the Taggert farm. We did not have far to go to make sure, and a good part of the distance was across farms, so we concluded to hunt bear a while, and give the old doe a rest for a short time. As Mr. Dingman said, the bear made straight for the laurel patch.

There was not more than 15 or 20 acres in the patch, so we thought that we would circle it and make sure that the bear was still in the laurel. We found that the bear was there all right, so Mr. Dingman selected a place where he thought the bear would come out when he was routed from his nest, while I was to follow the trail and drive out the bear. I followed until near the center of the patch, when I came onto a small open place forty or fifty feet square. This open space was covered with a heavy growth of wild grass which partly held the snow from getting close to the ground, and I could see the trail of the bear through this grass and loose snow very plain until nearly the opposite side of the open space, and there I could see a bunch of snow. I was sure that it was the bear that made the bunch.

I thought the matter over for a minute, then concluded to back out and go after Mr. Dingman, and see what he thought would be best in order to make a sure thing of Bruin's capture. Mr. Dingman thought the best thing to do was to go up town and get plenty of help so as to thoroughly surround the laurel, and make sure of Bruin. I objected, as I thought it best to try our own luck, and if we failed we could still get plenty of help. We followed my track back to where I had turned, and concluded to both fire at the bunch at the same time, hit or miss as luck would have it. When we fired at the bunch there was a shaking of snow, and bruin rolled out but was unable to rise to his feet. On examination we found that one ball had entered his shoulder. It was a short job to get bruin out to the road, and take him up to town where we sold him to Mr. Stebbins, a merchant, and then we made tracks back to see if we could find the broken legged doe. We found by circling the thicket that she was there, and we had the good luck to get her. We drove her out, and thus ended one of the liveliest day's sport that we ever had.

CHAPTER XXI.
Dog on the Trap Line.

Now, we will say first that there is as much or more difference in the man who handles the dog as there is in the different breeds of dogs. I have heard men say that they wanted no dog on the trap line with them, and that they didn't believe that any one who did want a dog on the trap line knew but very little about trapping at best.

Now those are the views and ideas of some trappers, while my experience has led me to see altogether different. One who is so constituted that they must give a dog the growl or perhaps a kick every time they come in reach, will undoubtedly find a dog of but little use on the trap line. I have known some dogs to refuse to eat, and would lay out where they could watch the direction in which their master had gone and piteously howl for hours. I have seen other dogs that would take for the barn or any other place to get out of the way of the first sight or sound of their master. This man's dog is usually more attached to a stranger than to his master. The man who cannot treat his dog as a friend and companion will have good cause to say that a dog is a nuisance on the trap line.

I have seen men training dogs for bird hunting, who would beat the dog most cruelly and claim that a dog could not be trained to work a bird successfully under any other treatment. Though I have seen others train the same breed of dogs to work a bird to perfection and their most harsh treatment that they would use would be a tap or two with a little switch. I will say that one who cannot understand the wag of a dog's tail, the wistful gaze of the eyes, the quick lifting of the ears, the cautious raising of a foot, and above all, treat his dog as a friend, need not expect his dog to be but little else than a nuisance on the trap line.

Several years ago I had a partner who had a dog--part stag hound and the other part just dog, I think. One day he, my partner, asked if I would object to his bringing the dog to camp, saying that his wife was going on a visit and he had no place to leave the dog. I told him that if he had a good dog I would be glad to have the dog in camp. In a day or two pard went home and brought in the dog. Well, when he came, the dog was following along behind his master with tail and ears drooping, and looking as though he had never heard a kind word in his life. I asked if the dog was any good and he replied that he did not know how good he was. I asked the name of the dog. He said, "Oh, I call him Pont." I spoke to the dog, calling him by name. The dog looked at me wistfully, wagging his tail. The look that dog gave me said as plain as words that that was the first kind word he had ever heard.

We went inside and the dog started to follow, when his master in a harsh voice said "get out of here." I said, "Where do you expect the dog to go?" I then took an old coat that was in the camp, placed it in a corner and called gently to Pont, patted the coat and told Pont to lay down on the coat which the dog did. I patted the dog, saying, "that is a good place for Pont," and I can see that wistful gaze that dog gave me now. After we had our supper I asked my partner if he wasn't going to fix Pont some supper. "Oh, after awhile I will see if I can find something for him." I took a biscuit from the table, spread some butter on it, called the dog to me, broke the biscuit in pieces and gave it to the dog from my hand, then I found an old basin that chanced to be about the camp and fixed the dog a good supper.

After the dog had finished his supper I went to the coat in the corner, spoke gently to Pont, patted the coat and told Pont to lay down on the coat. That was the end of that, Pont knew his place and took it without further trouble.

The next morning when we were about ready to start out on the trap line I asked pard what he intended to do with Pont. He said that he would tie him to a tree that stood against the shanty close to the door. We were going to take different lines of traps. I said, "What is the harm of Pont going with me?" "All right, if you want him but I don't want any dog with me." I said, "Am (that was pard's given name, for short), I do not believe that dog wants to go with you any more than you want him." Am's reply was that he guessed he would go all right if he wanted him. I said, "Am, just for shucks, say nothing to the dog and see which one he will follow." So we stepped outside the shack and the dog stood close to me.

I said, "Go on Am, and we will see who the dog will follow." He started off and the dog only looked at him. Am stopped and told the dog to come on. The dog got around behind me. A said, "If I wanted you to come you would come or I would break your neck." I said, "No, Am, you won't break Pont's neck when I am around, it would not look nice."

I started on my way, Pont following after I had gone a little ways. I spoke to Pont, patted him on the head and told him what a good dog he was. He jumped about and showed more ways than one how pleased he was. He showed plainly the disgust he had for his master.

It so happened that the first trap that I came to was a trap set in a spring run, and it had a coon in it. I allowed Pont to help kill the coon, and after the coon was dead I patted Pont and told him what great things we had done in capturing the coon, and Pont showed what pride he took in the hunt, so much so that he did not like to have Am go near the pelt. I saw from the very first day out that all Pont needed was kind treatment and proper training to make a good help on the trap line.

I was careful to let him know what I was doing when setting a trap, and when he would go to smell at the bait after a trap had been set, I would speak to him in a firm voice and let him know that I did not approve of what he was doing. When making blind sets, I took the same pains to show and give him to understand what I was doing. I would sometimes, after giving him fair warning, let him put his foot into a trap. I would scold him in a moderate manner and release him. Then all the time when I was resetting the trap I would talk trap to him, and by action and word, teach him the nature of the trap. Mr. Trapper, please do not persuade yourself to believe that the intelligent dog cannot understand if you go about it right.

In two weeks Pont had advanced so far in his training that I no longer had to pay any attention to him on account of the traps and the third day that Pont was with me he found a coon that had escaped with a trap nearly two weeks before. My route called me up a little draw from the main stream, and I had not gone far up this when Pont took the trail of some animal and began working it up the side of a hill. I stood and watched him until the trail took him to an old log, when Pont began to snuff at a hole in the log, and he soon raised his head and gave a long howl, as much as to say "he is here and I want help." After running a stick in the hole I soon discovered that the log was hollow. I took my belt axe and pounded along on the log until I thought I was at the right point and then chopped a hole in the log. As good luck would have it, I made the opening right on the coon, and almost the first thing I saw on looking into the log was the trap. Pont soon had the coon out, and when I saw that it was the coon that had escaped with our trap, I gave Pont praise for what he had done, petting him and telling him of his good deed, and he seemed to understand it all.

Not long after this Am came into camp at night and reported that a fox had broken the chain on a certain trap and gone off with the trap, saying that he would take Pont in the morning and see if he could find the fox. In the morning when we were ready to go Am tried to have Pont follow him but it was no go, Pont would not go with him. Then Am put a rope onto him and tried to lead him but Pont would sulk and would not be led. Then Am lost his temper and wanted to break Pont's neck again. I said that I did not like to have Pont abused and that I would go along with him. When we came to the place where the fox had escaped with the trap Am at once began to slap his hands and hiss Pont on. Pont only crouched behind me for protection. I persuaded Am to go on down the run and look at the traps down that way while Pont and I would look after the escaped fox.

As soon as Am was gone I began to look about where the fox had been caught and search for his trail, and soon Pont began to wag his tail. I began to work Pont's way and said, "has he gone that way?" Pont gave me to understand that the fox had gone that way and that he knew what was wanted. The trail soon left the main hollow and took up a little draw. A little way up this we found where the fox had been fast in some bushes but had freed himself and he had left and gone up the hillside. Pont soon began to get uneasy, and when I said, "hunt him out," away he went, and in a few minutes I heard Pont give a long howl and I knew that he had holed his game. When I came up to Pont he was working at a hole in some shell rocks. I pulled away some loose rocks and could see the fox, and we soon had him out and Pont seemed more pleased over the hunt than I was. There was scarcely a week that Pont did not help us out on the trap line.

Not infrequently did Pont show me a coon den. I had some difficulty in teaching Pont to let the porcupines alone, but after a time he learned that they were not the kind of game that we wanted, and he paid no more attention to them.

I have had many different dogs on the trap line with me. I can say that to any one who can understand "dog's language," has a liking for a dog and has a reasonable amount of patience and is willing to use it, will find a well trained dog of much benefit on the trap line, and often a more genial companion than some partners. But if one is so constituted that he must give his dog a growl or a kick every time he comes in reach, and perhaps only give his dog half enough to eat and cannot treat a dog as his friend, then I say, leave the dog off the trap line.

WOODCOCK AND HIS OLD TRAPPING DOG PRINCE.

CHAPTER XXII.
Two Cases of Buck Fever.

I have heard many hunters say that they had never had a case of buck fever, and that they could shoot at a deer with as little emotion under all circumstances as they could at a target. Now this is not the case with me, for the conditions under which I am working makes all the difference imaginable with my nervous system. I never saw but one place that I did not get the buck fever when deer hunting and that was in Trinity and Humboldt counties, California. There I saw deer so thick and tame that it was no more exciting than it would be to go into a drove of sheep in a pasture and shoot sheep. If by chance you failed to hit the deer the first shot it was only a matter of a few minutes when you would have another opportunity to kill your deer. So there was no cause to get the fever, but such has not been the case in Eastern States, for many years at least.

About 1880, a man by the name of Corwin and I were camping on the Jersey Shore turnpike in Pennsylvania. We had just gone into camp and as I usually make it a point to first get plenty of wood cut for the camp at night, so that when I come home in the evening I will not have to go out and cut wood, I had been cutting wood and fixing up all day until four o'clock in the afternoon, when I suggested to Mr. Corwin that we go out and see if we could find some signs and locate the deer so that we would know where to look for them early the next morning. We followed down a ridge for some distance without seeing any signs of deer but about the time that it was getting dark so that we could not see very good and we were about to go to camp, we came onto a trail of a number of deer. As it was so dark we left the trail and went to camp being careful not to start or alarm the deer. The next morning when we got up we found that a snow had fallen of some 8 or 10 inches and knowing that this snow would cover the trail of the deer so deep that there would be no following it until we could start them out of their beds, we concluded that one of us should go down the ridge opposite or west of the ridge where we had found the trail of the deer. It was decided that I should take the ridge opposite where the deer were thought to be, and Mr. Corwin was to warn me by firing two shots in rapid succession if he started the deer without getting a shot at them.

I was familiar with the woods and knew about where the deer would run when started up from any particular point. I had gone down the ridge until I thought that I was below the point where the deer would have crossed had they done so during the night, or if Mr. Corwin should start them. I had neither heard anything from Mr. Corwin nor seen anything of the deer trail. I had given up hope of Mr. Corwin starting the deer so they would be likely to come my way.

I had struck the trail of a single deer that was going down a short sawtooth point or a short spur of the main ridge. The track had been made during the night when it was still snowing and in some places it was hard to follow the trail owing to so much snow falling. The track led down this spur in the direction of low hemlocks. I was working my way very carefully thinking that the deer had gone down into those low hemlocks to get shelter from the storm and were lying down in the thicket. The thicket was just over a little cone or ridge so that I could not see the surface of the ground and I was dead sure that I would catch my game lying in his bed.

In a moment a dozen deer came into sight as suddenly as though they had come up out of the ground and I was suddenly taken with one of the worst fevers that any man ever had. I at once began firing into the bunch. The deer seemingly did not notice the report of the gun but kept steadily on their trail. I knew the condition I was in and that I was shooting wide of the mark. I then singled out one of the largest deer, a good sized buck, and tried to pick out a spot on the back of his shoulders as though I was shooting at a target. I could not keep the gun within range of the deer by ten feet, so when I thought the gun had jumped into line, I pulled the trigger. The deer made no alteration in its course or speed but kept steadily bounding along. The deer were not more than forty yards from me. I dropped on one knee and leaned the gun across my knee, grabbed a handful of snow and jammed it into my face, then placed the gun to my face and began firing at the deer again with no better results.

When the bunch of deer were nearly a hundred yards away and they had all passed over the brow of the hill, except one large doe that was a little behind the rest, the fever left me as suddenly as it came on. I pulled the gun onto her and fired. She staggered, gave a lunge down the hill and fell dead. I could have told within an inch of where the ball struck her before I went to the deer. I could not have told within fifty feet of where my other shots went.

I followed my drove of deer a short distance to make sure that I had not wounded any of them and then I dragged the doe down into the hollow to dress and hang up. Pretty soon Mr. Corwin came to me and seeing only the one deer asked me if that was the only one I had killed with all that shooting. Mr. Corwin said that he had counted nine shots that I had fired. When I told him the story he had a hearty laugh of half an hour and said that I was lucky that I did not die in a fit.

Now boys, you who have never had the buck fever can laugh at me all you like, but those who are over fond of the chase and get the buck fever will sympathize with me. Had I been expecting and looking for this drove of deer at the time instead of only one deer I should not have been attacked with this case of buck fever.

Now, I will tell you of another case of buck fever from a cause entirely different from that just related. I was following the trail and there was just enough snow on the ground to make the best of still hunting. The wind was blowing just strong enough to make a noise in the tree tops overhead to drown any noise that the hunter might make by stepping on a dry limb, and every once in a while there would come a snow squall that would be so dense that you could see scarcely fifty feet.

I had trailed the doe along the side of the hill for some distance. She was feeding alone and I was working along very carefully, keeping along the ridge several yards above the trail, to always be on advantage ground. I had not seen the trail of any other deer during the morning although it was in the height of the mating season, or as us common folks call it, the running season. I was trailing the doe along through a small basin where the timber was nearly all hardwood, beech and maple, and the woods were very open. I was quite positive that the doe was not far in advance for she had just been feeding on some moss from a limb that had blown down from a tree and the tracks were very fresh. About this time one of those snow squalls had come up. I was standing by a large maple tree waiting for the squall to pass by so that I could look the ground over well before I went any farther.

After the squall had passed I looked the ground over closely but could see nothing of my deer. Forty or fifty yards farther along the side of the hill and below me there was a very large maple tree which had turned up by the roots. This tree hid from view a piece of ground close to the log. I could see that the trail led directly up to the tree. I could see a slight break in the snow on top of the log that I took to be made by the leg of the deer in jumping the log. I could see nothing of the trail beyond the tree so I worked very cautiously along until I could see past the root of the tree and as I suspected, there stood my game with head down, apparently asleep and standing broadside to me. I drew the gun onto a point just back of her shoulders and let go and the deer dropped almost in her tracks.

I cut the deer's throat and began to skin out the foreparts. I had only partly gotten my work done when another one of those snow squalls came along. I was bending over the deer, busy at work when I heard a slight noise, and straightened up to see what had caused it. I looked none too soon to save myself from a terrible thrust from the horns of a large buck deer, for as I straightened up the deer shot past me like a shot from a gun, barely missing me and landed some six or eight feet beyond me. I had stood my gun against the log 8 or 10 feet from me. I sprang for my gun but

I was trembling so that I could do nothing and I could scarcely stand on my feet. The buck stood for a moment looking back over his shoulders. Every hair on his back stood up like the hair on the back of an angry dog and I well remember the color of his eyes which were as green as grass.

The deer stood and gazed at me for a moment then slowly walked off. The deer had gone some distance before I could control myself sufficiently to shoot. The buck had followed the trail of the doe up to the fallen tree and had caught me skinning her and it angered him. Instead of running off he was determined to attack me and the only thing that saved me from being severely hurt was my straightening up just at the right time to miss the thrust of the buck and the deer's missing me was what caused him to leave me.

This was the worst case of buck fever that I have ever had and I do not care to ever experience a case of that kind again.

CHAPTER XXIII.
Partner a Necessity.

As I promised to give some reasons why a partner is necessary, and as I have trapped many seasons both with and without a partner, I should know something about the subject. A writer, some time ago, in Hunter-Trader-Trapper said that it took some trappers fifty years to learn what others learned in a week. Now, I fully agree with this writer, for it only took me about three seconds to learn that a partner was necessary, and it came about in this way.

I had several bear traps set near what is known as the Hogsback on the old Jersey Turnpike Road in Pennsylvania. The traps were strung along the ridge that divides the waters of the East Fork and the West Fork, which are tributaries of the west branch of the Susquehanna River and were setting from one and a half miles to four miles of the wagon road, and about nine miles from any house.

The time in question was the last days of October or the first of November, and the day a very warm one for that time of the year. I had been walking very fast, in fact where the ground was favorable, I would take a dog trot. I wished to make the rounds of the traps and get out of the woods that day. When I came to where the second trap had been set, I found it gone, clog and all. The place where the trap was setting was in the head of a small ravine and near the edge of a windfall, just on the lower side of the bait pen, and but a few feet from it lay the partly decayed trunk of a large tree. I jumped on to this tree to get a good look down into the windfall to see if bruin was anywhere in sight. I had scarcely got on the log when I received a reception which I think was something equal to that the Russian Naval Fleet met with in the Corean Straits. I had jumped square into a colony of large black hornets, and they did punish me terribly in three minutes' time. My feet were swollen so that I was obliged to remove my shoes and my entire body was spotted as a leopard with great purple blotches and the internal fever which I had was most terrible. I thought that every breath that I drew was my last. I was two miles from the wagon road and nine or ten miles in the wilderness. No one knew where I was, nor where the traps were set.

I thought no more of the bear. I only thought of reaching the wagon road. I began one of the worst battles of my life, but after a struggle of three hours I got to the road more dead than alive. But here fortune favored me for soon after a man by the name of White (one of the county commissioners who had been in the southern part of the county on business) came along. He took me home where the doctor soon got me on my feet again.

I told my oldest brother where he would find the trap, so he took a man and team and went early the next morning and got the bear all right. It was four or five days before I felt able again to go into the woods and look at the traps, but when I did, I found a small bear, (a cub) dead and the skin nearly worthless. This was 45 years ago, but I am still working at the same old trade, in a small way.

At another time and previous to the time mentioned, I, with a partner, was trapping on the headwaters of Pine Creek. We had been in camp about a week, when one day we had been setting a line of traps about three miles from camp. It was in November and the weather was very disagreeable, yet we were hustling for we knew that the snow would soon be on us, and then we wished to put in all the time we could hunting deer.

On the day in question Orlando (that was my partner's name) long before noon was complaining of a bad headache, and said that it seemed as though every bone in his body ached. I tried to persuade him to go to camp but he insisted on setting more traps. About three o'clock in the afternoon he was obliged to give up, and said he would sit down where he was and wait until I could go further up the stream and set a couple more traps. I said no, we will go to camp, so we started. We were about three miles from camp, but Orlando could only go a few steps when he would be obliged to rest. He soon became so weak that I could only get him along by partly carrying him. He was several years younger than I, but he was somewhat heavier, so he was rather more of a load than I could well manage.

I kept tugging away with him, and about 9 o'clock in the evening I got him to camp, where I fixed him as comfortable as I could, then I began a race of about eleven miles to Orlando's father's house. The distance was about one-half of the way through the woods and it took me until 12 o'clock to make it, but we soon had a team hitched to the wagon and were on the way back to the camp where we arrived about 3 o'clock in the morning. We could only get within about one and a fourth miles of the camp with a wagon, so we had to leave it there and go on with only the horses. When we got to the camp we found Orlando no better, so we got him on to one of the horses and by steadying him the best we could, managed to work our way back home. We arrived there about 8 o'clock in the morning and found a doctor already waiting.

To make a long story short, it is sufficient to say that Pard had a long run of typhoid fever, and if he had been in the woods alone he would have surely died. I could relate other incidents where a pard did come in very acceptable.

As it is a necessity to have a partner, it is also necessary to have a good one, for the successful trapper has no idler's job on his hands. You should always have a partner who is able to read and write and should have a pencil and paper in your pocket, for it often happens that you wish to leave a message at a certain place where Pard and you expect to meet on the trap line. Then each one takes a different line of traps, and circumstances has happened since you left camp in the morning that it changes the entire program. It also often happens that you get into camp at a different time than what you expected and wish to go out again and take up another line of traps, and you should try to keep one another informed as to about what section you are working in.

Always endeavor to carry out the plans as near as possible the way they were planned before leaving camp in the morning. Of all things, do not accept of a man who is lazy or void of manly principles as a partner, for sooner or later you will drop him. Then it will make no difference how much you have done for him or how much you have befriended him in times past, he will do you all the dirt he is capable of doing.

If you want to know all about a man, go camping with him. Probably you think you know him already, but if you have never camped on the trail with him, you do not. It may be that he is your near neighbor or he may have been a partner in business, but if you have not camped with him, you have yet to learn him. It is not a hard job to believe a man a good fellow when at home, but when you have camped with him on the trail, then you will know him. When your companion wishes to annoy any game, which you may find in your traps for the mere purpose of hearing the animal moan with pain; will shoot birds and animals just for the purpose of killing if you have a team with you, and your companion will ride up the steep hills where other men would walk; will neglect his beasts of burden in any way, this man you should never choose as your camping or trapping partner. But when you find one who will never wantonly torture a dumb animal and is kind to his beasts of burden, always giving it all the advantages and kind treatment possible, this man you needn't fear to accept as a trapping partner for in this man you will find "a friend indeed when in need."

CHAPTER XXIV.
A Few Words on Deadfalls.

Comrades, as I have been asked to give my idea on the deadfall as a practical trap in taking the fur bearing animals, will say that I do not consider it a useless contrivance as some of the boys of the trap line claim. On the contrary, I consider it to be a very successful trap in taking many of the fur bearers such as will readily take bait including the skunk, mink, coon, opossum, rabbit, muskrat, etc.

It is not to be supposed that the fox, coyote, wolf, etc., can be taken in the deadfall; neither is it supposed to be as convenient or as successful a trap as the steel trap. Yet, under favorable conditions I prefer it to the steel trap in trapping some animals, and it is certainly a little more humane in its operation as it usually kills its prey almost instantly, therefore it saves the animal much suffering.

Now there are many kinds of deadfalls, the most of which have been shown from time to time in Hunter-Trader-Trapper. Were I up on drawing, I would illustrate some of the deadfalls which I consider the most successful, but I am not, so enclose photo. I will mention some of the deadfalls which I have seen in use in different parts of the country, some of which were good, but the majority I have seen in general use I did not like mostly on account of the length of time that it took to construct them, and the manner in which it was necessary to place the bait.

I prefer a deadfall so constructed that several different kinds of bait can be used at the same time, therefore the trap is ready for more than one kind of an animal and also a trap that is readily constructed. In the South we see many deadfalls. The most common deadfalls used are those made by placing a bottom log about six or eight inches in diameter and five or six feet long. The drop was about the same size as the bottom log, only much longer and stakes were split from the pine logs and driven into the ground the entire length of the bottom log on both sides of the log. These stakes or boards were long enough to come above the drop log when the trap was set. The drop log was placed between the two rows of stakes and above the bottom log. The common figure 4 trigger was used and placed about midway of the bottom log and raising the drop log six or eight inches from the bottom log. This made a runway that enabled the animal to enter from either end of the run and the animal necessarily was on top of the bottom log and directly under the drop log. The bait was fastened to the spindle. This deadfall may work well on mink, skunk and opossum, but I hardly think it a good trap for other animals and it requires too much time to construct it.

GOOD SMALL ANIMAL DEADFALL.

Another deadfall that I saw in common use on the Pacific Coast as well as in other sections of the country was the ordinary string deadfall. It is hardly necessary to describe this trap for every boy who works a trap line knows how to make them. The trap is made by using a bottom log three or four feet long and a drop log of the same size, but much longer. If the trap is not heavy enough of its own weight, place logs on the drop log until it is sufficiently heavy to kill the animal. Four stakes are driven, two on either side of the log and close to the bottom log and about two feet apart and driven so that the top or drop log will work easily between the stakes. Two of the stakes, the ones driven on the side where the bait pen is, had a crotch or fork and a stick was placed in these crotches. A string was tied to the drop log and to a stick of the proper length so that when the drop log was raised up eight or ten inches from the bottom log and the string passed over the stick in the crotches, one end of the trigger stick would rest against the stick placed in the crotches. The other end would slightly catch onto another stick, laid directly under the one that rests in the crotches and resting against the forked stakes and about two inches from the bottom log. This stick is called the treadle, as the animal going into the bait pen to get the bait must step on this treadle, pushing it down, which will release the trigger spindle and allow the drop log to fall.

The bait pen is usually made by driving stakes in a circle from one of the trap stakes to the other stake on the same side of the bottom log. This style of a deadfall is alright as to handling bait, but I do not consider it a sure trap, as often the animal will set off the trap before it is far enough under the drop to make a sure catch. I prefer a trigger that will cause the animal to get at least one fore leg over the bottom piece before the trap is sprung.

In making this style of a deadfall it is not necessary to use a string and the forked stakes with the cross stick in the forks; all that is necessary is to have two upright standards, one locked on to the other by just a notch cut in the standard that the drop rest on and catch the other end of the standard resting on the bed place. This standard is made slightly wedge shape so as to rest firmly in the notch in the upper standard. The notch should be about two-thirds the distance from the lower end of the stick up and just long enough to come down and rest against the side of the crossbar or treadle, which, as before stated, should be about two inches above the bed piece.

The stone deadfall with the figure 4 trigger, I have found in common use in nearly all sections where large flat rocks were to be had to use in making the trap. This stone deadfall is alright in mink trapping and smaller animals but it is not favored much in coon trapping. There are many other styles of deadfalls which I will try to describe later.

As to animals taking bait, will say, I have never had much trouble in getting meat or carnivorous animals to take bait, but sometimes it is necessary to use a different bait than what they will take at other times. This, undoubtedly, is owing to what the animals have been accustomed to feeding on. If the animal is fed on a certain kind of food and will no longer take readily to it as a bait, then use something different. For instance, I found it difficult on the Pacific Coast in the vicinity of Vancouver to get mink to take flesh as a bait, while they readily took other baits. When the mink will not take bait readily, then of course the deadfall does not make a successful mink trap. While the deadfall cannot take the place of the steel trap, yet a well constructed deadfall under some conditions has advantages over the steel trap. Often a deadfall can be set in a thicket of evergreen trees or under a single pine, hemlock or other evergreen tree, or it may be protected by building a frame of poles above the trap and cover with boughs to partly protect the trap from the heavy snows. Now you have a trap that will work alright, where a steel trap would freeze down from sleet or other causes and would not spring; nor will Johnny Graball carry off a deadfall.

No, boys, do not shun the deadfall when trapping skunk in a section where material is convenient to build it with, and especially if you are near your trapping grounds so that you can go out at times and put up a trap or two so as to have a good line of deadfalls ready when the trapping season arrives.

CHAPTER XXV.
Advice from a Veteran.

In trapping, cultivate the habit of taking great care in making sets. Always leave the surface level. As you cannot tell what particular animal may come your way, prepare for the most cunning. Note the surroundings of your set and use such material for covering as may be found there so that all may appear natural. Never stake the traps down for a dry land set, but select for a drag an old limb or root; not one fresh cut if avoidable. Obliterate your tracks; John Sneakem will not then catch on so quick. Above all things, never molest another's traps.

The jump-trap as now made by the Oneida Community has thicker jaws than the old style and therefore it is not so liable to foot the animal. I find it a good trap to use.

For mink, a good set is close to a bank and near the edge of the water. The bait if any is used, should be fresh muskrat, rabbit or chicken. All are good. If you wish for scent, the musk from the animal you are trapping is preferable.

One famous trapper says, "any fool knows enough to catch a muskrat." I doubt whether this man himself, knows how to trap them successfully. Of course, everyone knows that muskrats should be trapped along streams or swails where you find their works. For bait use carrots, cabbage or sweet apples. I like sweet apples best, and so do the muskrats. Set the trap in about two inches of water, fasten the chain at full length to a sunken limb, drive a stake on either side of the chain near where it is fastened and you need not fear that the rat will "foot" himself. He will soon become entangled and drown.

Another good set for rats is by scooping a piece out of a sod and placing it on a stone or root just under the water. Set trap on sod, fasten the chain as before and scatter bits of apple on the sod.

* * *

Now, boys, as many of you are about to seek new trapping locations, and as I have had more or less experience in trapping from the Atlantic to the Pacific, and as I get many letters from brother trappers as to different trapping locations, I thought perhaps that it would not come amiss to give you a little of my experience in regard to this matter. I would advise that before you go to a new location in other states from those in which you are familiar with the game laws, that you first write to the State Game

Commissioner of the state that you intend to trap in, enclosing 10 or 15 cents in stamps, and ask for a copy of the game laws, or for the information that you desire. The address of the Game Commissioner is usually at the capital of the different states. Advice on game laws is generally so meager that it is often misleading, and one relying on newspaper information, often runs up against problems that he would not have undertaken had he known the exact truth of the matter. The game laws of the different states are changed so often that the only way to get reliable information is to go direct to headquarters. Now, some states have local laws, county laws, and some states have even township laws.

I will also speak of writing to trappers for information as to the quantity of the fur bearing animals and game in their locality as another way to get posted.

Now, while I hope that the average trapper is as truthful as mankind generally, I am aware that a trapper will sometimes exaggerate as to the amount of game in his locality. If the person whom you make the inquiry of, is not particularly interested in trapping, or knows but little about trapping and wild life, he is liable to think there is much more game in his county than there really is. And on the other hand, if the party makes a business of trapping, he is quite liable to think that game is less plentiful than it really is. It is a good plan to write to two or more parties in the same neighborhood, on this matter, if you can, and then draw your own conclusion as to the scarcity or plentifulness of the game in that section. But the better way is to go and prospect the country and acquaint yourself with the locality, for you remember the old adage, "If you would have your business done, go and attend to it yourself; if not, send some one."

* * *

I have read with interest the discussion of the many different makes of guns, the different calibers for large game hunting, etc., and as I am not well up on "gunology," I have listened and wondered why there was so much agitation on the gun question. I believe that nearly all of the modern guns that are manufactured today are good--at least sufficiently good shooters for all practical purposes. Shotguns can be bought at $3.00 or $4.00 that do good work. Perhaps there is not a man in the country who has carried a gun as many days as the writer, but what has done more target shooting than I have.

Back in the 70's when men hunted deer in this section for the money that was in it, I often did not take my rifle down to shoot from one season's hunting to the next, unless by chance something in the way of game came into fields near the house. I was always in love with my gun and if I did not like it I would get rid of it at the first opportunity. I am still of the opinion that a gun is similar to a man's wife, you must love them in order to get the best results.

I always wanted as good a gun as there was on the market. By this I do not mean the highest priced, nor the highest power gun, but the gun that would do the business. A man by the name of Orlando Reese and I were the first to buy Winchester rifles in this section, and I think in this county. The guns were the common round barrel .44 caliber and we paid $60.00 apiece for them. The same kind of a gun can now, I think, be bought for $12.00 or $14.00. Previous to the time I bought the Winchester, I had been using a Henry rifle for a time, but it was not a good gun for hunting purposes. A few years later the .45-75 Winchester came into use, so I sold my .44 and bought a .45-75. I did not like it so I sold it and bought a Colts, which was a good gun, but one day I was doing some fast work on a bunch of deer and in my haste I did not work the lever just as I should and it jammed. This made me rather angry, so I sold it and got another .44 Winchester, which I used for a long time, but I disposed of it very unexpectedly.

I was coming out from camp after a new stock of provisions. My partner, Amersley Ball, was with me. We had not gone far after getting in the wagon road when we met a man by the name of Lyman who was on his way to the Cross Fork of Kettle Creek, for the purpose of inspecting the timber lands and wanted a gun to carry with him. Before Mr. Lyman was hardly in speaking distance he yelled at me and asked what I would take for my gun. Thinking that he was only joking I said $40.00.

Mr. Lyman came up to me, took my gun from my shoulders, looked at it and asked me if it was alright. I replied that if it was not I would not be carrying it.

Mr. Lyman replied, "I guess that is right," and taking a check from his pocket dropped down on one knee, filled it out for forty dollars and handed it to me, so I was without a gun right in the midst of the hunting season.

My protest was of no use, as Mr. Lyman took the gun and went his way, laughing at me. I received a little more for the gun than the usual price at the time, but there was no dealer at our place who kept the Winchester in stock. The dealers were always obliging and would take your order and get you a gun for a small profit of about sixteen dollars. I had no time to wait for a gun to be ordered, so I began to look about to find some one who had a gun for sale. Mr. Wm. Thompson, the publisher of a local newspaper in our place had bought a new .38 caliber Winchester to use in his annual outing and said that he would have no further use for a gun until another season that if I would give him $35.00, I could have his gun. I gave Mr. Thompson the money and the next morning we went back to camp.

After we had arrived at camp, I crossed the divide from the Sinnemahoning side of the Pine Creek side to hunt. I had not gone far after reaching Pine Creek before I struck the trail of five or six deer. After following the trail a ways I concluded that the deer would pass around the point of the ridge and pass through a hardwood balsam on the other side of the ridge.

I climbed the hill and made for the balsam in hope to head the deer off. I had only reached the brow of the hill so that I could look into the basin when I saw the deer. I thought to myself, there is a good chance to try my new gun, for I had not yet shot it. I drew on a large doe that was in the lead of the bunch and cut loose. The doe made a leap into the air, made a jump or two down the hill and went down, while the rest of the deer made two or three jumps up the hill towards me and stopped and looked back down the hill in the direction of the doe that I had shot. I pulled onto the shoulders of a buck, the largest deer of the bunch, who gave his tail a switch or two, wheeled, made a few jumps down the hill and fell, while the rest of the bunch made a lively break for other parts. I continued to scatter lead as long as I could see them.

I ran down to the deer that I had killed, cut their throats, removed their entrails, climbed some saplings, bent them down, cut off the tops and hung the deer on them. Getting a pole with a crotch at the end to place under the sapling, I pulled the deer up the best that I could and started on the trail of the others. I did not follow the trail long when I saw one of them had a broken leg. The deer with the broken leg soon dropped out from the others and went down the hill, crossed the hollow and went into a thick hemlock timber and laurel.

As it was nearly night, I left the trail and went home to camp. The next morning, Mr. Ball went with me to help get the wounded deer. We did not follow the trail far until we saw the deer fixing to lie down. I backed up and went up the hill above where we thought the deer might be lying. While Mr. Ball waited for me to give the signal to come. Mr. Ball had not gone far after I had howled, letting him know that I was ready, when out of the laurel came the deer. Mr. Ball was close, so that we both got a shot, killing the deer almost before it was on its feet.

Now I was so infatuated with my new gun, that it was a case of love at first sight. This was in the late 70's. I have used several different makes of guns. I also had a .30-30 Savage, which I considered a good gun for big game, and in fact, I can say that the most of the guns that I have tried were all good. I however am still married to my little .38 Winchester. I can say that in all these, considerable more than thirty years, I have never run up against a subject but that this little Winchester was equal to the emergency.

Now I wish to ask, why it is that a hunter cares for a high power gun that will shoot into the next township and kill a man or a horse that the hunter was not aware of existing, when a gun of less power will do just as good execution in deer hunting? The ammunition for the gun of lower power costs much less and there is far less danger in killing a man or beast a mile away. We hear men talk of shooting deer 200 and even 300 yards. In the many years that I have hunted deer, I believe that I have killed two deer at a distance of from 50 to 75 yards, to one a distance of 100 or 150. I believe most deer hunters will agree that there are far more deer killed at a distance of 50 or 60 yards than over that distance. I think that if those hunters who kill deer at a distance of 100 or 200 yards will take the trouble to step off the distance of their long shots, instead of estimating them, they will find that 100 yards in timber is a long ways. Yes, boys, 20 rods through the timber is a long ways to shoot a deer. Why? Because the deer can not often be seen at a greater distance, where there would be any use of shooting at all, and the little .38 will do all of that and more too.

* * *

Perhaps the average beginner at trapping makes his greatest mistake in listening to those who have had more experience in handling the pen than the trap. For instance, someone advised readers to use a No. 2 or 3 Newhouse trap to catch marten and said that marten frequented marshy places. Now if they had asked the editor of Hunter-Trader-Trapper, he would have told you that the Pine Marten frequented the higher and dry grounds in dark, thick woods and that it was their nature to run on old down trees and to run into hollow stubs, trees, etc., and that these were the places to set your traps. Unless you were in a country where the snow fell very deep, then you should use the shelf set. He would have also told you that the No. 1 and 1 1/2 Newhouse trap was plenty strong enough for the marten, that many use No. 0.

SPRING SET FOR FOX.

The average trapper also makes a mistake in listening to some one's ideas about scents in trapping the animal, instead of going to the forest, the field and the stream and there learn its nature, its habits and ways, and its favorite food. He also makes a mistake by spending his time in looking after scents, rubber gloves to handle traps with and wooden pincers to handle bait, instead of spending his time in learning the right way and the right place to set his traps. For one little slip and the game is gone if the trap is not properly set. It is like hunting in the days of the percussion cap gun. I have tramped all day long over hills and through valleys to get a shot at a deer, and just at night get the coveted opportunity, taking every precaution to see that there was no bush or obstruction in line. I would take deliberate aim, holding my breath that my aim might be sure. I trick the trigger, flick went the hammer, up goes the deer's tail and away he bounds beckoning me to come on. Come on, and my day's tramp has been in vain all on account of a damp gun cap. Now in these days of fixed ammunition, such mishaps rarely occur.

It is so in setting the trap, one little misfit and the game is gone. In the Hunter-Trader-Trapper, I read, undoubtedly written by a trapper of many years experience, telling the true way of setting the trap in front of a V shaped pen. He said that the trap should always be set so that the animal had to pass over the jaws of the trap and not between them. Now mark my mistakes, for of late years I have been very particular to set the traps so that the animal passed between the jaws, not over them for I reasoned like this: I thought that the animal might step on one of the jaws and turn the trap up without springing it. In so doing be frightened away, or that the animal might have ball of foot resting on the jaw of the trap, while it set the trap off with its toes, or the ball of the foot might rest on the latch, while the trap was sprung with the toes on the pan. In either case, the animal's foot would be thrown entirely from the trap or so that it would only get slightly pinched, which would put a flea into the animal's ear that he would never forget.

In days long since past, I was not particular how I set the trap, just so I got it planted, but in those days I also made the mistake of running after scents. We make a mistake in thinking that the fox is more sly in some states than in others.

Not long ago, I received a letter from a friend in Maine, asking if I did not think that the fox was harder to trap in some states than others. Now the states that I have trapped in are rather limited, but I have trapped in Wisconsin, Michigan, and Pennsylvania, mostly in Pennsylvania. I have also trapped in one or two other states, and wherever I found the fox, I found him the same sly fox. In order to trap this animal successfully it was necessary to comply with the natural conditions.

We make mistakes in not handling our fur properly; in not removing all fat and flesh from the skin in not stretching the skin on the proper shaped stretchers. Stretchers for most fur that we case should not taper more than 1/2 to 3/4 of an inch from shoulder to hind legs.

We make mistakes in setting our traps too early, for one prime skin is worth more than three early caught ones. We make mistakes in not having one, and only one, responsible and honorable party in each large city to ship our furs to; by giving one party a large trade should give the trapper the full market price for his furs. It would also have a tendency to make the buyer honest and honorable, even though he was not built strictly that way in making. All trappers should know the address of the party agreed upon in each city. This would give the trapper a chance to ship to the party most convenient to the trapper.

The worst mistake of all mistakes is in one who uses poison to kill with. Let me tell of an instance that came under my observation the spring of 1900, I believe it was. I had an occasion to go into the southern part of this country, my road lay over the divide between the waters of the Alleghany and Susquehanna, about five miles of the road lay over a mountain that was thickly wooded and no settlers. While crossing this mountain I saw the carcasses of four foxes lying in the road. On making inquiries I learned that a man living in that neighborhood was making a practice each winter of driving over the roads in that section and putting out poisoned meat to kill the foxes. I chanced to meet this man not long ago. I said, "Charley, what luck did you have trapping last winter." His reply was, not much only got one or two foxes. Old Shaw has dogged them out of the country (referring to a man who hunted with dogs). I said, "Charley, don't you think that poison business had something to do with it. He replied, "Oh, h--l there will be foxes after I am dead." This man called himself a trapper, and is quite an extensive fur buyer. Thomas Pope says, "Man's inhumanity to man, makes countless thousands mourn." But, in this case, I think it is the dumb animal that mourns and not the man. The trapper who makes the greatest mistake of his life is the one who does not subscribe for the Hunter-Trader-Trapper.

* * *

In a former article I undertook to give the most practical way of killing a skunk, as I have found it, but owing to a mistake, it left the method of killing rather hard to be understood, so I will try again. I do this, owing to the many requests that I have from trappers to give a method for killing skunks, without the skunk scenting themselves as well as the trapper. Practically, there is no way of killing a skunk without causing the skunk to discharge his scent. Their scent is a skunk defense, and they will use it when in danger.

Now my way of doing the job is to go at it without hesitation. We have an old adage, "If you would grasp a nettle, grasp it as a man of mettle." Now my plan is to wear clothes on the trap line to be discarded as soon as the day's work on the trap line is finished. When I come to a trap that has a skunk in it, I approach the skunk, advancing a single step at a time, with a good strong stick about four feet long, with the stick drawn up in readiness to strike as soon as close enough. Now when I am close enough to make the blow sure I strike the skunk a hard blow across the back, and immediately after, I place my foot on the skunk's back, holding the animal tight to the ground. At the same time giving the skunk a sharp rap or two on the head with the stick to make sure that it is dead. Then pick up the skunk and remove it a little to one side of the place where it was killed. Rip the skunk across from one leg to the other close to roots of tail, skinning around the scent glands at the roots of tail, so that the glands can be easily cut out and thrown away or saved for bait, as the trapper wishes. Now proceed to skin the skunk. By following these directions, the trapper will not suffer any great inconvenience from the animal's scent.

Now if the trapper is a little timid, he can carry some kind of a gun of small caliber and shoot the skunk in the head. But if the skunk does not use his weapon of defense, then it is a different skunk than I have been accustomed to meet with. If the trapper uses a clog instead of a stake to fasten his trap with, and his traps are close to water, he can use a long pole or a hook and gently drag the skunk to the water and drown it. Then the water will carry the fluid or scent as discharged, away.

Now if the trapper is very timid and has plenty of time, I would advise that he provide himself with a light pole ten or twelve feet long, split at one end and take a quart tin can with sockets or brackets soldered onto the sides of the can, so that the can may be placed in between the split at the end of the pole. The two prongs placed into the sockets on the can so as to hold the can firm. Now fill the can part full of cotton and prepare yourself with a bottle of chloroform (not brandy). Now with this outfit the trapper will proceed to follow along his trap line, and when he finds a skunk in his trap he will cautiously approach the skunk after he, the trapper (not the skunk) has well saturated the cotton in the can from the chloroform from the bottle. Then gently work the can up to the skunk's nose and over its head, when the chloroform will soon do its deadly work. After the skunk is dead, the trapper should remove the scent glands as before described, lest the scent may be squeezed from the glands in skinning the skunk.

Another reader asks what kind of a gun he shall take with him to hunt deer, as he is contemplating going on a deer hunting trip next fall. Now I would say any kind of a rifle that suits you. But if you should ask me what kind of a gun I use, I would not hesitate to say that I prefer the 38-40 and black powder. This gun shoots plenty strong to do all the shooting as to distance or penetrations that the deer hunter will require, and there is not near so much danger of shooting a man or domestic animal a mile away that the hunter knows nothing of, as is the case with a high power gun. Besides, from an economical point, the ammunition for the 38-40 black powder gun costs only about one-half that of the smokeless or high power guns. However, if the hunter thinks that he must have a high power gun in order to be a successful deer hunter, he will find the 30-30 or similar calibers good for large game, and it is not heavy to handle.

CHAPTER XXVI.
The Screech of the Panther.

Some time ago, a writer to the H-T-T, whose name I have forgotten, gave his views in regard to this subject, and requested that the readers give their experiences and ideas on the matter. A year or so ago, I wrote to a sporting magazine (now defunct) giving my views on this horrible screech of the panther.

I have camped in the wilds of California, Oregon, Idaho and Washington. Sixty years ago, in my childhood days, it was an everyday occurrence to hear some one tell of having a panther follow them through a certain piece of woods, and tell of the horrible screams that the panther gave while following them. And still to this day, there is, occasionally a person who reports of hearing that terrible screech of the panther here in old Potter, notwithstanding that there has not been a panther killed in the county for upwards of fifty years, though twice within fifty years, I have been frightened nearly out of my boots by that terrible screech.

On one occasion I was watching a salt lick for deer; I was on a scaffold built up in a tree thirty or forty feet from the ground. The lick was in a dense hemlock forest. It was well along into the night--I was listening with all my energy, expecting to hear the tread of a deer, but, so far I had heard nothing but the rustle of the porcupine and the hop of the deer-mouse and the jump of the rabbit on the dry leaves. Still, I was listening intently for that tread of a deer which sounds different from that of any other animal, when, with the suddenness of a flash of lightning that terrible screech of the panther came within six feet of my head.

Was I frightened? I guess yes. And had not my gun been tied to a limb of the tree to keep it in place it would have gone tumbling down the tree to the ground.

Glancing up in the direction from whence that terrible scream came, I could plainly see the outline of a screech owl.

On another occasion I had started about midnight from home to go to my hunting camp. About five miles of the distance was along a road with heavy timber on each side. The night was warm for the time of the year, with a slight mist of rain. I was hustling along the best I could to reach camp by the time it was daylight. I had my rifle and a pack-sack with a grub stake to last for a week, on my back. When again, with great suddenness that terrible screech of the panther sounded in the trees over my head. The screech was so sudden and so sharp that I came near dropping right through to China. After recovering my breath and gazing into the timber for a moment, I again discovered one of those frightful owls.

Every close observer, who has put in a great deal of time in the woods in the night, away from a fire and noise, knows that an owl will alight within a few feet of them, and they will not be aware of the presence of the owl when it approaches them. This noiseless movement of the owl is said to be from the large amount of down that grows on the wings of the bird.

As I stated, I have camped in several states west of the Rockies, and have from childhood until late years almost continually been in the woods, and the only screech of the panther I ever heard came from the owl.

My father moved from Washington County, York State, into this county about a hundred years ago, when northern Pennsylvania was an unbroken wilderness, and the few settlers who lived in these parts were compelled to go sixty miles to Jersey Shore to mill. This trip was made down Pine Creek, and usually with an ox team, and those who made the trip were obliged to camp out every night while making the trip for there were no settlers living along the whole route. The road was merely a trail cut through the woods.

Father often made this trip down Pine Creek to Jersey Shore, camping out each night. I have often heard him say that he never head any kind of a noise that he thought came from a panther--and panthers were plentiful in this section in those days. Father laughed at the idea of the panther screaming, when he heard people telling of hearing them.

However, regardless of what my father and other early settlers of this section, who were not possessed of strong imaginary minds have told me, as well as my own experience, I have evidence that the panther does scream and scream terribly, too.

A neighbor of mine, by the name of Mr. Mike Green, a man about fifty years old, after reading the article which I mentioned at the beginning, came to me and said that I was away off in regard to the panther not screaming. He told of two occasions where he had had adventures with panthers and they screamed fearfully. One of Mr. Green's adventures happened in Clearfield County, this state, the other in West Virginia.

Mr. Green stated that he was driving a team, hauling supplies for a lumber camp, when on two occasions he was out on the road until late at night with his load of supplies some of which consisted of several quarters of fresh beef. He heard the panther scream out in the woods and narrowly escaped the panther by whipping the team and driving rapidly into camp, the panther following him, screaming at every jump.

A few nights later the panther again attacked Mr. Green near camp. He heard it scream and again made haste to reach the camp. When near camp the panther made several attempts to leap onto the wagon, but owing to Mr. Green's rapid driving the panther failed to reach the load.

Later, Mr. Green was lumbering in West Virginia. The teamster who was hauling camp supplies the same as Mr. Green had in Clearfield County, was killed by a panther. Mr. Green heard the panther scream and when the teamster did not come, he with others from the camp went in search of the man, and found him dead. The men in camp made up a purse to pay the burial expenses, Mr. Green contributing to the fund.

I have often been going along the road at dusk through the woods and had an owl follow along for some distance, flying from tree to tree, alighting on trees near me, and would often give one of those screeches, which no doubt has often been mistaken for the scream of a panther, when this trick of the owl occurred when too dark to be seen.

* * *

The screech of the panther I believe to be all imagination. Years ago it was an everyday occurrence to hear some one tell of a panther screaming in a certain locality and tell how it (the panther) had followed them and how they escaped by running their horses, and how the panther screamed in a tree right over their head, and how they could see the panther's eyes shine.

Now I know that one cannot see an animal's eyes shine unless the animal is in the dark and a light shines directly in their eyes.

It is not always these stories are told to misrepresent facts, but it is often the case of imagination or being mistaken. One of the large owls has another cry or call besides the well known hoo-hoo-hoo, which the deer still-hunter often imitates when he wishes to inform a companion just where he is without fear of alarming the deer. The writer has often seen, just at twilight, or nearly break of day, one of those large owls follow along some distance in the woods, flying from tree to tree, lighting on the lower branches of the trees, only a few feet above my head, apparently doing this from curiosity. Frequently the owl would give a screech which was similar to that given by a woman who has been suddenly frightened. Undoubtedly this screech of the owl has often been taken for that of the panther. Owing to the great abundance of down or fine feathers on the quills of the wings of the owl, the owl can light within six feet of a person's head, and if the owl was not seen, you would not know of its presence, for you could not hear the flight of the owl.

While I have not had as much experience in the haunts of the panther as some, yet I have been all through the Pacific Coast States and a good part of the mountains, and have never heard what I thought was the cry of a panther, or a mountain lion.

My father often told me that he had never heard anything that he called a screech of panther and did not think that a panther ever made any such screeching noise as is claimed, yet in my younger days it was a frequent occurrence to hear some one tell of hearing a panther and how a panther had followed them through a certain piece of woods. Even to this day we occasionally hear of some one being followed by a panther and how they had heard a panther screeching on a certain hill.

CHAPTER XXVII.
Handling Raw Furs and Other Notes.

Boys, as you are nearly all in from the trap line and the trail, (May, 1910), I am going to take the opportunity to give the younger trappers (and some of the older ones, too) a drubbing. I would like to see every trapper get all that his furs are worth and I would not like to see one-half the value of your furs go, simply because you neglected to skin and stretch your catch as it should be.

During the past winter I was in town one day and met a fur buyer and he asked me to go over and see his bunch of furs, saying, "I am going to ship the furs tomorrow." I went with the fur dealer and found that he had a lot of stuff, several hundred dollars worth of furs, consisting of fox, coon, skunk, mink, and muskrat, some wildcat. A good part of this bunch of furs had been caught at least a month before it should have been. Of this unprime fur I will have but little to say. I am sorry to know that any trapper will throw away his time and money by trapping furs before the fur is in reasonably prime condition.

This dealer had many coon and skunk that had from one-half to a pound of grease left on the skin. I asked the dealer if he was going to ship those pelts with all that grease on. His reply was, that he was going to ship the furs just as they were and added that he did not pay anything for that fat, and only half what the skins were worth if they had been handled right. I suggested that he would have to pay express charges on that grease. The dealer said that he could not help that, signifying that he had made that up in buying the furs. I called the dealer's attention to a very good black skunk skin, that had been badly skinned and stretched and asked what he paid for such a pelt. He said that he did not remember, but he knew that he did not pay $3 for a hide that looked like that. Now this skunk skin was spoiled so far as the looks went, if not in real value, and it at least gave the dealer a good excuse to put that pelt in the third or fourth grade. The trapper, in skinning this skunk, had ripped down on the inside of the forelegs and across the belly three or four inches up from the tail. The proper way being to begin at the heel, ripping straight down the leg and close to the under side of the tail. Then carefully cut around the roots of the tail and work the skin loose from the tail bone until the bone can be taken between the fingers on one hand and with the other hand draw the tail bone clear from the tail.

In this pelt the tail bone had been cut off close to the body and left in the tail. In stretching this skin the trapper had made a wedge-shaped board. The board was at least four inches wider at the broad end than it should have been and then sharpened off to a point. I think it best to make the stretching board in width and length in proportion to the animal, slightly tapering the board up to where the neck of the animal joined to the shoulders, then taper and round up the board to fit the neck and head of the animal. The tapering from the shoulders to the point of the nose of course would necessarily be longer on a board for a fox or mink than that of a muskrat or coon, which would need to be more rounding. There are some good printed patterns for stretching boards for sale.

I have noticed that some trappers have holes in the broad end of their stretching boards and hang up their furs while drying with the head of the animal hanging down. Now I think that is a wrong idea. It is not a natural way for the fur on the animal to lay, pitching towards the head of the animal, and especially if there is any grease, blood, or other matter that would dry, causing the fur to stick out like the quills on a fretful porcupine.

Now, boys, let us get into the habit of getting more money out of our catch of furs by removing the greater part of the fat from the skins; also by taking a little more time to skin and stretch the furs that we catch; also by doing less early and late trapping, when the fur is not in a fairly prime condition. I am pleased to see so many of the trappers in Pennsylvania advocating a closed season on the furbearers of this state, though I think that they seem to be in favor of a longer open season than will be to the trapper's advantage.

*   *   *

Comrades of the trap line, are you awake to the conditions under which we must work? The dog man has no use for the trapper and his traps. Now comrades, while I am a lover of the dog, and have used him on the trap line and trail, I have, nevertheless used the dog for a different purpose than it is ordinarily used by the average sportsman. I hope the trappers throughout the country will arouse themselves to the conditions and not allow the legislation of their respective states to pass laws to put the trapper in the hole, at the pleasure of the dog man, as has been done here in Pennsylvania. (This was written Spring of 1912.)

I believe that the dog man and the trapper, are each entitled to equal privileges--the dog has no better friend than the writer. Though we do not blame our brother trapper, who will not put up as good a scrap in defense of his traps and his sport and occupation, as does the dog man in defense of his dog, and his way of enjoying an outdoor life. But comrades, we are all men and sportsmen in our way, and let us be reasonable in this matter;

but brother trappers, let us not take a back seat because we may not be possessed with as large an amount of worldly goods as some of the dog men may be.

Express your views upon this matter of the trappers' rights through the columns of Hunter-Trader-Trapper. Also with our respective representatives that they may not pass game laws that the trapper is compelled to ignore, as is the case here in Pennsylvania. Here they ask for a bounty on noxious animals, yet, the law forbids the setting of a trap in a manner that would take anything more wary or greater than the weasel. Was this law enacted wholly for the benefit and pleasure of the dog man?

Now I wish to speak of another matter that I think is greatly to the interest of the trapper, and that is, early and late trapping.

No, no, I do not mean morning and evening--I refer to trapping early and late in the season. And while I do not approve of putting out traps too early in the season, it is far better that we begin trapping in October, than it is to continue trapping until into March, for such animals as mink, fox and skunk begin to fade, or become rubbed, while the mink that is caught in October, has nearly its full amount of fur. Still, the flesh side of the skin is a little dark, which gives the dealer a chance to quote the skins as unprime, notwithstanding the pelt has its full value as to fur purpose. And as to furs caught in March, the dealer has a chance to quote "springy."

And brother trappers of the States, do not put off your shipments of furs until late in March. It has been my experience where furs are shipped late in the spring, the returns are marked "springy," "rubbed," etc., notwithstanding the skins, or at least part of them, may have been caught in December or January.

Comrades, let us work for our own interest, for no one will do it for us. And, Comrades, you are certainly aware that the dog man is playing every card to put the trapper in the hole.

* * *

Comrades of the trap line and trail, I wish to ask your ideas as to whether it is advisable to stick to the taking of the fur and game late and early, all the year around. We know that we all like the sport, and the trapper is a little greedy, as well as people of other occupations. But, is it wise to take a mink, fox or other fur bearing animal so late or early in the season that the skin is not worth more than one-third of what the same skin would have brought in a prime condition?

On the 18th day of March, 1912, a neighbor, who had put in many a day on the trap line with the writer, a man who with his three younger brothers makes a business of trapping every season and makes good money, came to my house with a female fox skin that he had just caught. I glanced at the skin and remarked that the skin was of but little value. My friend replied in an angry tone, "No. It ain't!" And that is not the worst of it--she would have soon had five young foxes. I said, "You will keep it right up, won't you, Fred." "No, I am done now," he answered. But I said, "Fred, that is what you say every year."

The skin was large for a female fox, and had it been caught any time from November to the last of January, it would have brought five or six dollars; but the best that he could get for the skin was three dollars. This is only one case of many, which came under my observation, and especially in the case of taking skunks after they are so badly rubbed that they will not bring more than half the price of prime skins.

Now in the case mentioned above, of the female fox, the loss in the price of the skin was small compared to that of the young foxes whose skins would have been worth, next November, or December, in the neighborhood of twenty dollars. In this particular case, my friend would have got the most of those young foxes if not all of them, for the fox den was on his premises, and not far from his house.

Now, comrades, let us stop this catching of unprime furs--it is our bread and butter. Let us stop wasting it, for there are but few trappers, who have any more of this world's goods than he needs. Let every trapper do all that he can to put a stop to this waste of fur by catching the fur bearers, when their skins are not more than one-half their value--and many are taken that are practically worthless. We must do all that is in our power to stop a wasteful slaughter of the fur bearing animals, for they are already becoming far too scarce; both for the trappers' benefit, as well as those who wear the finished goods.

Comrades, instead of slaughtering the fur bearers during the season of unprime furs, let us look up our trapping grounds, for the coming season, and have all preparations made, and our plans well laid. Then when the season of prime furs arrives, let us take to the trap line and follow it diligently for two or three months, then drop the fox, skunk, mink, coon and opossum and put in more time on beavers, otters, and muskrats.

This applies to the middle, northern and southern states, while those in the far north, can, of course, continue to take the fox, mink, etc., longer, but it is not good policy for the northern trapper, even to keep up the good work so long as to "kill the goose that lays the golden egg."

* * *

I notice that some of the comrades are complaining that they do not get a square deal from some of the fur buyers. Shame! shame! brothers. Do you not know that the Fur Dealer is not even making a living profit out of your pelts? That is the reason why there are so many in the business. And do they not always urge the trapper to send in his furs early for fear there will be a drop in the price, and the poor trapper will lose on the price of his furs? Now, boys, can't you see that the average fur buyer is awfully good to the poor trapper? But comrades, are not we, the trappers, partly to blame for this unfair deal? Are we careful that our furs are at least fairly prime and carefully cured and handled? Are we always careful when making our estimate to give a fair grade ourselves?

This, comrades, we should always be careful to do, and then we should never ship our furs only to parties who are willing to hold them until they have quoted what price they can pay for the bunch. If the prices are not satisfactory, the fur dealer should have agreed with the shipper before the furs were shipped to him to pay one-half of all express charges, and either return the furs to the shipper or to any house in their city that the shipper may designate.

Now, comrades, make some such bargain with your dealer, and if you do not get a square deal do not be shy in giving the transaction with the dealer's name.

* * *

Comrades of the trap line, come down to camp and let us talk over this question of the fast disappearance of the furbearing animals. The fact of timber becoming scarce has made nearly every one timber-mad--no, that is not right, I mean money-mad--and they wish to secure this money through the fast increasing value of timber. In the late sixties, right here in sight of where I am sitting, I saw as nice white pine cut and put into log heaps, burned up for the purpose of clearing the land, as ever grew.

Now, boys, I liken the trapper and the dig-'em-out and the dog-hunter to our ancestors in the wasting of timber, only our ancestors at that time could not see the value of the timber that they were wasting. The trapper, the dig 'em-out and the dog-hunter are all money-mad, made so by the high prices of fur. But unlike our ancestors, the trapper, dig'em-out and dog-hunter should be able to see the folly in taking the furbearers when in an unprime condition, because we all know the difference in the value of a fox, a skunk, a mink, or the skin of any other fur-bearing animal taken in September or late in the spring when unprime, than the same skins would be worth if taken in November or any month during the winter.

I trapped in three different states in the South last season (1912) and I met with trappers and dog-hunters who admitted that they trapped and hunted in September. We saw one trapper who had four large mink also quite a bunch of other furs, consisting of coon, muskrats, civet and skunk; the trapper said that the mink were caught last September or the first of October. He wanted six dollars for the four mink. Just think of those four large mink being offered for six dollars and he could not get a buyer at that price. The rest of his early caught furs ranked with the same grade as the mink. Comrades, just think that over and see how foolish we are to begin trapping so early in the season. These same mink, had they been caught the last of November or in December, would have been worth, easily, six or seven dollars apiece. This same party had two mink that he had caught the first of November and he asked five dollars apiece for them and they were not near as large as those caught in September.

Now, brothers of the trap line, the most of us will admit that we are not overstocked with worldly goods and we are not to be blamed for getting a little money-mad; but when we get so money-mad that it makes us so blind that we not only destroy our pleasure but we throw away from twenty-five cents on a muskrat and four to six dollars on a fox or mink we should stop and think!

While out in camp on our fishing trips this summer, let us invite all of the boys of the neighborhood to come and let us talk this matter over with them and show them how lame we are to indulge in this early and late trapping and hunting of the furbearing animals. Let us induce the boys to become readers of the H-T-T, one of the greatest sporting magazines of the world, and through the columns of this magazine, put up their fight for the protection of the furbearer and the song birds. Unless the trapper puts up his own fight for the protection of the furbearers, they will soon be exterminated. The dog-man is now trying to place a tariff on the trappers' bread and butter in placing a bounty on the furbearer to induce the money-mad trapper to destroy the furbearer during the summer when their fur is worthless.

Also, let us have a little chat with the dig 'em-outs or den-destroyers. Boys, what is the difference how the skunk or coon is caught, whether by the steel trap or by dig'em-outs or by the dog; if the animal is caught is it gone, isn't it all the same? Well, it looks to the fellow up the tree as though there was quite a difference. Now comrades, if we dig out a skunk, that den, that habitation is gone, is it not, and there is nothing left to induce other skunks to frequent that location. Now, as to hunting the coon and possum with the dog, two-thirds of the time the coon or possum is treed in a den tree or rock and the tree is cut down and the rock or other den is destroyed and you will get no more coon or possum at that place. If this work of destroying the dens of the skunk and the coon is thoroughly practiced, the dens will soon be gone and with the disappearance of the dens the skunk and the coon also disappear. If the dig'em-out or dog hunter, when he found that he must destroy a den in order to get his game, would leave it or get the animals in some other way without destroying the den, then there could be no objection to the dig'em-outs or to dog-hunting.

Now, comrades, I will give some of my own experience in regard to this destroying of den trees. I trapped for a short time around a slough or pond in Alabama two years ago. The large timber in the vicinity of this pond was mostly oak and lumbermen were cutting this timber and taking it out. Coon were quite plentiful around this pond when I first began trapping there but I soon noticed that signs were fast disappearing and I could not think what the cause was. I went to another pond or rather a swamp about two miles from this pond where I again found coon quite plentiful.

Not long after I had moved my traps to this other slough a party of negroes came to my camp; they had five dogs. I inquired what luck they were having and they complained that since the timber had been cut around Swan Pond there were no den trees for coon or possum and they were all gone. When these colored people told me what the trouble was I could readily account for the fast disappearance of the coon signs about the pond. I went to the same pond again this past season and while I found a few signs I did not consider it worthwhile to put out a line of traps so I went on to the swamp and put out my traps. It made me two miles further travel in that direction but it paid me just the same.

Comrades, let us induce all the boys to come to camp where we can consult with them and let us get a move on us and locate our trapping grounds and make all preparations for the trapping season. This will enable us when the fur is prime to make more money in two months than we do in four months when we indulge in this September and unprime fur trapping. At the same time we will be able to lift our traps while there is still some of the furbearers left and we have not "killed the goose that lays the golden egg."

CHAPTER XXVIII.
The Passing of the Fur bearer.

Well, boys, I suppose you are well pleased with the bounty law in this state, (Pennsylvania) as it now is? While it is doubtful if I shall ever again be able to follow the trap line, I am nevertheless as much, and perhaps more, interested in the welfare of the trapper, than when I was able to follow a line of traps.

I am inclined to think that the present bounty law (1907) will not only be a damage to the trapper but also to the state. People who never thought of trapping before are now preparing to trap, and some are already at it, and their cry is, Bounty! Bounty! It reminds me of John Chinaman when gold was discovered at Cripple Creek, Colorado. All John could say in his rush for gold, was Cripple Creek, Cripple Creek! Fortunately the greater part of this class of trappers will catch but few of the shyer animals (and the best fur bearers).

It was the Game Clubs that asked for and received the Bounty Law. Now if the bird hunter will leave his trained bird dog at home, and walk up to the birds he shoots, he will get plenty of exercise, and the game birds will soon be more plentiful--but I suppose this would not be sportsmanlike.

I am well acquainted with a man who is a member of a Game Club; also a game warden. A neighbor of mine who is a good trapper was visiting me a few days ago and he told me of a little matter that took place between the game warden and sportsman in question, and himself. My neighbor said that he was at the place of business of the Game Warden ----, and he said to my neighbor, "There are three traps you can have for I have no use for them. My dog got in one of them, and I brought the things home with me. I should have thrown them in the river."

When my neighbor came to look at the traps he found his own private mark on the traps, so he said to the warden that they were his traps, for there was his own private mark. The warden replied that he couldn't help that, and that there were three more over at the house that he could get if he wanted to. When my neighbor went to get the other traps he found that they were not his traps, but he knew by the mark on them the traps belonged to his neighbor, so he told the warden about it.

Now the intention of the true sportsman is to kill two birds with one stone through the Bounty Law; destroy the fur bearer, and by so doing, do away with what I have heard many a true sportsman call a nuisance--the trapper and his traps. Apparently this state or its lawmakers, look upon the game business and the fur industry in a very different light from what many do.

Many states throughout the Union are enacting laws to protect the fur bearing animals of their respective states, and are only placing bounties on such animals as are of little use as fur bearers, and are destructive to stock. No doubt but that these states look upon the hundreds of thousands of dollars put into the pockets of their citizens through the trapper and his products, the same as they would upon equal amount of money brought into their respective commonwealths through any other industry. I believe it would have been well to have had a bounty of $2.00 on a wild cat, and 50 cents or $1.00 on a weasel, and the same on hawks.

I would like to have a little private talk with the trappers of Pennsylvania. I do not wish to go away from home to give advice, for usually unsought-for advice will reach about the same distance that the giver's hat rim does. Boys, remember that this is private--just between you and I. When we get ready to set our traps about the first of November, let's try to--Oh, well, you kick, do you? You say that the bounty trapper will have everything caught before the first of November. That is true to a certain extent, but we can't help that, for you know we are not true sportsmen, so all we can do is to stick to common sense.

What I was about to say, boys, when we set our traps about the first of November, was, let's try to set our traps so as to avoid catching our neighbor's cats and dogs. If by mistake we should catch a neighbor's cat, in freezing weather, and the cat's foot is frozen, kill the poor thing at once and don't let it out to remain a poor cripple the remainder of its life. And say, boys, don't you think it would be a good idea to get the consent of the farmers to allow you to set traps on their premises, wherever you can do so? And don't you think it would be best to be very careful to not break down the farmer's fences and leave their bars and gates open when we pass through them tending our traps? In fact, we should be very careful and do as little damage as possible, for you know we trappers are not true sportsmen. The true sportsman can buy or lease lands and have their private game preserves, so let us try to keep on the right side of the farmer or there will soon be a time when we will have no place to set our traps.

***

Certain game club men who are headed by a certain M. D. are circulating a petition to both branches of the Legislature and the Governor, to have a law passed to abolish bear trapping in Pennsylvania. This M. D.'s excuse is a plea of humanity, claiming that many bear are caught and allowed to remain in the trap until the bear gnaws or twists off his foot and often the bear is caught the second time and another is taken off, when the bear is destined to go through life on two feet. Now in all of my more than fifty years of bear trapping, I have never known a bear to gnaw his foot in the least degree. Neither have I had a bear twist off his foot when caught in a trap that has a spread of jaws no larger than 12 inches, which will catch a bear through the thick of a foot. The Newhouse No. 5 bear trap which is the most common trap used in bear trapping, has a spread of jaws of 11 1/4 inches.

The law which is now (1910) in force in this state provided that a bear trap must be looked to at least every forty-eight hours. Under these conditions, there is no danger of a bear twisting off a foot. It is true that if a trap is used with a grasp high enough to catch above the foot and the bear is allowed to remain in the trap for a long time, they will sometimes twist off a foot.

But this sympathetic M. D. makes no mention of the bear that is wounded by a gunshot, escapes and lies for weeks, and then dies or recovers as the case may be. The wounding of a bear from a gunshot is far more liable to occur than it is to take a bear's foot by being caught in a trap.

This sympathetic doctor makes no mention of the farmer who has a number of sheep killed by bears, which is almost an every day occurrence during the summer season in any section where bear frequent.

Now, Brother Trappers, it is not the great sympathy that these gentlemen club men have for the bear. No, not in the least. What these gentlemen want is to drive the lowly bear trapper out of business, so that those very sympathetic gentlemen may more easily kill a bear without losing too much of their precious sweat, and not be compelled to get too far from camp and the champagne bottle.

Now, Brother Bear Trappers, my object in writing these few lines is to ask you and each of you to write your respective representative at once, advising him that you are opposed to any law to abolish the trapping of the bear.

I believe that I was the first to advocate some remedy against the wasteful slaughter of the fur bearing animals through the medium of our favorite magazine, the Hunter-Trader-Trapper. I urged that the remedy was with the large raw fur dealers by refusing to accept skins that were not in a reasonably prime condition. Since my writing, other more capable writers have taken up the matter and have advocated a remedy from the same standpoint.

Now by close observation I have become satisfied that there is no use of looking further in that direction for a remedy of this wasteful slaughter of the fur bearing animals. The city fur dealers receive the goods which consist of all manner of skins and all grades from good to poor and worthless. In most cases the dealer received the goods from local dealers who have gathered the furs up from among the trappers, paying such prices as he thought would leave a fair profit on the whole bunch. In most cases paying more for the poorer grade than it was really worth, while paying far less than the prime skins were worth.

WOODCOCK ON THE TRAP LINE 1912.

Now the dealer was hardly to be blamed for this sort of transaction, for it was the only way that he could make a deal with the trapper. The city dealer is in the same fix as the local dealer. He quotes furs from number one down to number four and trash, making up on the better grades what he may have lost on the poorer. Thus you see there is no one out anything except the trapper, who will insist on trapping too early in the season, as well as too late in the spring of the year.

Now we will say to the brother trappers of Pennsylvania and other states as well, that we are at the parting of the ways, allowing us to use the term. We must do something desperate if we wish to save the fur bearers from becoming extinct and save the trappers' pleasure and what profit he may derive from the business.

Now the only remedy is a closed season on all fur bearing animals. If we are to derive any special benefit from a closed season, the open season must be made short, for every trapper of much experience knows that the fur bearers of Pennsylvania have become extremely scarce in the past few years. In fact in some parts there is but little stock left to build on. I would say that not more than two months of open season should be allowed, if we get real benefit from a closed season, and taking the whole state into consideration, I believe that November and December would give the best general satisfaction.

Now, brother trappers, do not be hard on me because I advocate a shorter season to be open than some trappers seem to be in favor of. Well, we had the bounty law and we all have seen the results. I would like to say here that the bounty law is still doing its work of annihilation. The law is still in force as it appears on the face of it, but nevertheless there has been no appropriation made by the legislature to pay the bounty. Some trappers do not know but what they will get the bounty until they present these certificates for payment, then to learn that there is no bounty for them. Other persons and would-be trappers are getting the certificates and holding them, thinking that there will be an appropriation made to pay this bounty. In this they will also find their mistake.

Now, brother trappers, we all know that the Lord helps him, who helps himself and if we would save the fur bearing animals from complete annihilation we must each of us do our part and not depend on some one else doing the work. Let us all who would have a closed season on mink, fox, skunk and muskrat get a petition to that effect and circulate it. Get your merchant, doctor, and every other business man in your neighborhood to sign the petition and as many others as we possibly can.

Now, my dear friends, let us remember that the gentleman sportsman will not help us in this matter and if we would have a closed season we must push this matter ourselves. In my upwards of fifty years on the trap line and the trail, I have always done my part (as I saw it) to stop wasteful slaughter of game and the fur bearers and I will do the very best that I am able in this matter, although I realize that my days on the trap line are few.

Now, comrades, on the fourth of July (1910), the primaries to nominate candidates to represent the people of the commonwealth of Pennsylvania, will be held. Let every trapper of the state, who is interested in the matter of a closed season on our fur bearing animals get out and talk with their candidates whom they wish to represent them at the next assembly. Let him know that you wish a law passed at the next legislature giving a closed season on fur bearing animals. We should bear in mind, that writing and talking without action will not do. We must get busy at once if we would accomplish anything.

CHAPTER XXIX.
Destruction of Game and Game Birds.

Of late (1908) there has been much writing and law making in an attempt to preserve the game of this commonwealth, and it reminds one of the old adage of "Locking the Barn Door, after the Horse was Stolen." At the last Assembly of the Pennsylvania Legislature, there was a Bounty Law passed with an appropriation of $50,000 to pay the bounty on the different animals. The appropriation was exhausted almost before the trapping season had begun, or at least should have begun, so far as the trapper's interest was concerned. Now, I wish to speak of the bounty as to fox and mink, and I wish to speak of an incident that came under my observation.

A neighbor of mine makes a business of trapping each fall; there were three in the family, who trapped last fall. They caught 11 fox, 4 mink, 8 coon, 2 weasel and 1 wildcat. This catch was all made before the 20th of October and sold for $34.45, or including bounty, $66.45. Now, had this same fur been caught in November or December, the fur alone would have brought at least $68.00, and the taxpayers would have been $32.00 ahead.

I also know of another party who dug out two nests of young mink and got nine young ones. The old mink escaped. I asked this man why he did not let them go until fall or winter, as these dens were near his mill? He informed me that he never fooled away any time trapping and had he left them go until fall the mink would have been gone and now he was $6.50 ahead. Now, this man had actually destroyed at least $30 worth of furs to get $6.50 in bounty.

While I think that the bounty on wildcats and weasel is all right, I do not think a bounty on fox and mink at all necessary. The high price their fur brings will induce the trapper to take all that the bounty would induce him to do, and at a time when the fur will bring more than a great deal of early caught furs would bring, including the bounty.

It is quite doubtful as to mink being very destructive to birds or their nests, and as to the destruction of poultry, it is a very easy and inexpensive matter for any poultry raiser to arrange his poultry house so as to take any prowling mink that should come about his premises.

Now, I would suggest to the bird hunter, or as he prefers to be called, "sportsman," that if he will leave his automatic gun and his bird dog at home, and merely take a good double-barrel breechloader and go into the bush, and "walk up" his birds, instead of having a dog to show the bird to him, he will do far more to protect the game bird than any bounty law will do! This the sportsman must do, or the game birds of this state will soon be a thing of the past.

About 1870, there was a move begun to check the slaughter of the deer in this state, but it was only in a half-hearted way. The writer circulated the first petition to get the law enacted prohibiting the hounding of deer. After some years the law prohibited the chasing of deer with dogs, but the law could not be enforced for the very reason that these same sportsmen wished to hound deer. He would go on to the streams where there were but few inhabitants, and hire all of the people living in the neighborhood to take their dogs to the hills and start them on the trail of deer. The "sportsman" would lay in ambush and shoot the deer when they came to water, providing they were able to see the sights on their guns sufficiently clear to get a bead on the deer.

These "sportsmen" would pay the natives a good sum for their services and would often buy hounds at high prices and bring them to the locality where they intended to hound deer and pay some one living in the neighborhood a good price to keep their dogs from one season to another. These "sportsmen" were sure to make the constable, whose duty it was to report this violation of the deer law, a present of a fine fishing rod or some other article which might be a ten or twenty dollar bill.

Now, under these conditions it was next to impossible to get any one who knew anything about the transaction to make a complaint, or even be a witness against those transgressors of the deer or hounding law. But in time the law was made sufficiently stringent as to virtually put a stop to this most cruel practice of deer hunting.

But now another bad thing came into vogue. Non-residents were allowed to go into the woods where they would camp from the first day of the open season for deer until the close and often some days after. Now, "the horse has been stolen." The deer in this state are virtually gone. "The door has been strongly locked, but it is now too late." This game rule applies to the game fish of the state and unless there are laws enacted which will apply more closely to the preservation of the game birds, than a closed season and a bounty or scalp law, the game birds will soon go the way of the deer and the game fish too.

I wish to say a word to our friends on the Pacific Coast as to the slaughter of game and especially that of deer. I saw a slaughter of deer in nearly all of the states west of the Rocky Mountains that was cruel. In California, in 1904, I saw men kill deer seemingly for no other purpose than the desire to kill, or as I put it, the desire to murder. I saw deer killed when the slayer positively knew that there could not be any use made of the carcass. I saw deer killed when only a fry would be taken from the ham, the remainder of the carcass left to lay without even the pretense of dressing. It was a common occurrence to kill deer for no other purpose than to feed dogs.

One day I was standing by a man on a sand bar on the bank of a river when we noticed a doe a few rods away looking at us. The man drew his gun to his shoulder in the act of shooting and I exclaimed, "My God, man, you are not going to shoot that deer, are you?" My words were not out of my mouth when the gun cracked. The deer was mortally wounded and ran directly towards us, making desperate efforts to keep its feet. It fell dead within ten feet of where we were standing. I walked away. The slayer of the innocent creature stood and gazed at it a moment and then with his foot he pushed it off the bar into the river. I hope I may never see another such sight. It was June and the doe was heavy with fawn and this man knew that he could make no use of this deer whatever.

I saw much wasteful slaughter of deer but none quite so inhuman as the one mentioned. The game laws of the Pacific Coast were not enforced. When well back in the mountains it was a rare thing to hear the game laws spoken of, not even by the game wardens. Now I think that all who are lovers of the woods and fields should join in a general move to protect this wasteful slaughter of all game and game birds, no matter whether we are the so-called "pot hunter" or the "gentleman sportsman," but none will regret this unreasonable waste of game more than those who are living back in the mountains, where game is most plentiful, when it is gone. Nor none will get more benefit and pleasure from the very fact that they are living in a game section, yet these are the ones who do not seem to care how great the slaughter, apparently never taking it into consideration that the present rate of slaughter will soon leave their game laden section as bare of game as that of the older settled countries.

Comrades, let us all join in the preservation of what game and fish there is left, whether we may be called pot hunters or gentlemen sportsmen. I would be the last one to wish to deprive any trapper or camper from making good use of game at any time when in camp, but let us be careful about the waste of it.

***

Comrades of the trap line, you of course are aware that a trapper is considered of small account by those who make or cause to be made, the game laws of this state (Pennsylvania), and brother trapper, are we not as much to blame as the ones who concoct the game laws to their own liking? The accompanying picture will show a part of the confiscation from the writer by the game laws of Pennsylvania and this same confiscation applies to every trapper in the state to a more or less extent. Had we presented our side of this question to our respective representatives in a clear and reasonable light would we not get a square deal? If not, then why not? We are aware that the man with the dollar has a great influence in comparison with the poor trapper, but are there not ten of the poor trappers to one of the dollar men and have we not the just and reasonable side of the question? Do not our representatives know that the raw fur industry of the state is of greater importance, financially, than the wheat crop of the state, for which the legislature does all it can in the way of appropriations to help the farmer to increase the yield of wheat? Had this been shown to the assembly, would it not have passed laws to protect the fur-bearers of the state, instead of bounty laws to exterminate the fur-bearer, and this act at the expense of the public?

Every dollar that is appropriated by the House of Representatives in the way of bounty on so-called noxious animals, must come from the pockets of the taxpayers, and is not a dollar saved in the way of protecting the fur-bearers of the state equivalent to a dollar produced from a bushel of wheat? Now, the dollar man will tell us that the fox and mink are very destructive to game and game birds. This, to a great extent, is a mere bugaboo, or an excuse to knock out the trapper. There is little doubt but that a fox occasionally kills a grouse or partridge or a rabbit. Admitting this to be the case, is not a good fox or mink skin worth ten times as much to the trapper as a partridge or rabbit is to the dollar man?

But that is not all, if it is the pleasure of an individual to amuse himself with the traps, why should he be deprived of that pleasure? It is certain that the trap will not cause any more harm in the way of damage or in a cruel manner, than a dog will. While the dollar man makes a plea in defense of game, it is generally known that his plea is in reality in defense of his manner of sporting, regardless of any desires that the poor trapper may have and there are certainly but few trappers but wish to see the game and game birds preserved as well as the dollar man does.

I doubt if there is a man in the State of Pennsylvania who has worked longer, or done more according to his ability, to protect and preserve game than the writer has, and as to the dog, he has no greater friend than the writer. As to the preservation of game and game birds, I believe in preserving it in a substantial way and not in a mythical manner, under the pretext of a bounty on noxious animals and then pass laws that do away with the trap, the most effective implement there is in taking that noxious animal. As the game and bounty laws of Pennsylvania stand today, it reminds one of the old lady who told the boy that he could go in swimming, but he must not go near the water.

Now, I believe in a bounty on wildcats, hawks and weasel, sufficient to induce the poor man to spend the time necessary to exterminate these animals when an opportunity comes to him, for the dollar man will not take the trouble to do so. But the only effective bounty law must be placed on the game man, in the way of cutting his bag limit of birds for a single day and the season in two, and placing a closed season of five years on deer. There is much said as to the rapid decrease of game. Now, so far as this applies to deer, and my observation extends over four counties of the state, at the present decrease (1913) of the deer, there will not be a deer left in these four counties at the end of five years and the deer law is being continually violated. In order to enforce the game laws of the state, the laws should be as near equal as possible, in giving each man his way of enjoying his manner of out-door sport, either in fishing, hunting or trapping. We are aware that there must be a limit to man's idea of sport. There are plenty of men, for instance, who enjoy the use of dynamite in fishing, in killing all the fish in the stream, small fish along with the large ones, also all kinds of fish that happen to be in the pool where the dynamite is used. It may be the pleasure of other sportsmen to kill birds of all kinds and also deer at any and all times of the year. This kind of work can not be allowed. In order to enforce the game laws, the laws must be in harmony with the greatest number of people possible, and not enact game laws that deprives a goodly portion of the people (I refer to the trapper) of their pleasure simply to gratify a certain class of sportsmen.

The game wardens will then find it hard enough to enforce the law. Say, comrades, I wish to call your attention to an article in the December number of H-T-T, 1912, by Mr. J. R. Bachelder. Mr. Bachelder is an old and respected man and one of the rural mail carriers of Cameron County. Mr. Bachelder describes how the trap law of Pennsylvania has deprived him of the only pleasure that he was able to enjoy in the open, that of tending a few traps.

And comrades, we of the trap line and trail, who are not blessed with the dollar and the automobile, will soon find that our pleasures in the open, like Mr. Bachelder's, are laid by for all time. If the club man, through his leasing policies and the trespass law that he has before the House of Representatives, becomes a law, we can go away back and sit down.

But, comrades, I consider that we are to blame to a large extent for these "one man" game laws. Had we come out at the right time and fought for our rights in the open instead of slinking back in the dark, whining, I believe that the law, as applied to the trap, would be different and I should not violate the game laws after passed, no matter if they are not wholly to my liking.

The professional sportsman makes a great talk about the amount of birds that the fox destroys. Now, the facts are, one weasel or snake will destroy more rabbits or birds and birds' eggs than a dozen foxes. The fox gets the greater part of his food from the field mouse. This fact any close observer knows.

* * *

Brother trappers, you are aware that the nations--the United States, Great Britain, Japan and Russia, have taken the fur seal under their protection, and will protect the seal and sell their skins. I wish to ask you, brother trapper, if your wife, daughter or sweetheart wears furs made of the seal skin. No? Well, your wife, daughter or sweetheart does wear furs made from the fur bearer that runs on the hillside back of your house. Then, why do you stand for a bounty on these animals from which the furs are made for your wife, daughter or sweetheart to wear, to hasten the extinction of these fur-bearers, while the millionaire gives the word to the government, and the fur-bearer of the millionaire is protected at the expense of the people? Say, you wives, daughters or sweethearts of the trapper, do you stand for this kind of a deal?

A few words in regard to the protection of the game and game birds: I think that every lover of outdoor life should be willing to have a reasonable number to the bag limit of either game birds or game animals, and lend a hand in protecting the game to the amount of the bag limit.

Oh, you find fault with the game laws--you say that the laws are not just to all alike. Well, in one sense of the word this is true. The state law confiscated your traps, then placed a bounty on noxious animals, and then fines you heavily if you set a trap in a way so as to be able to catch one of these noxious animals (queer laws); but, nevertheless, we should try to protect our game if we are to have any left. At the rate the game is being slaughtered at the present time, there will not be a deer left in the State of Pennsylvania, and but very little game of any kind.

You say that it is a hard matter to protect the game--that is true; for it is hard to get local game wardens that are of much account. A man of much principle and business qualifications will not accept the position, as he does not like to arrest a neighbor for fear of hurting his regular line of business. The State Game Wardens are not acquainted with the different game localities, and with the people who have but little or no regard for the game laws of the state.

I will give an instance which came under my observation the past season: The game laws of Pennsylvania prohibit the use of buckshot in deer hunting, and the law also prohibits the killing of does. Now, a man who was hunting deer with a shotgun loaded with buckshot, was looking at another hunter's gun, which was a .32 Special Winchester; the shotgun man noticed the small caliber of the Winchester, asked the party who had the rifle (knowing nothing of the shooting power of the Winchester), if he expected to kill anything with that little thing, and at the same time stating that good buckshot gun was the thing to hunt deer with. When asked if he did not know that the law forbade the use of buckshot in deer hunting, he replied, "Oh to ---- with the law!" They knocked me out of my bear traps, and the next thing they will do is to pass a law to prohibit hunting with a gun that costs less than $500.00.

At the same time, and in this same place, a party killed a large doe that had its tail entirely shot away and several buckshot were found in its body.

I will tell a little joke that was got off on one of the State Game Wardens as told by himself in the hotel at this place, which is a fact, and took place in these same woods: The Warden was telling a crowd at the hotel how his attention had been called to a doe that some one had killed and hung up in a certain place in the woods. The Warden said he went and found the deer and watched for ten days, but no one came for the deer. A party standing by said to the Warden, "Oh, that is a way we have of fixing you fellows--we kill a doe, hang it up on the outskirts of the deer hunting grounds, then give you notice of it, and while you are watching the dead deer, we are killing the live ones." The Warden, after listening to the man's story, remarked, "Well by Jonathan! that is one on me--come on."

The above joke was actually got off here at the hotel in this town.

The number of bears killed in this part, fall of 1911, notwithstanding that the use of steel traps is prohibited, was larger than has been in years. A party of thirteen from this place went into the woods on the Trout River, and during the ten or twelve days they were there, they killed seven bears--five in one day. And there were several deer killed.

Now comrades, while we can't all agree on the justification of the game laws, we should all join hands and try to protect what little game we have left by getting the bag limit materially cut down, and give fifteen days more time to the hunter. Then stand by the law, or soon the game will all be gone with the exception of a few cotton-tails and what game is on private reserves, and posted lands.

CHAPTER XXX.
Southern Experiences on the Trap Line.

Comrades of the trap line, I am not able to report a large catch of furs the past season, 1910. I did not catch much fur, but say, boys, I had a good deal of experience nevertheless. I will try to tell of conditions as I found them in North Carolina.

I first stopped in Lee County, where I met Mr. A. L. Lawrence, one of the *Hunter-Trader-Trapper's* most ardent friends. After stopping here a few days and seeing some of the sights in Lee and Moore Counties, Mr. Lawrence, now my friend and partner, a gentleman whom I had never known before, started for Bladen Co., N. C., where we expected to be kept up a good portion of the night in order to keep up with the skinning and stretching of the numerous furbearing animals caught during the day. Well boys, I will say that we were not troubled in this matter at least.

While there is more fur in that section than in the north, there are also more disadvantages to be met with, than we have here. The majority of people that one meets with in the South are very kind and obliging. Nevertheless you will find it somewhat difficult to find suitable grounds to set your camp, providing the parties are aware that your intentions are to put out a line of traps. Remember that nearly every farmer has a drove of hogs that run in the woods, and the feeding grounds of the razorback is in the bottoms along the creeks and rivers. Naturally the farmer is a little fearful of his pigs being caught, so he says that the better way is to keep "shet" of the trappers, especially those that are strangers to the neighborhood. This is not the only way that the razorback gets in his work, and a good bit of work they get in too. The razorback is a powerful hunter, and it does not require a powerful animal scent to draw the razorback to the trap. To avoid the porker the trap must be set three inches below the water or six feet above the ground. As foxes are not given to tree climbing as a usual thing the trapper is sorely tried to devise schemes to take the fox in a section where the razorback is getting in his work. He is found in most places in the South, although there are some counties and even townships that have a stock law.

The great difficulty with a non-resident or a stranger in getting a site to camp on, is that he must be where he can use the water from some one's well, as springs are not very plenty. The water in the branches, small streams or rivers are not such that a trapper should use; there is such a heavy drainage from swamps that are full of decayed vegetation, so that the trapper would soon be looking for a doctor rather than for opossum and coon.

On South River near Parkersburg, we got a good place to camp, and the people were very kind and neighborly. Mr. Green, the postmaster at Parkersburg, and his family, with whom we stopped a short time before going into camp, were very kind and generous. The young ladies, daughters of Mr. Green, gave us some fine music on the piano, accompanied with singing during the evenings.

About eighteen or twenty miles from Parkersburg on Turnbull Creek where we expected to do the greater part of our trapping, and where mink and coon were quite plentiful with considerable otter signs, we were unable to get a place to camp. The people objected to outside trappers infringing on what they apparently looked upon as their individual right.

At the junction of Cape Fear and Black Rivers in Bladen and Pender counties, there is a section of low swampy country, which is a wild country where there is deer and bear as well as furbearers such as otter, mink, muskrats and coon. The latter are quite numerous. There is also wild turkey, quail and ducks on the river. Now this section of the country had a colony of mixed whites and colored people (Mulatto) who lived in these swamps, other people rarely going into that locality.

We were informed that there was a good deal of illicit or Blockade Whiskey as the natives call it, made in these swamps. It is said that it is not safe for strangers to be caught in their domain too often. I found that one needs nearly double the number of traps to trap in the swamps or bays, as these swamps are called by the natives. There is so much ground that is covered with water so near alike that the animal has no regular place to travel, as is the case along the open streams. Instead the animals have vast areas of ground to travel over that is partially covered with water, so that the mink or raccoon travels anywhere and everywhere, as it is all alike to the mink and coon. Consequently the trapper needs more traps in order to make the same number of catches as would be possible in a locality where the streams did not spread over such a large scope of land.

While the trapper in the South has but little snow or ice to contend with, he will not find it all milk and honey, for the swamps are not a paradise with the gall berry brush, the bamboo briers, saffron sprouts and holly brush. As for game birds, they are not so plentiful, but quail in places are found in good numbers. Wild turkeys are found in small lots scattered all over the country, but by no means plenty: doves are quite plentiful.

As for fur bearers there are quite a number of opossum. Coons are not found late in the season to any great extent only in the swamps where they are quite plentiful. Grey foxes are plenty. There are many hunters in the South who hunt with dogs, and they do not take kindly to any other way of taking the furbearers. Otter signs are seen on nearly all of the streams but by no means are they plenty, and every slide is closely watched by trappers living nearby. The ever present razorback is an obstacle in the way of otter trapping, for the trap must be set under the water, and this is not always practical in otter trapping.

We must not close this short letter without stating that our friend and partner, Mr. A. L. Lawrence, who was a native of Randolph County, N. C, was an expert trapper, and especially on mink. Mr. Lawrence was a good cook as well as a good trapper. Mr. Lawrence was hard to beat on baking opossum and bread making, but when it came to boiling water without burning it, your humble servant could hold him a close second.

Say boys, I forgot to say that you will find Billy the Sneakum just as numerous in Dixie as he is in Pennsylvania.

* * *

Comrades of the trap line, I am not in condition to write much at this time owing to my health, but, later I hope to be able to give a fuller account of my trapping experiences of 1912 in Alabama, northern Georgia, northwestern North Carolina and southeastern Tennessee. And Comrades, right here I wish to say that through the above mentioned sections of the south, I found nearly every trapper a reader and lover of the *Hunter-Trader-Trapper*, and many of these readers seemed like old neighbors to the writer, when he met them.

Well boys, during all of last year, my health was such that I never again expected to hit the trap line, but as the frost began to turn the leaves of the timber on the hillsides, the trap fever became so high that I was compelled to take a half dozen traps and take to the brush. The first night I got two foxes, the second night I got another fox, three skunk and wife's pet cat. The catching of Timy (the cat) caused wife to put up such a fight, that I was compelled to pull the traps, pack my outfit and start for Alabama.

Now boys, I am not going to tell you entirely of my own experience, but of the experiences of other trappers and hunters as told me by them. One trapper told of the killing of a bear in the thick cane brakes in the swamps of the Mississippi. It was against the game laws of Mississippi to kill bear at that time of the year, and as these hunters could not resist the taking of this bear, they put up a job on the bear. There were four of the hunters going through the thick cane brake, when they saw the bear coming toward them. The head man pulled his hunting knife, and told the other hunters to lie down, he dropping to his knees, knife in hand. When the bear was close up to him he sprang up and shouted "boo". The bear raised up on its hind feet and the hunter seized the bear and plunged the knife into it. The other hunters sprang to their feet, gun in hand and shot the bear. The party who told me this bear story, said it was a put up job, so as to make it appear that the bear was killed in self defense.

A PARTY OF VISITORS AT E. N. WOODCOCK'S CAMP ON THE BANKS OF THE ETAWAH RIVER AT DIKES CREEK, GA.

I know of many excuses to avoid game laws, but this one beats them all. I have had a good deal of experience in game hunting, but never had the luck to have a bear run on to me in this manner.

I will tell a panther story, which a man told me that happened some year ago, in North Carolina, near the Tennessee line. The man was in a small shack, and he often heard panthers screaming about the shack, and finally one night when he had some fresh deer meat in the shack, the man was awakened by some animal trying to pull up a roof board. The roof of the shack was not more than six or eight feet from the ground floor, and soon the panther raised up a board sufficient to run a foot down through the crack. The man stood watching the game, and when the foot came through the crack, the man seized the panther by the foot, and a terrible fight began. The hunter finally cut a foot of the panther off, and stabbed it with his knife until he killed it. The hunter had a rug made of the skin of this panther, which he intends to keep in the family for all time to come. I think that this hunter is doing the right thing in so doing.

I will now give a little of my own experience, but it is not in the way of an adventure with either a bear or panther, but, no doubt, I was just as nervous for a time as those who had the reported adventure with the bear and the panther.

The last days of December, 1912, I went into camp about twelve or fourteen miles from Crandel, near the Tennessee line. Early the next morning after going into camp, a man came to the camp and asked many questions as to what I was doing. How long I was going to be there? Where I was from? Also many other similar questions, and then went away. That evening four or five men came to my tent, and asked about the same questions that the man in the morning had asked.

When I stepped outside of the tent next morning, there were three or four bunches of hickory withes standing against the guy ropes of the tent. I did not know what those hickory withes meant, but surmised that some jealous trapper had put them there as a warning for me to get out. But it was not long after daylight, when a man came to camp, and said that I was suspicioned of being a spy in search of blockaders. I told this man that there could be nothing farther from it, that that would be the last thing I would mix up in, even if I knew of any such business, that I was simply a trapper and had no other business there.

The man, said that he knew that as soon as he heard my name for he had known of me for the past four years, ever since he had been a reader of the H-T-T. This gentleman told me not to worry, but to stay in my tent a day or two before going out to set my traps, and everything would be all right. I hardly knew what to do, but as it was raining I could not well break camp that night. Five or six men came to camp. Some were those who had been there before, and questioned me as to my business there. But now they were acting entirely different. Now these gentlemen rushed in with hands extended to shake hands and welcome me and offer me any assistance that they were able to give, and nearly all of them offered me a drachm of corn juice. I stayed a few days longer in camp there, and each day friends grew more numerous and corn juice more plentiful. I stayed a day or two and saw that friends were going to be so numerous that it would be next to impossible for me to get out on the trap line for some days at least, so broke camp and pulled for Pennsylvania.

CHAPTER XXXI.
On the Trap and Trot Line in the South--Fall of 1912.

Well, comrades of the trap line, as I see so many interesting letters from trappers in the H-T-T, the best of all sporting magazines, I will relate some of my experiences in the South, season of 1912. During the latter part of the winter and the greater part of the summer, my health was so poor that I never again expected to be able to enjoy the pleasures of the trap line. But as time passed and I was able to get out into the fields and wander about, I became stronger from day to day until in the last days of October, when the frost began to crisp the air and the leaves on the trees on the hillsides became a golden hue, it drove the trapping fever into me to such a degree that I was unable to resist the temptation any longer.

I took six or eight traps and went to the brush within sight of the house. I was obliged to use a good, strong staff to climb the hill with and could only take a few steps at a time, without stopping to take my breath. But, boys, I found this sort of exercise better for me than the doctor's medicine that I was taking. My first night's catch was two fox. Many of the readers of the H-T-T will remember of seeing my picture with the two fox in the December, 1912, number. The next two nights I got another fox and three skunk and wife's pet cat. The cat business put it up to me and I was compelled to lift my traps and take for other fields. Had I been able to traverse the hills and woods of old Potter County, I could have done far better than I did in the South.

My trapping fever had now reached such a high mark that I could no longer stave it off and not being able to travel the hills and streams of this section, hit my feet for Alabama, where I could do the greater part of my work from a boat. After reaching Tryanna, I made a trip up Indian Creek every day by boat to a fish trap dam, which I was unable to get the boat over so was compelled to leave it at the dam and hoof it up the creek to the end of the line. On the way back down the creek each day I would gather up a boat load of drift wood to last for the day. The water being at a very low stage, it caused several rapids, which made it tight nipping to paddle the boat over. I had occasion to stop paddling often as I was continually making sets for mink, rats, coon and opossum, first on one side of the stream and then on the other, so that I had abundance of time to rest. But, comrades of the trap line, this kind of work is much better for an old played-out trapper than pills.

While I found trapping conditions here in Alabama different than they were a year ago, I nevertheless got a mink, rat, 'possum or coon nearly every day, but two mink at a single round of traps was the best that I did at any time. There was no otter or beaver in this part of Alabama and but very few fox or skunk, and I found far more trappers than there were a year ago. Many of the trappers were from other states, and last season I did not see or hear of a colored man trapping, but this fall I heard of the dark man and his works daily. One of the worst and most foolish things that the trappers did was their early trapping before furs were any where near in a prime condition. This unwise work was indulged in by the white trappers as well as the negroes.

I was unable to get out into the swamps or sloughs to any great extent and it is in the swamps that the coon are found more plentifully. The mink does not take to the swamps as readily as the coon, nevertheless he is found in the swamps as well as along the rivers and smaller streams. If we could only keep down the trapping fever and the desire to get that mink before the other fellow did, it would help us out in a financial way. We saw many mink that were offered for sale here that were over three feet from tip to tip, from 75 cents to $2.00, and the skins went a-begging at that price. Now, comrades, just think of the difference in what those skins would have brought when in a prime condition. The price then would have been from $3.00 to $7.00, and this same rule applied to the coon and muskrats and other fur bearers, and you are aware that the fur bearers throughout the country are rapidly becoming scarcer each year. While I found more mink, coon and muskrats here in Alabama than I did in either Georgia or North Carolina, yet I did not see mink, coon or rat signs in comparison to what they were a year ago, and I do not believe that there was one-third as many mink, coon or muskrats as there was last season. Opossum seem to hold their own fairly well.

Well, comrades, the picture here shows the greater part of our Alabama catch of furs. I trapped in Alabama about three weeks when I went to Georgia, where I expected, from what I was told, to find far better trapping than was to be had here in Alabama, but I was sadly disappointed.

* * *

Leaving Tryanna, Alabama, by wagon, I went to Farley, eighteen miles. There I took a train to Huntsville, then by the Southern R. R. by the way of Chattanooga to Dikes Creek, Georgia, where I went into camp. I camped at this place about two weeks, building two boats, one a good large boat, sufficient to move my whole outfit from point to point, as I moved down the Etowah River, then the Coosa River. The other boat was much smaller, being suited to the trap and trot line. Boys, you who have trapped on the rivers and large streams of the South, know that the traps and the trot line go hand in hand and with only two or three trot lines, to one who is onto the job, you will find them quite profitable as well as a pleasure. In most places you will find ready sale for the fish you catch at 10 to 12 cents a pound. If one runs his trot lines two or three times a day and takes in from 20 to 100 pounds of fish, it is a little item along the financial trail. But, boys, there is a knack in running a trot line in a successful manner as well as a trap line. Where the trot line is run in connection with the trap line, it makes quite an addition to the trapper's job, for he will be out as late as 9 or 10 o'clock before going to bed to run the trot lines, take off the fish and rebait the lines. It is also necessary to put in any spare time that happens your way in digging wigglers, hunting crawfish and other bait.

E.N. WOODCOCK AND SOME OF HIS 1912 CATCH OF ALABAMA FURS.

The boat is an absolute necessity in trapping in the South, as the most of the fur-bearers are found along the rivers and large streams. It is next to an impossibility to make a successful set for mink and coon along the soft, slippery and sloping banks without the boat. And boys, the conditions on the trap line in the South are altogether different from what it is in the North on the clear, gravelly and rocky streams of the North and East sections. It requires a trap one size larger in the South in successful trapping than it does in the North and East. This is owing to the soft, muddy, clay banks and streams. Another thing that is a necessity along the rivers and streams of the South is the trap stake, while on most streams of the North the clog or drag is far better than a stake.

I did not find the fur-bearers in Georgia as plentiful as I expected, from what I had been told and trappers were numerous, many of them in house boats. I expected to find some beaver on Pumpkin Vine Creek, a branch of the Etowah River, but they failed to show up on investigation. There is but very few otter in northern and central Georgia and in Georgia, as in Alabama, many trappers began trapping in September. The best catch in one night at our camp was while we were camping at Coosa, on the Coosa River, but it was nothing in comparison to what we did in Alabama last season in a single night's catch. The catch at Coosa in one night was two mink, three coon, three rats and two opossum. This was done with about 20 traps. It was raining at this time, so we kept this bunch of furs three days and until there had been several more pieces added to the bunch. We wanted to get a picture of this bunch of furs and the camp at this place but it continued to rain and we were compelled to skin the animals and let the pictures go.

The steamboats are a serious drawback to the trappers on the river in the South. The average trapper plans to get out on his line and fix up as many of his traps as he can after the steamboat passes. On most rivers there is not more than one or two boats passing daily and on some of the rivers, boats do not make more than one or two trips a week. It was the intention of the writer when going to Georgia, to work the trap line all winter, going nearly the entire length of the Alabama River, to the Mississippi line, but met with unexpected conditions that I was unable to endure and was compelled to give up the greater part of the trip, which was a sad disappointment. But comrades, you know that there are but few trappers but what meet with disappointments at times.

The game laws of Georgia are a little hard on the trapper and fisherman. The non-resident trapper has to pay a license of fifteen dollars and the local trapper a license of three dollars. (This alludes to the laws of 1912.) That is not the worst part of it. In fact, the license fund, if justly used in the protection of game and game birds and the propagation of game and birds, I would not object to the license.

The hard part of the game law of Georgia is the trespass part of it. The trapper must have a written permission from the land owner to trap or fish on any man's land and where the river is the dividing line between different parties owning the land, the trapper or fisherman must have the written permit from both land owners, even though he does not leave his boat to set a trap or place a trot line. Now it is a very difficult thing for a stranger to learn who owns the land and often the owner of the land lives in some city of the North, or elsewhere. Now here is where the shoe pinches the hardest. The fine for trespassing on a man's land is $40.00 and it is the duty of the game warden to arrest any one he finds hunting, trapping or fishing on any man's land without a written permit. Here is the worst of all. The game warden must make the arrest without any notice from the land owner and if the game warden fails to make the arrest, he is liable to the same fine as the one who is doing the trespassing. This is a law that the average land owner never asked for.

I had men come to me every day and offer me the privilege of trapping or hunting on their land without any request on my part. I found the majority of the people of Georgia very kind in regard to this trespass matter as well as other matters. It was only a few sporting "Nabobs" that concocted this stringent part in the trespass law, contained in the game laws of Georgia.

Most other states of the south have as trespass laws, that the land owner must order the arrest. The laws of Alabama allow or at least can not stop the trapper or fisherman from trapping or fishing so long as he keeps within the boundary limits of the river, which is sufficient to give the trapper or fisherman ample ground to camp on.

After leaving the Coosa River I went into the extreme northern part of Georgia where I camped for about three weeks and never met a more friendly class of people than within the vicinity of Oakman and Ranger. After leaving this section, I went into camp near Crandel, Ga. From there I went into the Fog Mountains, where I found game fairly plentiful but owing to bad weather and the condition of my health, did not hit the trap line very heavy.

CHAPTER XXXII.
Trapping in Alabama.

Well, comrades of the trap line, as I am getting well up to the seventy notch, and as the chills of zero weather chases one after the other up and down my spinal column, like a dog after a rabbit in a briar patch, and as I am unable to shake off that desire for the trap line, I concluded to go south again to trap. I began an inquiry in several different sections, in states of the South, and finally decided upon Alabama, where a gentleman and a brother trapper by the name of Ford had invited me to come. On the last days of October, 1911, I arrived in Alabama where I met Mr. Ford, whom I found to be a gentleman in all respects, and a member of the M. E. Church.

My first day's outing after reaching Mr. Ford's place was on the Tennessee River, raising fish nets, and putting out a few mink traps to ascertain what the complexion of the inner side of a mink's coat was. I got a mink the first night, which I found to be of fairly light color, but not quite light enough to my liking. The setting of more traps was delayed for a few days and we spent the time in tending the fish nets.

I have whipped the streams and drowned earthworms for brook trout and other fish, from my childhood days to the present time. I had never done any fishing in large rivers with nets, so you can imagine my feelings when one net after another was raised which contained many fish of different kinds, such as yellow cat, channel cat, buffalo, pickerel, pike, carp, suckers, black bass (called trout in the South) and many other kinds. These fish ran in weight all the way from one-fourth pound up to twenty pounds each, and occasionally a buffalo or yellow catfish much larger. Mr. Ford informed me that often on trot lines they got sturgeon, weighing more than one hundred pounds.

We intended to put out a trot line and catch a sturgeon that I might get some oil. It is said that the oil from a sturgeon is a sure cure for rheumatism in the joints, but it rained so much, keeping us busy adjusting our traps, that we did not get any time to get the bait and put out the trot line. So I did not get to see one of those large fellows.

Mr. Ford pointed out corn and cotton fields where the corn and cotton was still ungathered and told me that he had trot lines set out all through these fields last spring and caught hundreds of pounds of fish--it hardly seemed possible as the water was then fifteen of twenty feet below the banks of these fields. But in December when it began raining nearly every day, and the water rose so suddenly that I was obliged to leave many of my traps where I had set them around ponds and banks of streams and in the swamps, I could then readily see that it was perfectly possible for the fish to get out into the corn and cotton fields to feed.

The rainy season set in nearly a month earlier this season than usual, causing the rivers and streams to rise so as to flood the whole bottoms (it is called the tide by the people in Alabama).

I will not give my views of the country and conditions in northern Alabama--it would not look well; it is sufficient to say that the greater part of the land is owned in large tracts by a few men and leased out at from $3.00 to $4.00 per acre. Corn and Cotton are the main crops. Any land lying above the overflowing sections requires heavy fertilizing in order to make a crop. The fertilizer is the commercial sort, and all the crop will sell for is put onto the land in the way of fertilizers. These lands are mostly leased to colored people--in fact, I was told that the landlords did not care to lease to white men.

The poor white man in northern Alabama is worse off than the colored man, for he is looked upon as neither white nor black. In this section the population is largely of the colored class. All of the landlords have a store, so as to furnish their tenants with goods of an inferior quality at exorbitant prices.

There is no good water to be found in that part of Alabama. The water that the people use is something fearful--of course the wealthy class have cisterns. The soil is mostly red clay, and terrible to get about in when the least damp. The roads are only names for roads.

South of the Tennessee River is what is called the Sand Mountains; the soil is of a sandy nature, freestone water, and the people are all white--in fact, it is said that they will not allow a colored man to live there. I heard it stated that they would not even allow a negro to stop over night in that section.

The Sand Mountain region is a piney country with a sandy soil. The land is not as fertile as the bottom lands along the Tennessee River, but they produce a finer grade of cotton, which brings a cent or two a pound more than that of the bottom lands.

As to game in north Alabama, there is but little large game to be found. In the extreme northern part of Madison county, well up to the Tennessee line, there are a few deer and wild hogs; it was said that there were some bear, also plenty of wild turkeys. There were plenty of ducks, and a good many quail.

There is still some lumbering being done, mostly in oak of different kinds, though a good part is white oak. The logs are cut and hauled to the Tennessee River and taken by steamboat to Decatur in Limestone County, and worked up into lumber and manufactured articles. There is still quite large bodies of cugalo gum left in the swamps, though this timber is not yet used to any great extent.

I wish to say that if the trapper expects to ship his camp outfit by freight to any part of the South, he should start it from four to six weeks in advance of the time that he will arrive at the place where he will use it. The trapper, as a usual thing, is too shallow in the region of the pocket book to afford to ship an outfit of camp stove, cooking utensils, tent and a hundred traps or more of various sizes, by express. Of course, he can take his bed blanket and extra clothing as baggage in his trunk.

Now to make this matter plainer, I will give my experience of the last two seasons. In 1910 I trapped here in Pennsylvania the first two weeks of November before going south. So shipped my camp chest by express to Cameron, N. C, started it four days before I started so as to be sure that it would be there by the time I arrived. But when I got to Cameron there was no express matter for Woodcock.

Five days later while I was standing on the depot platform at Cameron waiting for the eleven o'clock express train, along came a freight train, stopped and put off my camp chest. Now, the express charges on this chest was something over ten dollars on 180 pounds.

The next season I concluded that I would not give the express company another rake-off, so started my camp outfit by freight for Madison, Alabama, four weeks before I started, so as to again be sure that it would be there when I arrived. Mr. Ford met me at the station nine miles from his place with a conveyance to take baggage and camp outfit to his place. And boys, imagine my feelings when I was again told by the station agent that there was nothing there for Woodcock. About a week later, I got the goods. So boys, take the hint and start the outfit well ahead if you wish to get it on time. I have had other similar experiences.

On our way back to Mr. Ford's place the day he met me at the station, he called my attention to several different places along the road to mink tracks in the ditches and in the road. I thought that it would be no trick at all to take three or four mink each night, but I was not reckoning on the disadvantages I had to contend with.

This section of the country is very thickly settled with colored people, and each family keeps from one to three dogs, which are out searching for food all the time. These people never think of feeding their dogs. Nearly every night these colored people are out hunting in droves of five or six, and with six or eight dogs. They think it no more of a crime to steal a trap, and anything found in the trap, than they would consider it a crime to eat a baked 'possum. A trapper must keep a good lookout when setting his traps to see that there is no "dark object" anywhere in sight. If there is, you may expect that that particular trap will be missing the next time you come that way.

In setting a trap, the first thing to do is to select a place where the trap is to be set, then look carefully around to see that no "dark object" is in sight; then go into the bush and get the trap, stake and everything that you will use in making the set. Then you will again look carefully for that "dark object," and will proceed to make the set, provided that yourself is the only human being in sight, stopping your work often to look about you. Do not think that this caution is not necessary, for it sure is. The writer had nine traps taken at one time within an hour after he had been over the line.

We went into our first camp, I think, on the 5th of November, at a place called Blackwell's Pond or Blackwell's bottom, I am not sure which. The first day after we got to camp, Mr. Ford went out and put out a few traps, while I stayed in camp and fixed up things.

The next morning we went out to look over the ground a little while. Mr. Ford went to the opposite side of the pond to set a few more traps, and see parties who owned land along the pond, for we found that the land had been posted "No Trespassing." When Mr. Ford came in that evening I think he brought in five rats. We set nine traps that day and went south along the pond to look over the grounds.

The next morning we had one mink and one coon in the nine traps. I think Mr. Ford brought in four rats and had one coon foot. That evening Mr. Ford went home to raise his nets, and when he came back he brought in two mink; I got two coon. Mr. Ford went home again and made arrangements for a team to come in and move us out to "pastures new." He also brought another mink, and I believe that we got two or three coons that night. I think we got nine rats, four mink and eight coons in the three nights with about twenty traps.

The land about this pond had been leased by Mr. Edmon Toney, a wealthy young man living near the place. While Mr. Toney is wealthy, he insists in indulging in the meek and lowly occupation of the trapper. We know Mr. Toney to be a successful trapper, for he caught, while we were in camp at that place, one of the wealthiest and most beautiful young ladies in that section. Mr. Toney is a reader of the H-T-T.

Our next camp was on Little Indian creek, at the edge of a large cugalo swamp not the pleasantest place that one could wish for a camp.

E. N. WOODCOCK AND SOME OF HIS ALABAMA FURS.

The next day after we went into Camp No. 2. I set a few traps near camp. Mr. Ford went down the creek toward his place and set a few traps, and went home to look after his fish nets, returning to camp that evening. Mr. Ford had warned me that the mink in that section would foot themselves equally as bad as muskrats, but as I had never been bothered with mink footing themselves, I paid no attention to his warning.

The next morning Mr. Ford stepped outside of the tent--it was about five o'clock and called to me, asking where I had set my first trap on the creek, and being told, he replied, "Well, you have caught a mink." When asked how he knew, he said, "Come out and hear him squall." I ate breakfast and hastened down to release the mink, but my haste was unnecessary for the mink did not propose to wait for me, I found only the mink's foot--the mink had gone.

I had never had a mink foot itself in this way before and did not think that the mink did, although here in Alabama, we had two mink to foot themselves in one night. Had I heeded Mr. Ford's warning, I would have been several mink pelts ahead.

While there was considerable fur to be found in the vicinity of Camp No. 2, it was a hard place to camp, owing to the scarcity of camp wood and the inconvenience of getting water, so we moved on to Beaver Dam creek, in Limestone county, where we were in hopes of finding a few beaver and quite a plenty of mink and coon. But we were sadly disappointed; we found but little to trap, but found trappers and trap-lifters in abundance, so made haste to get out of that country while we had our boats left. Our catch was only two mink, twelve rats, five coon and one or two 'possum.

We moved from this place back into Madison County and pitched our camp at a point known as the Sinks, where we did a better business. But the rainy season soon set in, so we were compelled to break camp and get out, leaving a good part of our traps where we had set them, now under several feet of water. We shall never see them again.

Well boys, you will excuse me from telling just how many coon we got in an hour and seven minutes. I can only state that during the five weeks that Mr. Ford and the writer were in camp that we got twenty-six mink. I do not remember the number of coons, opossums and rats caught.

CHAPTER XXXIII.
Some Early Experiences.

Comrades of the trap line and trail, as I have gotten too old, March 1913, and too nigh played out to longer get far out into the tall timber, I will, with the consent of the editor of the H-T-T, relate some of my experiences on the trap line and trail of some years ago.

A young man by the name of Frank Wright was hunting and trapping on the Crossfork waters of Kettle Creek. Frank was a young man barely out of his teens, and had been in the woods but little, but Frank was a hustler and was not afraid of the screech of the owl; the days were altogether too short for him.

We went into camp early in October as we had to do a good deal of repairing on the camp as the cabin had not been used in two or three years, and the porcupines got in their work in good shape. The cabin was built of logs and the "porces" had gnawed nearly all of the chinking out from between the logs and the mud was all gone from around the chinking. Some of the shakes were gone from the roof and the door which was made of split shakes.

First, we split out shakes and repaired the roof and the door. We then split chinking block out of a basswood tree to renew the chinkings that had been gnawed and eaten up by the porcupines. After the chinking was all replaced and fastened in place by making wedges and driving them into the logs, one at each end of each chinking block, we gathered moss from old logs and calked every crack, pressing the moss into the cracks with a wedge-shape stick made for the purpose. The calking was all done from the inside.

After the chinking and calking was done, we dug into a clay bank and got clay, which we mixed with ashes taken from the fire then added sufficient water to make a rather stiff mortar. We filled the spaces between the logs, going over every crack on the outside of the shack.

Now and again Frank would notice a mink or coon track along the creek, while he was gathering moss from the old logs. These tracks would drive Frank nearly wild, and he would double his energy so as to get the shack finished so we could hit the trap line.

After we got the shack in good shape, we went to work getting up a good supply of wood, sufficient to last through the season. We had an open fireplace, so we cut the wood about three feet long. The wood was now up near the camp door, ranked up in good snug piles. We then cut crotched stakes and drove them in the ground on each side of the ranks, and laid poles in, then placed cross poles on and covered with hemlock boughs.

Frank was so anxious to get to work on the trap line, that he at first objected to putting in so much time in getting up the wood, saying that we could get the wood at odd times. But when told that there are no odd times on the trap line, he then worked the harder to get the supply of wood, including a good supply of dry pine for kindling fires, which we got by cutting a dry pine stub.

The camp now being in good shape, we hit the trap line and began building deadfalls for marten. We went onto the ridges into the thick heavy timber, where the marten were most likely to be found. We would select a low hemlock to build the deadfalls under, so the trap would be protected from heavy falls of snow, as much as possible. Some of the traps we would drive crotched stakes and lay poles in them and then cover with hemlock boughs to keep the snow off.

After we had several lines of marten traps built, we went onto the stream and branches and built deadfalls for mink and coon.

Nearly every day we saw deer, but the weather was still too warm to keep venison any length of time, so we did not carry our guns with us. When Frank would see a deer he would make grave threats that he would carry his gun the next day. We were about two miles from the stage road. The stage made only one trip a week, so there was no way of disposing of a deer as long as the weather was so warm. It took but little persuasion to convince Frank that it would be poor policy to kill deer as long as we could make use of but a small part of a single deer.

After we had gotten out a good line of deadfalls for marten, mink and coon, and as it was now about the first of November and time to bait up the deadfalls, and set out what steel traps we had for fox, I told Frank that we would carry our guns with us and try to kill a deer for bait and camp use. Frank could hardly sleep that night; he was so delighted to think that the time had come to quit the monkey business, as he called it, and begin business.

We climbed the ridge where we knew there were some deer, following down the ridge, one on each side, along the brow of the hill. We put in the entire day without getting a shot at a deer. That night it snowed about an inch, so that in the wooded timber, one could see the trail of the deer in the snow; but in hemlock timber there was not enough snow on the ground, so a track could be followed. We had killed a squirrel or two, and had a little prepared bait, so we concluded to bait a few traps until we struck a deer trail.

We did not succeed in finding the tracks of any deer until well along in the afternoon. It so happened that I got a shot at a deer that was nearly hidden from sight behind a large tree. I shot the deer through, just forward of the hips. We followed it only a short distance when we found the bed of the deer, and there was blood in it, so it was plain to be seen in what manner the deer was wounded. All still-hunters (excuse the word still-hunt; the word stalking does not sound good to a backwoodsman) of deer know that when a deer is shot well back through the small intestines, that if conditions will allow, the right thing to do is to leave the trail for a time and the deer will lie down. If left alone for an hour or two the hunter will have but little trouble in getting his deer. So in this case, as we were not far from camp and it was nearly sundown, I told Frank that we had better let the deer go until morning, when we would have more daylight ahead of us, and we would get the deer with less trouble.

We started for camp and had gone only a short distance when Frank said he would work along the ridge a little and see if he could not kill a partridge.

FOOT OF TREE SET.

I went on to camp and when dark came I couldn't see nor hear anything of Frank. I ate my supper, and as I could get no word from Frank either by shouting or firing my gun, I climbed to the top of the ridge so I could be heard for a greater distance, but still I could get no answer. It had turned warmer and what little snow was on the ground had melted. I could not follow his trail in the dark, so went back to camp and built a good big fire outside of the camp in case Frank should come in sight, he might see the light and come in. At intervals of half an hour, I would call as loud as I could. I kept this up until midnight, when I lay down to get a little sleep, knowing that I could not help matters by staying up.

At daylight the next morning I was on the ridge at the place where I last saw Frank, and by close watch managed to follow his trail while he was in the hardwood timber, where there was a heavy fall of leaves; but when he struck into the heavy hemlock timber, I could no longer track him. However, I had tracked him sufficiently far enough to see that he had gone back to look for the wounded deer. I made tracks in the direction I expected the wounded deer would be likely to lie down. After some searching I found the bed of the deer, also tracks of a man, which I knew to be Frank. But I could only follow the trail a short distance from where he had driven the deer out of its bed. There were plenty of deer tracks all around, but knowing that the wounded deer would naturally work down the draw, I worked my way along the hollow, keeping a close lookout for any signs of the wounded deer that I might chance to cross. At different times, I found a few drops of blood, but no signs of Frank.

I had worked down the hollow some ways, when I ran onto the wounded deer; it staggered to its feet, but was too near gone to keep its feet. I finished it by shooting it in its head. I removed the entrails as quickly as I could, bent down a sapling and hung the deer up, and then made tracks down the stream the best I could shouting and occasionally firing off my gun.

We were in a big wilderness. No roads or inhabitants west of us for many miles, and this was the course I feared Frank was most likely to take.

I now began to think that I had a serious job on hands. I kept up the search all day without getting the least trace of Frank and returned to camp late that night.

Starting early the next morning, and taking a good lunch with me, I crossed the head of Winfall Run and over the divide onto the waters of the Hamersley, continuing to shout and occasionally firing my gun. I had worked down the run some six or eight miles, when I heard some one hollow two or three times in quick succession. I was quite positive it was Frank. It was miles from any inhabitants in a dense wilderness, and hunters were not common on those parts in those days. I immediately answered the call, and soon I could hear Frank coming down the hill at breakneck speed, giving tongue at every jump.

We at once started for camp, Frank eating the lunch I had brought in my knapsack, and telling of his trials, as we made tracks the best we were able to for camp. Frank, in telling his story, would cry like a baby, and then laugh like a boy with a pair of new boots. But he cut no more boy tricks.

We finished the season's hunt, catching a goodly bunch of fox, marten, mink and coon, as well as killing a good bunch of deer. Had fur and venison brought as much in those days, as at the present time, we would have bought an automobile, and put an end to this hoofing it.

CHAPTER XXXIV.
The White Deer.

I do not remember whether I have told the boys of the H-T-T the story of the white deer, which I had the good luck to get, and the picture of which was shown in one of the sporting magazines a few years ago. The picture was sent to the magazine by Mrs. Prudence Boyington, Roulett, Pa., who was the owner of the deer at the time, and I believe a daughter of Mrs. Boyington still has the deer.

It was in the spring of 1878 or 1879 that a doe and a white fawn were seen on the hill just south of Lymansville. The fawn and its mother were seen almost daily in some of the fields near the village, and often were seen in some one of the pastures with the cows. The fawn would run and play about like a lamb.

It was plain to be seen from week to week that the fawn was rapidly growing, and as the open season for hunting of deer drew near it was generally understood that the white fawn and its mother should not be killed. When the winter came on, the fawn and its mother were all at once missing. The general supposition was that they had been killed, but when spring came the doe and the white fawn (now a yearling deer) again appeared on its old haunts of the year before. They had merely gone back into the more dense woods to winter.

Along in June it was noticed that there were three deer instead of two. Another fawn had appeared on the scene, this time an ordinary spotted fawn. They were again daily seen during the summer the same as they were the year before. Now it had been strongly urged by the people all about the country that these deer should not be killed, and there was none that was more strongly in favor of this than I was. The deer were regularly seen again all summer and up to the last days of October, when they again disappeared and all were anxious for spring to come to see if they would return as usual. When spring came the deer came back as before, but in June "the whole bunch came up missing," and it was generally thought that they had changed their haunts or they had been killed. The latter was strongly suspected.

I had taken a scout through the woods on the hills back of the locality where these deer had been frequenting and had seen signs that convinced me that the white deer, at least, was still alive, although it had not been seen for a number of weeks. Here I wish to explain that Coudersport is two miles from Lymansville and it is on the hill between the two places that the white deer had been seen most, and it was in the former place that the loudest cry for the protection of this white deer came from.

Now about this time I had killed a deer in the big woods where several of us had been on a fishing trip and I took a piece of this venison to a friend in town. It so happened that one of the side judges of our court (Stebens by name) was at the house of my friend. A few days later I was in a store belonging to a brother of the Judge, when the Judge came in and accused me of killing the white deer. Of course I denied, and told the Judge that I would wager two dollars that the white deer was still living. The Judge said "Very well," and at the same time handed a two dollar bill to a man standing by, by the name of Abison, who was listening to our conversation, which was quite heated. I told the Judge at the very first opportunity I would kill the white deer.

The white deer was not seen in the woods any more, and I was charged with killing it. I said nothing in regard to the charge, for I had now made up my mind to kill it if I could. One day three or four weeks after I had made the wager, Mr. Abison came to me and handed me two dollars and said that the Judge had got his money and told him to give me my money back as he (the Judge) did not want to take the money, that I had killed the white deer all right.

Now I was quite positive that the Judge had learned that the white deer was still alive. I had heard that the white deer had again been seen in a field near town. Now this made me all the more determined to kill the white deer. I will explain that I had learned that several of the sportsmen of Coudersport, the Judge included, had had dogs after the white deer several times the previous fall, but it so happened that there were no watchers at the place where the deer came to the creek.

That fall as soon as the first snow fell I went after the deer. I did not strike the trail until quite late in the afternoon, and as the deer left the woods where it had been accustomed to staying and went into the big woods farther south, I left the trail for that day. I would have got a shot at the deer if my attention had not been called in the wrong direction by the chirping of several blue jays which I thought were excited over the presence of the white deer.

I was working the trail to the best of my ability and knew that I was close to the game, when my attention was drawn by the chirping of those blue jays which were down the side of a hill. I was working the trail so as to be on vantage ground and could see from where I was standing that the trail had turned slightly down the hill along the side of a fallen tree and in the direction of the chirping of the jays. This led me to think that the jays were scolding the deer, so I cautiously advanced a few steps down the hill, expecting every moment to see the deer. While I was watching down the hill, I heard a slight noise to my right and partly behind me. I looked in the direction in which the noise came from and was surprised to catch a glimpse of the deer jumping the log near where I had last seen the trail. The log hid the deer from my sight so that I was unable to get a shot at it. The deer had lain down close to the log, and had I taken a few more steps in the direction I was going instead of giving attention to the jays I would have seen the deer and made my word good the first time.

It was too late in the day to follow the trail farther at this time, knowing that the deer would run a long distance before stopping. As I had a team engaged to take me to my camp and I was anxious to get there on the first tracking snow, I concluded to give the white deer a rest a few days until I returned from camp in the big woods. I was in camp only a few days when the snow went off, so I came home. I had only been home a day or two when a man by the name of Hill came to my house in great haste. He had been cutting logs en a hill, and looking across onto a hill opposite where he was working, saw the white deer, so came to tell we what he had seen. I at once took my gun and started after the deer. I went up the hill in the direction that Mr. Hill had seen the deer until I was quite sure that I was well above the deer, then cautiously worked my way down the side of that hill. There being no snow on the ground and the deer being white, I soon discovered it lying in its bed. I cautiously crept up within shooting distance and fired, killing the deer instantly.

I will explain how it happened that these deer disappeared so suddenly at the time Judge Stebens accused me of killing the white deer and the wager was made between the Judge and your humble servant. A man by the name of Frank Williams had shot the deer breaking a foreleg at the knee joint, and this caused the deer to remain hidden away until it recovered from the wound. The leg or joint was stiff when the deer was killed and the force of the bullet was so spent that it lay against the skin after shattering the knee joint and I still have the ball which I took from the knee. I had the deer mounted and Mrs. Boyington took it as she was collecting freaks and curios of this country.

CHAPTER XXXV.
A Day of Luck.

Every hunter of long experience could tell of the ups and downs along the trail consisting of good, bad and indifferent luck and as usual tell of our hits and let others tell of our misses, I will tell of a day of good luck. It was in November and there was no snow on the ground. I was camping on the Holman branch of Pine Creek in Pennsylvania and one night, just at dark, a party of several men came to my camp and asked to stay over night. They stated that they were going to camp on the opposite side of the ridge on the Sinnamahoning waters. My camp was small but I made room for the hunters the best I could.

This party was going into a section of country where I had several bear traps as well as a good number of smaller traps set for fox, mink, marten and other fur animals. As I wished to look these traps over the next day before this party got scattered about the woods where my traps were, I got up early the next morning, ate a hasty breakfast and put a lunch into my knapsack and was ready to start out before the party of hunters was up. I cautioned the hunters to see that the fire was safe when they left camp and then started on my day's hunt without the slightest idea that I was starting on one of the luckiest days I ever had.

I had to climb a high ridge, then my route was for some distance on a long ridge, which I would follow for a distance of a mile and a half, when I dropped off the right hand side of the ridge into a ravine where I had a bear trap set. This ridge was a clean open one of beech and maple timber. I knew it would keep me busy the entire day to get over the trap line, the best that I could do, so had no intention of spending any time looking after deer. When I got to this open ridge, I took a dog trot along the ridge.

I was making good time when on looking ahead along the ridge I saw a good-sized buck come from the left hand side of the ridge. He would take a jump or two then drop his head to the ground and then take another hop or two and again drop his head to the ground. I knew that he was on the trail of other deer. I had hardly time to bring my gun to my shoulder when the buck wheeled and disappeared back over the ridge from where he had come. I started on a run to where the deer had gone out of sight, thinking that possibly I might catch him before he got out of range down the side of the hill. Imagine my surprise when just as I reached the top of the hill, where I saw the deer disappear from my sight, I almost ran against the buck. He had turned back to cross the ridge when I met him. He whirled down the hill but I was too close onto him and I caught him before he could get out of reach. I took out the deer's entrails and bent down a sapling and hung the deer up, then I crossed the ridge and started down the ravine to look after the bear traps.

I was hurrying down the hill near a jam of fallen timber, when all at once out jumped five or six deer from this timber. In an instant the whole bunch was out of sight behind the jam with the exception of one large doe. I could see, one of her hips standing out from behind a large hemlock tree. Without hesitating a moment, I fired at what I could see of the deer and it dropped out of sight as the gun cracked. I hurried through the jam of timber to where I saw the deer and there the doe lay, trying to get on her feet. I soon ended her misery by shooting her in the head. I soon had her entrails out and hung up as I had the buck. It was the trail of this bunch of deer that the buck was on when he ran into me.

After I had hung up the deer I hustled on down the ravine to the bear trap. When I got to the place where the trap was set it was gone. The trail led down the ravine and was easy to follow as I hurried along and I soon found a small bear tangled up in a thicket of small brush. It was only the work of a moment to fix bruin in shape to skin. After I had the hide off, I cut the bear up into quarters and hung the meat up in the trees. I toted the trap back up to where it was set and reset it then I went back down the hollow to where I had left the bear skin and took it on my shoulder and made tracks down the hollow to the main creek where I had a string of deadfalls set for mink and coon. The bear skin was about all the load I cared to tote, but I had not gone far down the creek before I had the skins of two good sized coon and one mink tied to my load. The coon and mink skins I could get in my knapsack so they did not bother much.

After following the creek a distance of about one mile I left the creek and went up a long narrow sawtooth point to cross the divide to the Cross Fork waters where I had some bear, fox and marten traps set. When I was about two-thirds of the way up this point I stopped at the side of a large rock which would shelter me from the cold wind. The point was covered with low laurel. I had been watching down the side of the hill to see if I could not catch sight of some animal on the move, but I had not got a glimpse of even a squirrel.

I had about finished my lunch, when I saw the motion of something move in the laurel, forty or fifty yards below me. I picked up my gun and stood watching, when I again caught sight of the animal and in a moment I saw the horns of a deer. I could get the outline of the deer's body so I said, "Now or never," and let go the best I could at the bunch, but when the smoke from the gun was gone, I could neither see nor hear anything but stood ready with my gun to my shoulder. I again saw a part of a deer move in an open space in the laurel. I again fired at the bunch with the remark that I guessed that I could drive him out of there after a while.

I left the bear skin and knapsack at the rock, knowing that the rock would be a good landmark to find them by and went down through the laurel to see what effect my shot had. When I got to where the deer were, when I shot, I readily saw plenty of blood on the green laurel leaves and I only had a few steps to go when I saw the buck lying dead. I cut his throat and stood waiting for the blood to stop flowing and saw a trail that was fresh. I could readily tell by the way the leaves and ground were torn up that the trail was of some animal that was having a hard time to keep on its feet. You can imagine my joy and surprise to get two deer so unexpectedly. I had only a few rods to go when I found a good big doe dead.

Well, you may guess that I lost no time in getting the entrails out of these two deer and swinging them up as I had the other two for it was getting well past noon. I would be a good five miles from camp when I got to my first marten trap.

After I got to the top of the divide, I made the best time that was in me. I looked at several fox and marten traps but none had been disturbed. When I got to the first bear trap on the divide I had an occasion to scold and scold hard, but all to no purpose. I found the limb of a tree jammed in between the jaws of the trap. Of course, I thought some hunter had done me the favor and having as hard a stunt ahead of me, you can guess that the trick was not pleasing to me. Well, here I learned how foolish it was to fly off the handle before you know what has been doing. Now, after a little investigation, I found that the limb had been broken from the tree by the wind and it so happened that it fell right onto the pan of the trap and sprang it. Setting the trap, I hurried on to the next bear trap and here I had another chance to be disgusted, even more than in the first case. This time it was a porcupine in the trap but there was nothing to be done, only reset the trap and hurry on again. None of the other traps were disturbed, neither the small traps nor the bear trap until I came to the last marten trap which had a marten in it. It was now too dark to see to skin it so I was obliged to dump the carcass into the knapsack and tote it along with the coons and mink pelts.

I had about one mile to go to reach the road, then four miles to camp and I often thought what a hunter and a trapper would endure and call it sport. It must have been nearly nine o'clock when I got to camp, where I still found the hunting party. They had taken a part of their outfit to their camp grounds and had worked on their camp until nearly night when they returned to my camp to stay for the night and get the balance of their outfit.

Well, I was pleased to find them still in camp for they volunteered to go with me the next day and help me get the deer and bear out to the road in return for venison and bear meat. This ended one of the luckiest and hardest day's work that I ever did on the trail or trap line.

CHAPTER XXXVI.
A Mixed Bag.

I promised some of my old trapper friends back East, that I would let them, who were fortunate enough to be subscribers to the H-T-T, hear from me. I will say that this is a mountain region of the first magnitude. A man that cannot mount a donkey and ride over a trail where the river is hundreds of feet below, or as it looks to be nearly under him, and the trail not more than twelve inches wide, hewn out of the solid rock, he had best remain in the East.

This is a sportsman's paradise, and the trapper will find here prey in the way of bear, both black and brown, fisher, mink, raccoon, fox, otter, panther, or as the natives call them, mountain lion, wildcat, skunk, civet cat and many other fur bearing animals and all quite numerous. Deer seem to be very abundant. I counted thirteen in a lick this morning, and it is not an uncommon thing to see from ten to twenty in the licks at one time.

The fishing is said to be the best in the spring and fall. It is not an uncommon thing to catch salmon, weighing from six to thirty-five pounds, and as it is only thirty-five miles to the Pacific Ocean, they are of the very best quality. Mountain trout are plentiful.

Another animal that is plenty is the mountain goat. Bear, mountain lion, and other signs are as numerous as those of rabbits in the East. I am not prepared at this time, to say how shrewd these animals are to trap, but if they take bait as readily as they are reported to, they must not be very hard to catch. There is a bounty of $4.00 on wolves and the writer has seen numerous signs of them.

Will say to my friends in the East that while on my way from the coast to the ranch, a distance of only fifty miles, and the most of the way over mountain trails, I stopped often to watch the deer feeding along the side of the trail. When they saw you they would trot off a short distance and begin feeding again.

Only last evening, Mrs. Evie Newell, shot and killed a large mountain lion that started into the yard after a pig. It seems to me panthers are thicker here than wildcats in Pennsylvania.

* * *

I have experimented with scents for years and have found scents of no particular benefit for trapping the fox. I have tried the skunk and muskrat scent, the matrix of the female fox taken at the proper time. I have had a female fox and have lead her to my trapping place, and I have tried many so-called fox scents and all to no purpose. Fox urine may, in some particular places, be used to some slight advantage. It is not so with other animals in regard to scents, for they do not use the same acute instinct that the fox does.

I do not wish to insinuate upon those that do use scent, but for me, I would not give a cent for a barrel of so-called fox decoy. I boil my traps in soft maple bark, hemlock boughs or something of that nature. I do not do this because the fox can be any more readily got into the trap, but because it forms a glazing on the trap and thereby prevents them from rusting and the trap will then spring more readily. It makes no difference how rusty the trap is, so far as catching the fox is concerned.

No boys, no scent for me, the fox soon learns to associate the scent business with the man, then you are up against it. With me there is nothing mysterious about trapping. It is simply practical ways of setting the trap, learned from many years of experience.

* * *

I have had fifty years experience as a hunter and trapper. I have netted wild pigeons in the Adirondack Mountains, in New York, to the Indian Territory, so you know that the articles in H-T-T are very interesting to me. I would say that no young trapper should be without this journal, although I would advise them not to take too readily to scents and decoys.

As to the discussions that have been in H-T-T, one writer says he has twenty ways to catch the fox; now I have just as many different ways as there are different conditions. I would say that no one can become a successful trapper until he learns to comply with the natural conditions, which will differ with almost every trap he sets when trapping fox, mink, etc.

I will tell my brother trappers what I have been doing this fall (1902) along the line of trapping. In August I took a trip through portions of Montana, Idaho and Washington, to look up a site to do a little trapping this winter. There is much more game here than in the East, but nothing like you hear talked of. I found the mountains too steep and the underbrush too thick and from what I could learn, I was afraid the weather was too cold for one of my age and condition of health, but, oh boys, what trout fishing I found in the Clearwater; this is a branch of Snake River and empties into that river at Lewiston, Idaho.

As I found things, I thought I would return to old Potter County, Pennsylvania, and have a little fun trapping the fox and skunk as that is about the only game there is in this section when we have no beechnuts, for that is the only mast we have here. We have no beechnuts this season and most of the fur bearing animals have migrated south of here where there are chestnuts, acorns and hickory nuts.

Brothers, I will tell you where my camp is, and you will always find the latch-string out. My camp stands at the very head of the Allegheny River, 1700 feet above sea level. From the cabin door you could throw a stone over the divide to where the water flows into the west branch of the Susquehanna. In a half hour a person can, from my camp, catch trout from the waters of the Allegheny, and the Susquehanna.

As we have no beechnuts we have no bears, so I have not set my bear traps. This will cut my sport considerably short. I have put out but about sixty small traps, so I spend my time about equally between camp and home.

I will send a picture of myself and my old dog Mage, who I believe knows more about trapping than some families. But poor old Mage is 13 years old and is following the down trail very rapidly. He is quite deaf and gets around with difficulty. Poor fellow, he is nearly to the end of the trail.

WOODCOCK AND HIS OLD TRAPPING DOG--MAGE.
THE BEST TRAPPING DOG THAT EVER TROD THE EARTH.

The furs shown in the picture are my first four days' catch with forty traps: 9 fox, 2 coon, 1 mink and 7 skunk. My catch to date, November 25, in thirteen days is 14 fox, 27 skunk, 9 coon and 1 mink.

* * *

Brothers, I will give some reasons why I do not write more of my experience as a trapper. First, I am not much given to writing. Second, my experiences in trapping are so different from so many trappers who write, that I thought it best to say but little or nothing about trapping. I could call myself, "Old Honesty," and then write or cause it to be written and published in some of the sporting papers, that I had caught 300 fox this season, as I see one trapper did, but I would not feel good about it after I had done so. Fifty-seven fox are the most that I ever caught in one season.

A brother was down to see me and I was pleased to meet him, I wish to say, brother trappers, that if you should have an opportunity to meet Brother Stearns, you will find him a gentleman in every respect. But, Brother Stearns and I could not agree on the scent question, and he did not like to believe that I handled my traps, bait and all pertaining to the setting of the trap, bare-handed. He went so far as to hint that I was cold-blooded, and even felt of my pulse to see if my circulation was all right. Hold on, I am mistaken, it was my hands that he felt of to see if they were not cold, but he pronounced them all right. He then related a story about an old uncle of his and a crow, but shook his head and said it did not do any harm to wear gloves if it did not do any good. That is all right, but we do not like to be carrying unnecessary weight.

One word with Brother Chas. T. Wells. No, brother, I do not go much on scents. Perhaps you would have caught more than 15 fox, but I do not like to own that you could have done so. Now the first ten days that I was in the woods, there were hundreds of head of cattle in the woods, and the woods were full of men gathering them up, and one could do but little or nothing in the way of trapping. Neither did the 15 include the five that were stolen, nor the two that broke the chains and went off with the trap. By the way, Brother Stearns could tell you of a chase I had with one of those that carried off a trap, the worst jaunt I have had in many a day. No brother, the only scent I use is the urine of the fox and I only use that in certain places. No, I believe that one good method is much better than scents in trapping the fox. If one wishes to use scents, they will find none better than some of those advertised in the H-T-T.

Now brothers, while I do not believe that any one man is so cute he cannot find his equal, I do not like to believe but that I can catch as many fox as the next one--all things being equal. For the last ten years I have not set traps over a scope of territory to exceed two or three miles square and if Brother Stearns had been on the ground that I trapped on, a few days before I began trapping, he would have seen but few fox signs. I usually trap on a different piece of ground each year. I know of some trappers here that begin trapping the first of September and they are good trappers too, but they are so greedy, they are willing to kill the "goose that lays the golden egg."

* * *

Several years ago, through the courtesy of Mr. John Shawl, one of the Tide Water Pipe Line Co's telegraph operators, I was allowed the use of one of their offices for camping purposes during the trapping season. Now, do not think that this office was located in a town, for it was not. On the contrary, it was located in the largest wooded section of this locality, and on the old Jersey Shore Turnpike. There was a path or sort of a woods road at the point where this office was located, leading from this road to another road, a distance of more than four miles and making a cut off for people who wished to go on to the waters of the Sinnamahoning or Kettel Creek in Northern Pennsylvania.

It was customary for me to stay in camp for a week or ten days and then go home and stay two or three days. One day on returning from one of my trips home, I had rather better luck than coming, getting 5 fox, 3 coon and 1 wildcat. I usually hung my furs on the side of the building close up under the eaves until I went home, then I would take them home on the following morning of the day I had caught them.

There was a rap at the door about five o'clock in the morning and on going to the door, I found two men with a lantern; one man of middle age, the other a young man. There had just been a fall of snow of about four inches, and the men were going onto the Cross Fork of Kettel Creek, deer hunting. They had stayed at a farm house on the other road and had started from this house between three and four o'clock in the morning. Seeing a light in the office, they thought they would come in and stay until daylight.

The old gentleman inquired what I was doing there. I informed him that I was trying to trap a little. He said that he should not think it would pay me, but if I could catch a fox it would be different, as he had seen several tracks along the road by the light of the lantern. He also told me that he had a recipe for making fox scent, that was a dead sure thing, and as I lived so far from his place, I would not be liable to interfere with his trapping, he would knock off one-half his usual price and sell me a recipe for five dollars.

I said I would see what luck I had while they were gone, and it might be possible that I would buy his recipe when he came back. He said, delays were dangerous, and that I was losing the greatest opportunity of my life, that he might not come back that way. I thanked him, but told him I would chance it.

It was now daylight, and as the hunters stepped outside they noticed the carcass of a wildcat, and I told them if they would step to the corner of the building, they would see what I got yesterday. They did so, and gazed for one second at the pelts, then the older of the two said, "Come, Charley, let's be going," and they left without even bidding me good morning.

Comrades you do not know how I enjoy your letters as given in this splendid magazine, especially so this winter (season of 1905-6) as I have not been able to trap. But I have no kick coming for this is only the third time in fifty years, but what I have been able to be out with the traps and gun.

I know that the readers of the H-T-T would be pleased to read articles from old veterans. The H-T-T has about reached the height of perfection so far as the trapper is concerned. There is none of the high top boot, fashionable, corduroy suits and checkered cap business about the H-T-T. Success to all.

* * *

Boys, you know how we all like to gather around a camp fire and talk over our hunting and trapping experiences, of how we caught a certain mink, fox, coon or bear, or how we killed a certain deer. So while we are out fishing I thought I would like to have a chat with the trappers. And boys, all you who have not camped out for a week and had a good time fishing, do not know how much you have lost, especially those who need the care of a doctor.

Yes, boys, take your camp outfit and go out into the woods among the hills, streams and lakes. There you will find one of the most competent doctors and nurses that ever treated the ills of human family. Do not forget to take a few copies of the HUNTER-TRADER-TRAPPER along and other sporting magazines, as well as some of the Harding Library, so while you are resting in camp you can visit with the trapper boys all over the Union.

This is May 20, 1905, and the second time I have been out camping and fishing this spring. Trout are not as plentiful as they were forty years ago by a great deal, but we still get all we can use, and that is plenty.

While you are out fishing do not forget to keep a lookout for signs of game you will be trapping next winter. You may see where there has been a litter of young mink, fox or coon reared. While these animals are of migratory nature, they will, nevertheless, visit their old homes frequently, so you will find these places a pretty sure place to make a catch next fall when you put our your traps. Do not forget that during the summer is just the time to fix some of your best sets for fox and other fur bearing animals.

As I have had many years experience in camping, let me say to those who have never camped, and who expect to camp the coming season, that now is the time to hunt up a partner and get acquainted. I have camped many seasons in large woods both with and without partners.